Carceral Entanglements

In the series *Critical Race, Indigeneity, and Relationality*,
edited by Antonio T. Tiongson Jr., Danika Medak-Saltzman,
Iyko Day, and Shanté Paradigm Smalls

ALSO IN THIS SERIES:

Joo Ok Kim, *Warring Genealogies: Race, Kinship, and the Korean War*
Maryam S. Griffin, *Vehicles of Decolonization: Public Transit in the Palestinian West Bank*
Erin Suzuki, *Ocean Passages: Navigating Pacific Islander and Asian American Literatures*
Quynh Nhu Le, *Unsettled Solidarities: Asian and Indigenous Cross-Representations in the Américas*

Wendi Yamashita

Carceral Entanglements

Gendered Public Memories of Japanese American World War II Incarceration

TEMPLE UNIVERSITY PRESS
Philadelphia • Rome • Tokyo

TEMPLE UNIVERSITY PRESS
Philadelphia, Pennsylvania 19122
tupress.temple.edu

Copyright © 2024 by Temple University—Of The Commonwealth System of Higher Education
All rights reserved
Published 2024

Library of Congress Cataloging-in-Publication Data

Names: Yamashita, Wendi, 1985– author.
Title: Carceral entanglements : gendered public memories of Japanese American World War II incarceration / Wendi Yamashita.
Other titles: Gendered public memories of Japanese American World War II incarceration | Critical race, indigeneity, and relationality.
Description: Philadelphia : Temple University Press, 2024. | Series: Critical race, indigeneity, and relationality | Includes bibliographical references and index. | Summary: "Utilizing a comparative racial methodology, this book interrogates how Japanese American community memory is invested in Asian American decriminalization and the forgetting of settler colonial landscapes so as to reveal how state power operates"— Provided by publisher.
Identifiers: LCCN 2024000399 (print) | LCCN 2024000400 (ebook) | ISBN 9781439920398 (cloth) | ISBN 9781439920404 (paperback) | ISBN 9781439920411 (pdf)
Subjects: LCSH: Japanese Americans—Forced removal and internment, 1942–1945. | Japanese Americans—Ethnic identity. | Collective memory—United States. | Memory—Social aspects—United States.
Classification: LCC D769.8.A6 .Y354 2024 (print) | LCC D769.8.A6 (ebook) | DDC 305.8956/073—dc23/eng/20240227
LC record available at https://lccn.loc.gov/2024000399
LC ebook record available at https://lccn.loc.gov/2024000400

9 8 7 6 5 4 3 2 1

For my grandmother, Mae Sumie Kanamori

Contents

Acknowledgments		ix
	Introduction	1
1.	From Distance to Proximity, Japanese Americanness and Blackness: The Limitations of Post-Redress Japanese American Incarceration Narratives	24
2.	The Intimate Connection among Truth, Memory, and Life: Refusal in the Densho Digital Archive	55
3.	The Colonial and the Carceral: Building Relationships between Japanese Americans and Indigenous Groups in the Owens Valley	84
4.	NSU Cultural Night and Generational Transmissions of Memory: Performative Disruptions and Other Futures	104
	Conclusion: The Shifting Futures of Japanese American Memory from 9/11 to the COVID-19 Pandemic	128
Notes		139
Selected Bibliography		163
Index		169

Acknowledgments

July 13, 2020. At the height of the COVID-19 pandemic, my maternal grandmother unexpectedly passed away. Four months later, my maternal grandfather passed away. Devastated, I struggled to finish this manuscript, paralyzed with a kind of grief and loss I cannot even put into words. How could I continue to write when my subject matter was so connected to what I had lost? How could I continue when the one person I wanted to read this book was no longer alive? As a Yonsei (fourth-generation Japanese American), I have always had a deep connection to my maternal grandparents and their siblings. Raised in a multigenerational household with my grandparents, I had the opportunity to know, understand, and love them in ways that I no longer take for granted.

This book explores the Japanese American community's anxiety about Nisei death, but it is also a deeply personal reflection on my own fears about the loss of the generation that raised me—a generation that kept us together, fed us, and shared stories with us so we could better understand ourselves. It is also a book that hopes for something more. Challenging community memory practices to consider more than just Japanese Americans is something I am seeing more and more of every day. I am grateful to the organizations out there doing that work: Vigilant Love, Nikkei Progressives, Tsuru for Solidarity, Densho, Florin JACL Sacramento Valley, the Manzanar Committee, and many more.

I would like to thank Temple University Press for their generosity in this process—in particular, Tony Tiongson and Shaun Vigil, whose patience and guidance were instrumental to my editing process. I have always felt a special connection to Temple University because it is where my grandfather attended (and later dropped out of) school and the reason my mother was born in Philadelphia. Thank you for seeing worth and value in my work.

This book would not be possible without the community spaces and people that welcomed me. To Gene Kanamori, who invited me to the community event that started this project—your activism and love for community inspire me and are woven throughout this project. While conducting my research, the Manzanar Committee included me into their organization, and I have learned so much about community building and grassroots organizing from them. I appreciate the work they do and feel lucky to be a part of it. In particular, I would like to thank Bruce Embrey, Gann Matsuda, Jason Fujii, Pat Sakamoto, Vicky Perez, Jenny Chomori, Kerry Cababa, Colleen Miyano, and Monica Embrey. I am immensely grateful to Sarah Ando for her beautiful and moving artwork that appears on the cover of this book—thank you for your generosity. I would also like to thank Emiko Kranz for her interview and insight as well as UCLA's Nikkei Student Union, whose Cultural Nights made research so fun. I am also grateful to the late Harry Williams, whose activism will never be forgotten. Thank you to Rose Masters, Alisa Lynch Broch, and Sarah Bone for sharing their brilliance and for their collaboration at the Manzanar National Historic Site. I am also grateful to the Nichi Bei Foundation and the Florin JACL Sacramento Valley, who have welcomed me as I transitioned to life in Northern California and allowed me to find a community.

I am indebted to my academic community. Grace Kyungwon Hong's unwavering support and mentorship are a gift that I deeply cherish. This book would not exist without her. I also offer thanks to Mishuana Goeman, Sarah Haley, and Valerie Matsumoto, whose generative comments on my dissertation shaped this book in so many ways. Thank you to the UCLA Gender Studies Department, Asian American Studies Department, and Asian American Studies Center for training me, financially supporting me, and/or employing me during my graduate studies. Thank you to Preeti Sharma, Dalal Alfares, Esha Momeni, Stephanie Santos, Rahel Woldegaber, and Rana Shariff, for their intellectual community, love, and support, and to Lisa Ho, who read early drafts of this book when I was too scared to let anyone else read it. I also am grateful to Nicole Horsley, who was instrumental in the writing of my book proposal and whose friendship sustained me when I felt so isolated in New York. I also wish to thank my Ithaca College students who inspired me in my first years of teaching: Katelyn Monaco, Hana Cho, Mark Gregory, Jaye Kayne, and Rebecca Steinberg. And I am grateful to my colleagues and friends in the Ethnic Studies Department at Sac State for their support.

And I offer thanks to those who have always taken care of me. Thank you to Cindy Huynh, Ed Amorim, Janice TiraTira, Peejay TiraTira, Jin Hua Dana Jiang, whose calls, visits, and friendships have carried me through this process and life in general. Thank you to Lisa Ho, David Chia, Chun Mei Lam, Raissa Diamante, Mary Keovisai, Mai Yang Vang, Jason Chan-Pierre, and Audrey Chan-Pierre for filling my life with so much laughter, food, puppies, and now babies. Thank you to Preeti Sharma for being my roommate and friend during much of this writing process. Thank you to Elaine Harada and Sharilynn Jung for creating a fun and safe space to exercise and for fostering a wonderful community. Thank you to Garon Yamashita, Diana Yamashita, and Kara Yamashita for housing me, feeding me, and being my emotional guardians. To my nieces and nephews, Ethan, Alexandria, Elizabeth, Alexander, and Lily, thank you for bringing so much joy to my life. To my cousins, Traci Murata, Eric Murata, Lance Kanamori, Jordan Kanamori, Cheryn Kanamori, Kelly Kanamori, Justin Shudo, and Miko Shudo, thank you for always believing in me and reminding me to have fun. Thank you to all my aunts and uncles who helped raise me and continue to lift me up. Thank you to my new family, Suk Hoan Hong, Myung Ok Hong, and Michael Hong, for welcoming me into their lives.

I am grateful to my parents, who emotionally and financially supported me in this process. I am thankful for their love and the encouragement to follow my dreams even when it did not make sense to them. Their strength, intelligence, and care for others continue to inspire me. Thank you to my partner, Steve Hong, for pushing me toward the finish line with so much laughter, silliness, and fun. You make our life together so lovely. And finally, thank you to my grandmother. I am grateful to have been raised by you, to have grown up in your home, to have eaten your food, but most of all for your stories—the ones that made me cry or hysterically laugh, the ones I wrote down, and the ones I will never share.

Carceral Entanglements

Introduction

Today, the young generation doesn't realize it, but we on a per capita basis are the most law-abiding people in the United States, we have the lowest crime rate, we have the highest intellectual rate per capita wise, and we're among the three ethnic groups with the highest per capita income. That's not bad, from internment camps.
—Daniel Inouye, Japanese American National Museum 2011 Gala Dinner

The inevitable passing of the generations has brought into question the ability of our Nikkei community [Japanese emigrants and their descendants] to maintain its vitality.
—Terasaki Family Foundation, signature sponsor of the Japanese American National Museum 2011 Gala Dinner

My project came to be at this very particular moment, at the 2011 Japanese American National Museum Gala Dinner titled "Continuing Family Stories: The Expanding Nikkei Community." When the late senator Daniel Inouye came to the stage to ask the audience for donations to bring buses of schoolchildren to the museum, several things happened. There was a staged conversation between Inouye and a young girl to whom he relayed his entire life story, emphasizing the importance of remembering Japanese American incarceration, to which she promised to "never forget." And after relating the aforementioned statistical information on Japanese Americans, he went on to say, "Today I stand before you when I was once declared an enemy alien on December the seventh, and today I am president pro tempore, third in the line for the presidency." And then he turned to the audience to say, "That's not too bad," to which the audience enthusiastically applauded. I remember feeling violently out of place in that moment. I did not join everyone else in clapping because I was forced to acknowledge the ways Japanese American memories were so intimately connected to justifying forms of racialized state violence and criminalization by touting our status as the "most law abiding" with the "lowest crime rate" even while acknowledging our own experiences of incarceration during World War II. Consequently, this book asks: How do these narratives of worth and success that make Japanese Americans legible to the state come to be? And what are the consequences of such narratives?

I begin the introduction with these two quotes and this personal memory because they are emblematic of two very important factors that shape contemporary Japanese American public memory in relation to incarceration. Inouye's speech and his political power as a Japanese American senator from Hawaii, embodied in his World War II veteran experiences, demonstrate how narratives of personal responsibility and heteronormative respectability embedded in Japanese American historical memory reinforce mass incarceration and settler colonialism. Connecting his ability to overcome racial violence as a Japanese Hawaiian through patriotic masculinity to his political ascendancy erases his settler status and his antiblack statistics as merely a celebratory multicultural success story.[1] The second quote exposes the generational anxiety surrounding the physical death of the Nisei, second-generation Japanese Americans, where historical legitimacy is intimately linked to the living witness of racialized harm. In many ways, the living witness is assumed to make Japanese American history legible to the state (which occurred historically through redress and testimony) and thus makes this history worthy of national remembering. These quotes alert us to what kind of narratives are being produced as well as how they are being reproduced, circulated, and consumed in public spaces of Japanese American memory. I argue throughout this book that death, both physical and historical erasure, has played an integral role in the memory practices of Japanese Americans. In particular, death is racialized for Japanese Americans in multiple ways at different historical moments and has impacted memories of incarceration. First, Japanese Americans were denied personhood during their incarceration via dislocation, dispossession, and detention. Second, prior to redress and reparations, Japanese American experiences of incarceration were absent from community and national memory. Japanese Americans had no language with which to talk about what had happened to them; incarceration was still remembered as a "military necessity" and therefore could not be articulated as racialized harm. Despite the promise of redress to resolve these memories of racialized harm, they continue to linger in the present and seep into how Japanese Americans remember today. Contemporary memory practices are shaped by this fear of disappearance from national historical memory and the denial of personhood. Entering national memory or the national archive promises a way of living beyond physical death. Consequently, as I explore in the following sections, for the Japanese American community, death, generationality, and normativity are intimately wrapped up in legitimizing Japanese American histories via their public memorializations. To be worthy of remembering and thus state recognition, Japanese Americans strategically construct narratives of ideal citizen-subjects that revolve around their performances of proper gendered and heteronormative behavior. As I discuss later, in the 1980s these narratives were being shaped by larger national discussions about welfare dependency in which certain groups of color were being racialized and gendered as deviant through a discourse of heteronormativity that criminalizes and punishes them for being poor.

I put these memorializations under a microscope to expose the dangers of benign narratives that shape Japanese American identity, community, and history. In these narratives, normativity is sustained by generationality wherein the future of Japanese American historical memory is no longer seen as precarious. The work of maintaining the legitimacy and visibility of Japanese American memory exposes how contemporary racial discourses maintain a neoliberal racial hierarchy that Japanese Americans willingly and unwillingly partake in but also disrupt at various moments. As I elaborate later, because of the impact that redress and testimony have made on the Japanese American community—its understanding of itself, its knowledge production and community spaces—memory becomes an important vehicle to examine. Embedded in memories of World War II are these logics of "success" wherein the state has made Japanese Americans visible in order to proclaim that racism is either not happening or officially over.[2] *Carceral Entanglements* examines the relationship among death, generationality, and normativity to understand how Japanese American memories replicate nationalist and neoliberal narratives of resolution and racial reconciliation that sustain settler and carceral logics.[3] My intervention into the literature on Japanese American incarceration is to critically think about the ways that history relies upon generationality to posit racialized normativity as resolution in the face of a haunting or always looming racialized deviancy that comes directly from their incarcerated pasts. Prior to and during World War II, Japanese Americans were outside the racial and sexual mainstream, which resulted in their exclusion from citizenship, immigration, and owning land and culminated in their removal and detainment from the rest of the population. This book draws on a queer of color critique of racialized normativity and nonnormativity to analyze how "racist practice articulates itself generally as gender and sexual regulation" or the "social formations that compose liberal capitalism."[4] Although Japanese Americans do not constitute recognizably queer subjects, I read for racialized memories that enable nonnormative discourses and narratives to emerge.[5] As an intervention, *Carceral Entanglements* attempts to locate Japanese American racial formations and spatial modes of enclosure via public memory alongside other racial formations such as Indigenous communities, settler colonialism, antiblackness, and the prison industrial complex. I see these disruptions to normativity as offering not just alternative memories and histories but as becoming moments in time where previously unimaginable alliances can occur. I theorize that these alliances are distinctly different from a progressive historicism that narrates Japanese Americans as proof of the advancement of racial progress and instead establish a different temporality. These alliances narrate their experiences of comparative containment (reservations, incarceration, prisons) as not just in the past but resonating in the present as well. This temporality renarrates containment as central to U.S. nation building and thus forces a questioning of the construction of the "criminal" and "criminality." And as I explore, this comparative temporality imagines and struggles for a future without racialized containment.

To do so, I examine Japanese American practices of public memory by examining museums, digital archives, pilgrimages, and student-run and performed plays as important sites where these narratives play out but are also disrupted.[6] As Roderick Ferguson argues, a "queer of color critique approaches culture as one site that compels identification with and antagonisms to the normative ideals promoted by the state and capital."[7] By examining these sites of public memory, we are able to see how Japanese Americans occupy this "contradictory location" produced by the state. *Carceral Entanglements* is interested in how memories of incarceration (the denial of citizenship and property rights) prevent Japanese Americans from completely partaking in the neoliberal racial order despite the privileges obtained from redress.[8] In other words, redress promised to protect Japanese Americans from the erasure that they experienced during incarceration, but only within the confines of a neoliberal order that justifies mass incarceration and settler colonialism by taking recourse to personal responsibility and heteronormative respectability. It is within this "contradictory location" that we can see what Lisa Lowe argues, that "culture is the material site of struggle" where "alternative forms of subjectivity, collectivity, and public life are imagined."[9] It is through an examination of culture that we can "question those modes of government" that regulate the citizen-subject. Thus, I argue that Japanese American public performances of memory are important sites of interrogation because the logic of redress, most visible in these memorializations, is arguably the epitome of contemporary neoliberal racial formation in the United States. My reading of these practices of Japanese American public memory is rooted in these cultural analyses, and I look for these contradictions and disruptions to explore the complicated and nuanced ways Japanese American identity, memory, and history function. Therefore, I also read these performances of memory against the grain as a way of examining both their limitations and possibilities. Reading for this "contradictory location" allows for a reading of incarceration that is both wrapped up in and subject to racialized harm in a neoliberal racial order.

My comparative racial project is not merely about Japanese Americans and their memories but is instead an interrogation of how the United States normalizes and justifies a neoliberal racial order. *Carceral Entanglements* is about the interlocking relationship that Japanese American incarceration memories have to the prison industrial complex and the settler colonial logics that at times unknowingly sustain it. A comparative project is necessary to understand how state violence is operating even as it is being disavowed.

The Heteronormative Logic of Generationality: Understanding Japanese American Historical Memory

Before moving forward, I want to explain how Japanese American historical memory is rooted in generationality. By using the term "generationality," I refer to two aspects unique to Japanese American history. First, due to immigration patterns and restrictions, Japanese American history, community identity, and memories are organized by generations: Issei (first generation, 1885–1924), Nisei (second generation, 1900–1945), Sansei (third generation, 1942–1975), Yonsei (fourth generation, 1975–2010), and so on. Each generation is narrated as having a particular set of collective experiences that revolve around historical events such as incarceration (Issei and Nisei) and redress (Nisei and Sansei). This periodization of Japanese American history (prior to World War II) is characterized by immigration, labor, and racial exclusion that "restricted and regulated the possibilities of Asian American settlement and cultural expression."[10] During these early waves of Asian immigration, "capital needed a cheap, manipulable labor force" unconcerned about the "'origins' of its labor force, whereas the nation-state, with its need for 'abstract citizens' formed by a unified culture to participate in the political sphere, is precisely concerned" with how to "maintain a national citizenry bound by race, language, and culture."[11] These contradictory concerns of state and capital then sought Asian immigrant labor and later sought to exclude them through exclusionary laws and policies.

Second, Japanese American history and generationality differ from those of other Asian immigrant communities at the time because loopholes in immigration restriction allowed for the creation of families, which was denied or made more difficult for other groups. For example, the Page Act of 1875 "prohibited the entry of prostitutes," and it was "enforced so strictly and broadly it served to not only exclude Chinese prostitutes but also to discourage Chinese wives" from coming to the United States because of the "rigorous interrogation and cross-examination by U.S. officials."[12] Chinese women's immigration to the United States between 1876 and 1882 "declined from the previous seven-year period by 68 percent."[13] This halting of Chinese women's immigration and the subsequent Chinese Exclusion Act in 1822 prevented the "formation of families and generations among Chinese immigrants."[14]

For Japanese immigrants, while the Gentlemen's Agreement of 1907–1908 restricted the immigration of Japanese laborers to the United States, there remained a loophole, which Japanese immigrants took advantage of, where "parents, wives, and children of laborers already in America would be allowed to emigrate."[15] According to Ronald Takaki, "Thousands of women also entered Hawaii and the mainland through the same opening—66,926 of them between 1908 and 1924."[16] In addition, 20,000 women immigrated through the picture bride system: arranged marriages that occurred through the exchanging of photographs where wives and husbands did not typically meet until the women arrived in the United States. This occurred until 1921 when Japan agreed to terminate picture bride emigration in the "Ladies Agreement."[17] Unlike Chinese male immigrants, who largely formed bachelor communities due to immigration restrictions, this large influx of female Japanese immigrants allowed for families to be established and entrenched within Japanese American history. In this way, Japanese American racialization is the "material trace of the history of this 'gendering'" of immigration restriction.[18] In other words, immigration restriction gendered Japanese American communities where the reproduction of family enabled by the loopholes of the Gentlemen's Agreement meant that Japanese Americans' access to a nuclear family model was a direct result of immigration law and policies. Consequently, heteropatriarchal relations were artificially constituted through immigration law that allowed the nuclear family to form for Japanese immigrants but not for others. Utilizing Michael Warner's theorizations of reprosexuality, "the interweaving of heterosexuality, biological reproduction, cultural reproduction, and personal identity," I argue that the reprosexuality of Japanese American history relies upon reproducing history via generations in order to maintain legibility, visibility, and vitality.[19]

In addition, the Nisei are a focal point of Japanese American community identity because of their experiences of incarceration. In 1900 "there were only 269 Nisei children," but by the eve of Pearl Harbor, "the Nisei outnumbered the Issei by two to one."[20] In particular, as children of the first generation, the Nisei were citizens by virtue of being born in the United States, while the Issei could not naturalize.[21] Historian Yuji Ichioka proposes that these generational categories "were fundamentally political constructs" in which the "production of differences between the Issei and Nisei rested with their citizenship status, which was in and of itself a product of racial formation under white American hegemony."[22] Citizenship is not only a marker of generational differences between Issei and Nisei but is held up as proof that incarceration is, in fact, a wrong. The Nisei's access to citizenship, as well as their age, is then central to historical retellings of World War II in which the Nisei serve as evidence and archive of state racialized harm.[23] In this way, World War II incarceration is central to these generational narratives that produce community identity and thus belonging.

Because the majority of the Sansei did not experience incarceration, the death of the Nisei, the impending loss of this entire generation, has produced an anxious Japanese American community constantly grappling with what it means to lose that connection to incarceration. That connection, established through generations, is personal and familial. Generations are also constructed within a familial discourse, one that centers the nuclear family as the proper site of historical memory and legacy. Japanese American history is reliant upon a kind of regeneration, a familial reproduction of their World War II incarceration history that ensures that history will be remembered by future generations.[24] However, often the narrative descriptions of these groups are presented progressively within an assimilationist timeline, from Japanese immigrants to each following generation being further removed from their cultural heritage and, more importantly, from histories and memories of incarceration. Japanese American authenticity of identity is often established through the "proper" remembering of incarceration that is exemplified in Inouye's "look how far we've come" speech. In addition, the Japanese American community is changing with the growth of Shin-Issei and Shin-Nisei (post-1965 immigrants) as well as multiracial Japanese Americans.[25] The fear of Nisei death is rooted in these generational categories and hinges upon a generational reproduction where the Japanese American community places a deep emphasis on familial responsibility to maintain its vitality. If the vehicle to tell Japanese American history relies upon the nuclear family and heteronormative transfers of memory, how does this affect which kinds of narratives are remembered and which are forgotten?

This is important because these narratives remember incarceration in ways that collude with state narratives of redemption that allow the United States to imagine itself as a liberal democracy where racism ceases to exist. The reproduction of generational and historical narratives is intimately intertwined with the reproduction of both the proper citizen-subject *and* the state as guarantor of rights. In this introduction, I explore how Japanese American memory practices are structured by the struggle for and subsequent success of redress as it relates to state redemption. But first, I explore how Japanese American incarceration operated via disposability and erasure to better understand not only how redress became so important to the Japanese American community but how death became central to their visibility.

Incarceration: Death, Disposability, and Erasure

After the bombing of Pearl Harbor, President Franklin D. Roosevelt signed Executive Order 9066 authorizing the mass forced removal and incarceration of Japanese Americans from the West Coast. At the time, incarceration was justified as a "military necessity" within a language of national security, but it was also conceptualized by the War Relocation Authority (WRA) as "protecting" Japanese Americans from the possibility of violent crimes and riots in reaction to Pearl Harbor and "anti-racist" in its benevolence to help Japanese Americans assimilate. As I discuss in the following section, the Commission on Wartime Relocation and Internment of Civilians during the redress and reparations movement found that the incarceration of Japanese Americans during World War II was a product of "race prejudice, war hysteria, and a failure of political leadership."[26] However, I argue that incarceration—its dispossession, dislocation, and detainment of Japanese Americans—is a condition of disposability and erasure central to carceral logics. Redress is supposed to correct this, or, as I argue, it offers protection from this erasure that Japanese Americans experienced during incarceration. However, these vulnerabilities seep into contemporary commemorations of incarceration, and rather than narrate World War II incarceration through a narrative of resolution, I draw on theories of carcerality to situate incarceration within a longer history of containment. To understand the United States as a carceral state is to think about how the United States uses imprisonment at different historical moments to punish those outside the racial and sexual mainstream. To renarrate incarceration within this longer history opens up the possibility of comparative racial analysis and solidarities.

Drawing from Clyde Wood's theorization of "racialized social-spatial enclosures," or the space used to "establish stable control over specific territories and their populations' which are maintained by a system of militarized regulation, physical boundaries and social, political, and economic traps," I argue that World War II incarceration is a formation of a racialized social-spatial enclosure.[27] Additionally, in her foundational text, *Golden Gulag*, geographer Ruth Wilson Gilmore defines racism as "the state-sanctioned or extralegal production and exploitation of group-differentiated vulnerability to premature death."[28] Incarceration made Japanese Americans vulnerable to premature death through a "racialized social-spatial enclosure." Incarcerated Japanese Americans were deprived of decent housing, education, medicine, and a sense of security—and in fact were experiencing a death that was physically apparent in their disposability. Incarcerees were forced to live in unlivable conditions that dehumanized Japanese Americans' sense of identity and self—from sleeping on hay in horse stalls at fairgrounds and racetracks to the lack of privacy in the latrines and barracks to the languishing away waiting to find out what would happen to them and the constant surveillance from the administration, block leaders, and military police. The living conditions of incarcerees make visible how containment was secured through the effacement of Japanese Americans. Disposable to national security, Japanese Americans were "vulnerable to premature to death."

Another example is the questionnaire issued by the WRA as a technology to determine the loyalty or disloyalty of Japanese Americans. These questions asked incarcerees if they would be willing to serve in the U.S. army and if they would forswear allegiance to the Japanese emperor by swearing qualified allegiance to the United States.[29] By answering yes to the first question, Nisei men (of eligible draft age) were being asked to be willing to physically die as the ultimate proof of their loyalty. For Issei, who were not eligible for citizenship, answering yes to the second question rendered them stateless. If incarcerees answered no to either of the questions, they were classified as disloyal, segregated from those who were deemed loyal, and transferred to Tule Lake. Here, Japanese Americans were made to prove that they were capable of being citizens within the WRA's conflation of culture and loyalty with their literal bodies. They either must die (from war), be stateless and have even less access to protection, or be punished through separation from other bodies.[30]

While I explore the significance of the Nisei soldier in relation to redress later in this introduction, here I want to explore how death and visibility intersect and were mobilized by the state during World War II as a means of propagating a disavowal of racism for a particular geopolitical agenda. As Takashi Fujitani argues, the Japanese American soldier was needed to visibly prove to the rest of the world that the United States was fighting for freedom and democracy and not for the preservation of Western dominance in the Pacific. In addition, the logic of total war and the concept of manpower utilization persuaded the War Department to completely reverse its earlier decision and admit Japanese Americans into the army.[31] The segregation of Japanese American soldiers into separate units and the publicization of their exploits during the war strategically put their bodies (lives and deaths) on display to showcase this disavowal of racism. In this way, America was truly democratic because it allowed these young men to die for the nation. According to the Commission on Wartime Relocation and Internment of Civilians, in its seven campaigns, the 442nd (Japanese American segregated combat team) "took 9,486 casualties—more than 300 percent of its original infantry strength, including 600 killed."[32] These high casualty rates make visible the ways Japanese American bodies were expendable in the war, both in terms of a larger ideological struggle and on the battlefield. As one soldier remarked, "it was a high price to pay," but "it was to prove our loyalty which was by no means an easy task."[33] Ironically, to prove they were worthy of life, they must at least have been willing to die. Pointing out the ways these interests converged is not meant to discredit the loss suffered by these men, but rather to highlight the ways the inclusion of the Nisei soldier allows for the complete transformation of the Japanese American from being a "symbol of racial discrimination into a living representation of America's denunciation of racism."[34] Their death (because it is tied up in this geopolitical agenda) allows for the Japanese American to be narrated within a story of heroism that affords a particular kind of belonging—where they are celebrated as America's "model minority."

Similarly, in her book *Ends of Empire*, Jodi Kim demonstrates that after World War II, both Japan and Japanese Americans underwent a process of "gendered racial rehabilitation" from "former enemy [and enemy alien] to proper Cold War junior ally" and "model minority" respectively.[35] More specifically, before World War II, Japanese American farming "successes" on the West Coast, despite the Issei being unable to own land,[36] were a threat to white economic security and therefore deemed punishable by forced removal and incarceration. As Kim argues, incarceration was then articulated as a space for producing "properly assimilated and anticommunist liberal" Japanese American subjects.[37] Japanese Americans could learn to be "productive subjects without 'damaging' the environment, becoming hyper-competitive in any field, or contributing to California's 'maladjustments.'"[38] Kim articulates the U.S. occupation of Japan in a similar fashion, where "these gendered valences" also occur "through the trope of domestication and its related trope of 'domesticity'" where a former enemy nation is "demilitarize[ed] and feminiz[ed]" to produce "a sense of diminished masculinity for (former) patriarchs."[39] Through an analysis of Japanese American cultural producers, Kim shows how occupation and incarceration are "linked U.S. imperial projects" of gendered racial rehabilitation.[40] In other words, the successfully rehabilitated Japanese American body becomes one of the central figures through which U.S. democracy and empire could find legitimacy in a postwar era. Both Fujitani and Kim demonstrate the ways Japanese American "success" is utilized by the state to justify international geopolitical and domestic projects. In this way, Japanese American bodies and memories have a long history of being used by the state to sustain whiteness and nationhood. During World War II, Native American men had the highest rates per population to enlist, with "99 percent of all eligible Native Americans" registered for the draft by January 1942. Additionally, African Americans continued to serve in segregated units, escaping poverty produced by Jim Crow segregation only to return to these racialized spatial enclosures after the war.[41] However, the Nisei soldier and the rapidly shifting racialization of the Japanese American (from "enemy alien" to "model minority") marked Japanese American soldiers differently as the United States' global and national agenda changed. Grounded in these historical moments, Japanese Americans are recognized by the state as models for their "success" as patriotic soldiers and properly gendered racial subjects who were "liberal capitalist consuming and producing subjects."[42]

Disposability enforced by the racialized spatial enclosure of World War II incarceration was closely tied to the erasure of Japanese American personhood and their experiences of racialized violence at the hands of national security. Incarcerees were imprisoned away from the West Coast, dispersed from the ethnic enclaves and communities that threatened white economic prosperity, and hidden from view on or near Indigenous reservations. They were erased from view, and Americans could imagine forced removal and incarceration as white liberal benevolence that helped Japanese Americans become proper citizen-subjects. In other words, the dehumanization of incarceration could be erased through gendered racial rehabilitation, signaling a shift in Japanese American racialization. During and after redress, rehabilitation was less about Japanese American subjectivity and more about the rehabilitation and redemption of the state—more specifically, about how a recognition of Japanese American incarceration history could offer the state evidence of itself as a true liberal democracy. Incarceration, redress, and Japanese American racialization became important to studying an emerging neoliberal racial order. In the next section, I explore how this shift from death and erasure to resurrection occurs through redress and how a comparative analysis of this historical moment is necessary to our contemporary understandings of race and race relations.

Redress and Neoliberalism

Japanese American public performances of memory are important sites of interrogation because the logic of redress, most visible in these memorializations, is the epitome of contemporary neoliberal racial formation in the United States. Grace Kyungwon Hong defines neoliberalism as "an epistemological structure of disavowal," or "a means of claiming that racial and gendered violences are things of the past" by "affirming certain modes of racialized, gendered and sexualized life."[43] Hong argues that a "new neoliberal order arose based on the selective protection and proliferation of minoritized life as the very mechanism for the brutal exacerbation of minoritized death" in response to the social movements in the 1960s and 1970s.[44] I argue that Japanese Americans are central to this disavowal in a neoliberal racial order and obtain "invitation into reproductive respectability, so as to disavow its exacerbated production of premature death."[45] In this section, I explore how the struggle to obtain redress and reparations shifted memories of incarceration from the private sphere to a public national stage that mobilized these incarcerated experiences in the name of "truth." First, I show how the creation of the Commission on Wartime Relocation and Internment of Civilians and its subsequent reliance on testimony not only allowed Japanese American memories of their incarceration to be heard but also established a particular way of speaking about racial injury. As I argue later on, this way of speaking could be heard because the new neoliberal order needed to protect certain minoritized life. Second, the intertwining of testimony and narratives of racial injury that developed out of redress provided Japanese Americans with a continued way to remember what happened to them during World War II. These narratives, while always in flux and never stable, do continue to exist in the present moment.

Japanese American redress and reparations are often articulated as a defining historical moment for many reasons. First, the Civil Liberties Act of 1988 gave Japanese Americans a national apology and monetary compensation of $20,000 to individual survivors for their unjust incarceration during World War II. Second, through the creation of the Commission on Wartime Relocation and Internment of Civilians, the Japanese American community was given the opportunity to speak about their incarcerated experiences on a national platform.[46] The resulting commission's report was "rooted in both its hearings and archival research" after holding twenty days of hearings and taking testimony from more than 750 witnesses, including "Japanese Americans, Aleuts who had lived through the events of World War II, former government officials, public figures, interested citizens, and other professionals who had studied the subjects of the Commission's inquiry."[47] As a result, redress and reparations provided the Japanese American community "with the possibility of remembering and reclaiming their silenced pasts."[48] Because the Commission on Wartime Relocation and Internment of Civilians required Japanese Americans to testify as witnesses to and victims of racialized state harm, testimony became an important strategy and way of speaking for Japanese Americans that continues to this day. I argue that the creation of the commission established a dialogue between the state (as perpetrator) and Japanese

Americans (as victims/witnesses). As part of the "evidence" to be examined by the commission to determine the facts and circumstances surrounding Executive Order 9066 and its effects, Japanese American ways of remembering their incarceration are shaped by how the state was willing to listen to them almost forty years later.

This logic of testimony that was established through these hearings relied upon a transparent way of articulating damages and violence that could then be recorded in the official report. In fact, because monetary compensation was being considered, economic calculations of property loss became a mode of speaking to the state. Economic loss was a tangible way to express how the Japanese American community suffered. In the Commission on Wartime Relocation and Internment of Civilians' report, *Personal Justice Denied*, a section titled "Economic Loss" is divided into subsections that address the economic impacts of incarceration on agriculture and fishing, small businesses, white-collar workers, automobiles, and property disposal. At the end of the section, the Commission on Wartime Relocation and Internment of Civilians reports that

> the loss of liberty and the stigma of the accusation of disloyalty may leave more lasting scars, but the loss of worldly goods and livelihood imposed immediate hardships that anyone can comprehend. Moreover, it was the loss of so much one had worked for, the accumulated substance of a lifetime—gone just when the future seemed most bleak and threatening.[49]

This is not to say that Japanese Americans did not articulate loss in other ways or that the commission only took into consideration economic hardships rather than what are repeatedly referred to as "scars" in the report. However, to justify monetary compensation, loss becomes synonymous with the material loss of these "worldly goods" and "livelihood." In this way, loss can be calculated, compensated, and thus resolved. In her book *States of Injury: Power and Freedom in Late Modernity*, Wendy Brown suggests that the emergence of identity politics is rooted in the discourse of injury, which simultaneously contests the nation-state while reaffirming white masculine middle-class ideals that are paradigmatic of citizen formation.[50] In the moment of redress, we are able to see the intertwining of Japanese American identity (and thus memories) with a discourse of injury that relied upon economic calculations of a liberal democratic, propertied subject who had "worked for" an "accumulated substance of a lifetime" that was lost. The loss that can be articulated within the testimony is the loss of a proper citizen-subject. Japanese American incarceration is then remembered as an interruption to that citizen-subject, and therefore redress would resolve racial violence through a return to that proper subjecthood.

In addition, these hearings assume the idea that history can be recounted and retold, that the state can hear and listen, and that visibility and audibility before the state are a sufficient means of redressing violence. As a consequence of this, the legibility of said experiences was often articulated within narratives of patriotism, loyalty, masculinity, and never forgetting. In another section, "Military Service," the report finds that the "Nisei had indeed distinguished themselves" and "the question of loyalty had been most powerfully answered by a battlefield record of courage and sacrifice."[51] This section also opens with a quote from former senator S. I. Hayakawa, notoriously known for his conservative leadership and repression of the San Francisco State College strike (1968–1969). Here, we can see how military service as proof of one's ultimate loyalty and patriotism was a strategy for obtaining redress:

> "We are good Americans," they said. "We are good neighbors. We are useful and productive citizens. We love America and are willing to die for her." These messages were communicated by the industry of workers and businessmen and farmers, by their service to the communities in which they live, by their behavior of good citizens, and by the war record of the 442nd.[52]

Nisei war veterans (both alive and dead) were *proof* that Japanese Americans were not only loyal but "good" citizen-subjects. In this way, Daniel Inouye (as a starting point) is an important figure and fixture within Japanese American historical memory to unpack, and his significance reveals the complicated ways masculinity and patriotism make Japanese Americans visible as deserving of redress. As a highly decorated World War II veteran who served in the famed Japanese American segregated unit, the 442nd Regimental Combat Team, Inouye and other Japanese American soldiers became emblematic of Japanese American suffering, loss, and death. As I have argued, these masculinist patriarchal narratives gained legibility during the Japanese American redress and reparations movement as a prime example of Japanese American heroic sacrifice. Patriotism via enlistment became the main avenue of demonstrating one's loyalty to the United States (a tangible means of resolving anti–Japanese American sentiments that culminated in incarceration) during World War II and long after (during the struggle for redress). This kind of patriotism gains cultural capital through these historical retellings that frame veterans as emblematic of worth. Redress in combination with patriotism, loyalty, and success promises to alleviate the terrors of racialized violence that continued to linger long after incarceration's official ending. Here, Inouye becomes another part of that promise of resolution. Inouye is often identified as a key player in the passage of the Civil Liberties Act of 1988. He is credited with establishing the Commission on Wartime Relocation and Internment of Civilians as a means of garnering political and public support for redress and reparations. In addition, Inouye is one of the key founders of the Japanese American National Museum and served for many years as the chairman of the Board of Governors. Going back to Inouye's narration that began this introduction, his body (the absence of his arm, which he lost in the war) and self-narration are emblematic of what makes Japanese Americans visible to the state. Inouye as decorated veteran, political leader for redress, and founder of the National Museum exposes how patriotism, loyalty, visibility, and historical legibility are intimately intertwined.

In addition to the official apology and reparations, the Civil Liberties Act of 1988 also included the establishment of the Civil Liberties Public Education Fund, a federal program dedicated to educating the public about Japanese American World War II incarceration "in an effort to remind Americans that such events must never be allowed to happen again."[53] Not only were memories of incarceration allowed to be spoken through testimony, but they were now an important part of the lessons to be learned. The discourse of "never again" establishes a progressive temporality that presumes state violence is not happening in the current moment but is in fact always on the cusp of occurring. This discourse is a deployment of Holocaust memorialization, most notably articulated by the United States Holocaust Memorial Museum, and provides an important lesson in the "fragility of freedom, the myth of progress, and the need for vigilance in preserving democratic values" while teaching about the "dangers of unchecked hatred and the need to prevent genocide."[54] Thus, Japanese American memories of incarceration are in direct relation to Jewish cultural narratives of genocide and the Holocaust that evoke a nationalism that positions Japanese Americans as a carceral exception. In other words, World War II incarceration is a "bad" mode of imprisonment that is most closely related to the Holocaust and not mass incarceration. This relationship to the Holocaust and the inherent distancing from mass incarceration through public memory demonstrates how visibility and legitimacy are often gained on a national stage.[55]

Within the Japanese American community, the Civil Liberties Act of 1988 is remembered as a "triumph for the Nikkei community as much as it was a triumph of our democratic processes" because like the "many gains of the broader civil rights movement [it] demonstrated the strength and resilience of American democracy."[56] "Never again" and celebratory commemorations of the Civil

Liberties Act situate the state as reformed into a benign entity. More important than resolving the racial traumas of Japanese American World War II incarceration, Japanese American redress provided the state with the opportunity to renew "their traditional commitment to the ideals of freedom, equality, and justice."[57] Thus, Japanese American redress and reparations become an important part of disavowing racism. Relegating racial violence (incarceration) to a past that is resolved (through redress) means that the state can legitimate itself as the arbiter of freedom, equality, and justice even as it continues to make those outside the racial and sexual mainstream vulnerable to premature death.[58]

Testimony, memory, and historical truth not only served an important function during the commission hearings but continued to have what Karen M. Inouye terms a long "afterlife."[59] While I am interested in Japanese American incarceration as "afterlife" and the concrete actions that "breathe life" into these memories, *Carceral Entanglements* critically thinks about how trauma became testimony and thus recognizable to the state to significantly change how "afterlife" exists in the present moment. Japanese American redress shifted the "afterlife" of Japanese American incarceration where loss, trauma, and racial violence could be packaged as accumulated and then resolved by an official state apology and monetary compensation. In the next section, I explore how the shift in speaking, visibility, and legibility had unintended consequences. During and after Japanese American redress, Japanese American history, memories, and bodies could be used as "evidence" that racism was officially over (something it would constantly need to prove over and over in a post–civil rights era). We can also think about this in the larger context of testimony that emerged in a post–World War II era as a way of redressing, for example, the Holocaust, colonial harm, and apartheid.[60] Testimony as a technology of neocolonial and neoliberal governance acknowledges and then apologizes for racialized harm in order to disavow it in the present. Allowing the victims of racialized and colonial violence to make their experiences legible to the state serves to resolve the past and absolve the perpetrator—an important technology of state violence.

Unintended Consequences: Redress as Disavowal in the Neoliberal Racial Order

With the passing of the Civil Liberties Act of 1988, the state could absolve itself of any responsibility and guilt because it had officially apologized for incarcerating Japanese Americans by giving living victims $20,000.[61] Because they had been awarded redress and reparations, Japanese Americans now had to present their historical memories of incarceration within a neoliberal framework that presented racialized harm as a thing of the past. That is, the "bargain" promised protection from precarity and erasure (experienced during incarceration) in exchanged for a sanitized history. In the struggle for redress and reparations, Japanese Americans had learned to make themselves visible to the state through testimony as those who were "deserving" of an official apology. As I argued in the previous section, this often occurred through masculinist patriotic retellings of injury or economic calculations of material loss that made Japanese Americans worthy of state recognition and apology. The "afterlife" of these particular narratives became useful when juxtaposed with other groups of color.

In a post-redress era, deservingness often rested upon proper gendered and heteronormative behavior of "success" as these ideal citizen-subjects who had been wrongly incarcerated while committing no real "crime." For example, when arguing for redress, the Japanese American Citizens League (JACL) stated that even though the Issei could not become citizens, "they worked to create exemplary communities" and "generally took care of their own problems so that the public records showed the Japanese had hardly a person on the public welfare list or police blotters."[62] The imagery surrounding who constitutes someone on welfare is racialized, gendered, and sexualized. This kind of imagery was constituted through works like Daniel Patrick Moynihan's *The Negro Family: The Case for National Action*. This discourse of the public charge revolves around the disciplining of the Black family that exists outside heteronormative nuclear family formations, which is seen as contributing to their low socioeconomic status. The JACL's seemingly innocuous statement in reality plays on this imagery to constitute the Issei and thus Japanese Americans as proper citizen-subjects who are deserving of redress because they do not rely on state resources for survival. Their value was established upon discourses of anti-blackness at a crucial moment where the state was legitimizing its transformation from a welfare state to a warfare state.[63] Here, I draw on Lisa Cacho's articulation of the violence of value where "human value is made intelligible through racialized, sexualized, spatialized, and state-sanctioned violences" and social value is both "contested and condoned through legally inflected notions of morality."[64] While Cacho looks specifically at the law, my work thinks about the ways forms of public memory also participate in the maintenance of these racialized value hierarchies.

Even the success of Japanese American redress itself provided the opportunity to deny African Americans and other groups of color reparations for historical racialized harm. Historian Alice Yang Murray writes that opponents of African American reparations rejected "the idea that one can determine the effects of slavery on later generations" and also contrasted Japanese Americans as "patriotic and hardworking" model minorities with "undeserving African American militants."[65] In addition, the Civil Liberties Act of 1988 intentionally awarded reparations to "former living victims" to then close off the possibility of other groups seeking reparations. The language of the "living victim" substantiates a progressive temporality in which past racial harm can only be resolved through life and privileges the "witness" to provide proof. It refuses to recognize the way that past racial violence and trauma can linger in the present and in the generations that come after. To acknowledge racial violence outside of the bodies of those who experienced it is to understand how systems of oppression (such as containment) shift and transform throughout history. To give reparations to groups whose "victims" are no longer living or did not necessarily live through an "event" would disrupt how the United States as a carceral state narrates itself as nonracist in a post–civil rights era.

For Japanese American redress, the state repairs damages from a historical event, one that is neatly contained in the past, that can then be assessed and later apologized for and perhaps even compensated. The past is an important component of reparations in the United States because it functions to narrate the state within a progressive temporality that posits neoliberal inclusion as an end point. Here, we can see how remembering Japanese American incarceration and reparations operates within the historical framework of carceral neoliberalism. Carceral expansion is legitimized in the moment of apology because it operates to disavow racialized punishment via containment in the present. Apology also serves as a technology of neoliberal and neocolonial governance to ensure that contemporary racialized harm cannot be recognized in the present.

However, other groups struggling for reparations do not necessarily draw on Japanese American redress as their ultimate goal and do not posit the state as the arbiter of freedom and democracy. Black and Native American reparative claims disrupt the temporality established by reparations. Both Black and Native American reparative claims challenge a bounded and progressive temporality where racialized violence cannot necessarily be redressed monetarily. For example, monetary compensation cannot repair "land theft, genocide, ethnocide, and above all, the denial of the fundamental right to self-determination."[66] Reparative justice for settler colonial violence means a restructuring of settler society through "the restoration of Indian lands."[67] The current model for redress, with its reliance on the state and capitalist exchange for past racial harm, is already rooted in settler structures of governance that exist by denying Native American self-determination. The struggle for Black reparations does not necessarily solely ask for monetary compensation but rather seeks reparations that "improve the lives of African descendants in the United States for future generations to come," foster "economic, social and political parity," and "allow for full rights of self-determination."[68] Thus, proponents of Black reparations recognize that reparations can and need to "be in as many forms as necessary to equitably (fairly) address the many forms of injury caused by chattel slavery and its continuing vestiges." Pointing to the continuing vestiges disrupts the progressive temporality established by Japanese American redress and holds the state accountable for racialized violences that exist in the present. In addition, reparations are an entire restructuring of U.S. society that cannot merely be repaired with monetary compensation.

The "success" of both Japanese Americans and redress allowed the state to simultaneously claim that racism was over via reparative resolution and continue to deny life-sustaining resources to people of color. *Carceral Entanglements*, then, seeks to place Japanese American incarceration and redress within a longer history of the carceral to disrupt the way the United States imagines itself as a nation of freedom and democracy in the neoliberal moment. In order to do this, I interrogate the contradictory location of Japanese Americans and their memories as simultaneous victims of carceral violence and those who gain privilege from redress. For example, geographer Ruth Wilson Gilmore argued that during the 1980s and 1990s, the contemporary prison system "was constructed deliberately—but not conspiratorially—of surpluses that were not put back into work in other ways."[69] What it did was "make use of a lot of idle land, get capital invested via public debt, and take more than 160,000 low wage workers off the street."[70] Through this shift from a welfare-warfare to a workfare-warfare state, "the new state built itself in part by building prisons" is where Gilmore locates the crisis of this particular historical moment. By connecting the prison to these state logics, Gilmore is able to show how the prison functions as a geographic "fix" for these economic crises stemming from the "crumbling foundations of [an] old order."[71] The buildup of what Beth Richie calls the "prison nation" also relies upon "the ability of leaders to create fear (of terrorism or health-care reform); to identify scapegoats (like immigrants or feminists); and to reclassify people as enemies of a stable society (such as prisoners, activists, hip-hop artists)."[72] Here, Japanese Americans were reclassified as "enemy aliens" during World War II, when racial fear was produced to justify incarceration. However, as I showed earlier, after redress, Japanese Americans became essential to the breakdown of the welfare state as they are positioned as "successful" in relation to the "failures" of other groups of color deemed racially and sexually deviant. Japanese American public memory is then intimately connected to racialized discourses and carceral logics (even as it struggles against them) by relying on generationality and normativity as vehicles of visibility. In the growth of the prison nation, Japanese Americans, in exchange for redress, distance themselves from other groups of color, which ends up sustaining the buildup itself.

Carceral Entanglements also thinks about the relationship between the colonial and the carceral—their similarities as well as their differences and how they sustain one another. Memory practices, such as the fight for official recognition of former sites of incarceration as having national significance, are predicated on Indigenous dispossession and containment by the National Park Service preservation in conjunction with reservations. Japanese American preservation is often rooted in settler colonial logics. As Patrick Wolfe explains, the increase of Indigenous people obstructed settler access to land that could then be turned into private property, a cornerstone of liberal democracy.[73] Preservation can only occur through a continued means of maintaining settler access to territory. To disrupt this disappearance of Indigenous peoples from the landscape (past, present, and future), I explore the complicated ways Japanese Americans who were organizing around carceral memories were confronted with their contradictory location as both settler and incarceree. To situate the Asian (and, in this case, the Japanese American) as a settler who benefits from U.S. settler colonialism is to look, as Alyosha Goldstein suggests, at these "complex reciprocities, seemingly opaque disjunctures, and tense entanglements" that offer us "new insights for anticolonial struggle."[74] And yet, at the same time, as I explore later, there exist slippages in memories of carceral and colonial confinement in which reservation and incarceration are comparatively placed together to challenge racialized punishment in its varied forms. Therefore, it is important to examine the relationship between Japanese American memories and those of other groups of color to understand how a settler state and a prison nation are maintained.

It is important to point out that while Japanese Americans occupy this contradictory location due to state racialized violence and a neoliberal racial order, not all Japanese Americans mobilize their memories of incarceration in this way. For example, Diane Fujino has done extensive work on the political organization, the Nisei Progressives (1949), who broke away from the "dominant narrative of postwar assimilation" in the early Cold War to develop a movement challenging "the transformation [of the Japanese American] from incarceration to integration."[75] The Nisei Progressives instead embodied a "deep solidarity in linking their liberty with justice for others in ways that often required a risk or sacrifice to direct self-interest."[76] *Carceral Entanglements* focuses on how the contradictory location continues to shape Japanese American memory today in order to explore futures that do not replicate the carceral and instead push for an abolitionist future.

Chapter Breakdown

Carceral Entanglements is organized by sites of memory significant to the Japanese American community and the preservation of World War II incarceration history. Each site is examined to understand how memory is reproduced (generationally or not) and read for moments of interracial solidarity and connection that either reinforce or disrupt the United States as a carceral state. Understanding how Japanese American memory functions in the maintenance of neoliberal race relations can help illuminate the dangers of Asian American inclusion and visibility in a post–civil rights era. It also provides continuous lessons for remembering and organizing across difference (time, space, etc.) through an axis of relationality that can position multiple groups of color together in the fight against racial punishment and containment.

In Chapter 1, "From Distance to Proximity, Japanese Americanness and Blackness: The Limitations of Post-Redress Japanese American Incarceration Narratives," I compare and contrast two events held or sponsored by the Japanese American National Museum: the 2011 Gala Dinner (that began this introduction) and the 2015 Los Angeles Day of Remembrance. Located in Little Tokyo, Los Angeles, California, this museum serves as an important community archive that legitimizes and makes visible Japanese American memory, culture, and community as historically significant. This chapter explores how narratives of death function within Japanese American memory to sustain narratives of progress or resolution by drawing on discourses of either antiblackness or multiculturalism. Despite the seeming difference between these two events, with the creation of distance or proximity to Blackness, both events failed to consider how Japanese American positionality and thus memories play a part in sustaining the carceral state even while attempting to uncover it. In this chapter, a convergence among history, family, and violence emerges in these narratives that make visible racialized subjects' reliance upon gender and sexual regulation. I argue that a queering of these heteronormative transfers of memory is about a refusal to rely upon cultural nationalist and masculinist narrative logics and reckon with the violence of the nuclear family.

Shifting to the virtual space of the digital archive, Chapter 2, "The Intimate Connection among Truth, Memory, and Life: Refusal in the Densho Digital Archive," explores Densho: The Japanese American Legacy Project to deconstruct how community remembering is inherently tied up in the biopolitical logic of life and death. Exploring Densho's website and promotional materials demonstrates how death haunts the archive in a variety of ways: it serves as part of its mission to document stories before they are gone forever while giving purpose to the stories that are meant to serve as lessons for younger generations. However, in many ways, death is constantly banished, as archiving becomes a way not only to provide "living proof" of Japanese American incarceration through the video recording of personal histories but also forms a way of living beyond death. There is an intimate connection among truth, memory, and life, which are seen as being sustained by the passing on of stories through a discourse of family and lineage that centers the importance of Japanese American incarceration to historical memory. But death, trauma, and forgetting manage to find their way into the oral histories and cannot be completely banished from the archive. In an examination of Densho's curriculum development, a component of its archive that offers concrete lesson plans for sixth-through-twelfth-grade educators, I argue that a centering of Japanese American incarceration is actually decentered when comparing World War II to other moments of racialized violence, opening up the possibility of learning about a longer carceral history that is central to the United States.

Chapter 3, "The Colonial and the Carceral: Building Relationships between Japanese Americans and Indigenous Groups in the Owens Valley," takes part in the growing dialogue that is thinking about the convergence of Indigenous nations and Asian American communities within the carceral state. Assessing the carceral state across diverse communities contributes to the conversation about the settler state, which uses multiple logics of containment, surveillance, and punishment to maintain its power. More specifically, I explore how the solar ranch proposed by the Los Angeles Department of Water and Power (LADWP) threatened not just the viewshed of Manzanar (a former WWII incarceration site now preserved by the National Parks Service) but exposed the layers of colonial violence in the Owens Valley, first by white ranchers and then by the LADWP, which diverted Owens Valley (where Manzanar National Historic Site is located) water to Los Angeles. In the fight against the LADWP, Japanese American and Indigenous peoples of the Owens Valley worked together for the first time to eventually defeat the LADWP, building important coalitional relationships. From my ethnographic fieldwork (participant observation and interviews), I discovered that this historic fight not only put these different groups in conversation with each other but also forced a recognition of the ways the colonial and the carceral sustain each other.

And finally, Chapter 4, "NSU Cultural Night and Generational Transmissions of Memory: Performative Disruptions and Other Futures," looks at how Nisei death informs a transfer of responsibility to younger generations of Japanese Americans to care for history and community when the Nisei are gone. For the Japanese American community, Japanese American youth are the "future" and are often positioned as the community's singular hope of surviving. In this chapter I look specifically at the Nikkei Student Union's Cultural Nights at the University of California, Los Angeles, to analyze how Japanese American college students engage with these generational transmissions of memory through the medium of performance. I argue that through performance (in particular script writing and acting), Japanese American youth grapple with the charges of generational responsibility, sometimes embracing it and other times rejecting it. These performative disruptions often highlight the limitations of the Japanese American historical memory that form community identity as a way of opening up spaces of connection.

And finally, I conclude by exploring how Japanese American organizing has continued to shift at various historical moments: from 9/11 to Trump's election campaign and presidency and the COVID-19 pandemic. I mark how memories of incarceration continue to move toward more interracial, intergenerational, and feminist discussions, solidarities, and possibilities.

1

From Distance to Proximity, Japanese Americanness and Blackness

The Limitations of Post-Redress Japanese American Incarceration Narratives

> Today I stand before you, Lane, when I was first declared an enemy alien on December the seventh, and today I am president pro tempore, third in line for the presidency. That's not too bad.
> —Daniel Inouye at the Japanese American National Museum 2011 Gala Dinner

> Every twenty-eight hours a Black man, woman, or child is murdered by the police or vigilante law enforcement. An estimated 25.1 percent of Black women live in poverty, this is higher than any other ethnic group. The average life expectancy for trans Black/ transgendered women is just thirty-five years.
> —Dr. Curtiss Takada Rooks, 2015 Day of Remembrance Los Angeles

I begin this chapter with these two different moments to mark the contrasting ways Japanese Americans remember their incarceration. Through a discourse of Japanese American "success," the late senator Daniel Inouye strategically garners donations from wealthy individuals and businesses in order to sustain Japanese American knowledge production via the Japanese American National Museum. In utilizing a narrative of "look how far we've come," Inouye ultimately distances himself from those who have remained racialized enemies of the state. This distancing from other groups of color legitimates Japanese American history and experiences often at the expense of other groups of color. On the other hand, Rooks makes visible the way the state devalues Black lives today and narrates through a discourse of proximity that Japanese Americans should care about police brutality, antiblack racism, and mass incarceration as former incarcerees. Highlighting the ways Black and Japanese

Americans' lives were once historically intertwined, the organizers of the Day of Remembrance event hoped to garner Japanese American support for Black lives. In this chapter, I argue that Japanese American public memory (such as these two Japanese American community events) not only produces knowledge about Japanese American history and identity but often unknowingly participates in neoliberal logics. These logics justify the death and destruction of "deviant" populations, including the structuring of feelings that allows state violence to persist. By contrasting the Japanese American National Museum's 2011 Gala Dinner with the 2015 Day of Remembrance Los Angeles, I examine how these opposing narratives both rely upon a discourse of generational responsibility that privileges heteronormative family formations where Japanese Americans are seen as "ideal" citizens performing "proper" gender roles. Taking seriously the limits of the previously mentioned strategies, this chapter considers Japanese American incarceration from a contradictory location: it is simultaneously a site where technologies of carcerality work to demonize and dehumanize Japanese Americans in ways that legitimize punishment and imprisonment as well as a site of rehabilitation and normativization. A queer critique of Japanese American incarceration history provides an alternative narrative to discourses of "never again" that positions abolition at the center of solidarity work.

The Japanese American National Museum as Community Archive

The Japanese American National Museum in Little Tokyo, Los Angeles, opened in 1992. The idea for a museum was generated by two distinct groups: businesspeople and World War II veterans. These two groups came together with a common vision "to ensure that Japanese Americans' heritage and cultural identity were preserved."[1] With the passing of the Issei and Nisei, they "realized that their children and grandchildren the Sansei and Yonsei were often unaware of the hardships and successes of earlier generations."[2] The National Museum as a community archive would ensure that their lives and experiences would be remembered long after they were gone. In her narration of the importance and significance of the National Museum, former executive president of the National Museum Irene Y. Hirano argued that "by placing the Japanese American experience within the context of American history and by working to improve the understanding and appreciation of ethnic and cultural diversity, the National Museum has striven to serve and enrich a global audience."[3] And not only does the museum interpret the past, but the "National Museum is also committed to building bridges among ethnic and cultural groups for the future," believing that their institution brings "together people in the telling of their stories."[4] In the present moment, the National Museum situates itself as an institution that reaches "across diverse ethnic communities nationally" while seeking "new global partners to explore the relevancy of history to current events."[5] After September 11, remembering Japanese American incarceration was discussed as even more important in underscoring the "need to ensure that the loss of civil liberties reflected in our history is not repeated." Hirano saw the post-9/11 moment as opening up conversations and bringing "together two communities affected and then intertwined by world events nearly sixty years apart."[6] In this way, Japanese American community and the knowledge produced by and about the community, often see the relevance and urgency in sharing the lessons of incarceration so that it may never happen again. By utilizing the logic of "never again," Japanese Americans are allowed to position themselves as model citizens who stand up for other groups of color experiencing similar injustices.

And yet, one of the main ways the National Museum financially sustains itself is through the monetary contributions of various museum stakeholders ranging from individuals to large corporations such as American Airlines or Wells Fargo. The annual gala dinner, as the largest fundraising event for the National Museum, is simultaneously a space of community celebration and business—an intertwining of Nikkei community vitality with money from wealthy donors who are encouraged throughout the night to support the museum in any way possible. Attendees can bid on donated items during the silent auction, purchase raffle tickets to win a flight to Japan, or, as I explore later in the chapter, place a bid to fund schoolchildren visiting the museum. The dinner is an important site of interrogation. Despite the apparent contradiction between the museum's mission of preserving marginalized history for public consumption and public good with its need for capital, it is the night of this gala dinner where these two seemingly opposing forces are visibly intertwined. In order to continue to exist, the museum must ensure financial security by featuring itself and, by extension, Japanese Americans as "successful" or "worthy" of one's monetary contribution. Quietly the museum takes on the work of "producing and managing forms of sexual and racial difference that meet the terms of capitalism and the state" in order to sustain itself where the "reproduc[tion] of categories of deserving and underserving" occurs along the "lines of legible and illegible identities."[7] In other words, the National Museum unintentionally does the insidious work of supporting state-sponsored forms of inequality and disenfranchisement even as it challenges them.[8]

At the Japanese American National Museum's 2011 Gala Dinner, "Continuing Family Stories: The Expanding Nikkei Community," the celebration was articulated as an opportunity to expand Japanese American histories by deliberately shifting the focus away from incarceration to the post–World War II era. Analyzing the way the Japanese American community is seeking to utilize a language of lineage and legacy that situates the past as a way of legitimating the present and a specific future, I explore the ways death (as the past that needs to be remembered) and education (about the past for the vitality of the future) are intertwined not only as a way of furthering the museum's mission but also as a means of interpellating Japanese Americans as proper, worthy citizen-subjects. By situating the dinner's theme, fundraising mission, and articulation of history within a larger context of Japanese American nationalist remembering, I point to the ways these modes of memory reproduce the kind of surveillance and carcerality that operated during wartime incarceration.

The Parameters of a Gala Dinner: The Temporalities of "Look How Far We've Come" and "Where We Are Going"

The focus on celebration and capital establishes very particular temporalities. The temporality of "look how far we've come" situates the community as "successful" while the temporality of "where we are going" envisions its "successful" future as a way to entice attendees to desire to be part of it through financial contributions. But this conceptualization of time through success also posits the past as the authority where the dead and the not-quite dead are resurrected back to life in order to serve "the purpose of glorifying the new struggles."[9] For example, the dinner begins with a tribute video remembering important community members with ties to the National Museum who passed away in the last year. The video is composed of small excerpts from previously recorded interviews conducted by the museum, and each clip provides a particular glimpse at what each individual was best known for. Included in this video was William Hohri, who filed the court case against the United States for redress; Frank Emi, a draft resister; Hisaye Yamamoto, author of *Seventeen Syllables*; Wally Yonamine, Nisei baseball pioneer; Toshiko Takaezu, artist and professor at Princeton University; and University of California, Los Angeles (UCLA) coach John Wooden, from the Japanese American basketball documentary *Crossover*. This featuring of death is sorrowful in its language of loss but also simultaneously brings that person back to life. By watching the interview clips, the deceased are resurrected even in the moment you are reminded that they are no longer here. And even as we are meant to mourn the loss of these important community members through this remembrance video, we are also expected to acknowledge what makes this community great. Those who are memorialized in this video are those whose contributions are worthy of our attention and remembrance. As the Japanese American community mourns these individuals, "they anxiously conjure up the spirits of the past to their service and borrow from them names, battle slogans and costumes in order to present the new scene of world history in this time-honored disguise and this borrowed language."[10] In other words, the dead are utilized by the community to situate the National Museum's recent or "new" knowledge production within a legacy of successful individuals. In this way, the dinner is a space where history's terrors are domesticated into safely consumable narratives and emotions.[11] The dinner as a performance of Japanese American identity demands a particular relationship to community and history that inherently expects a particular affective response from their dinner guests. The dinner aspires to make the audience feel a sense of belonging and community that should propel attendees to donate money that is also meant to legitimate a particular kind of knowledge production. It also situates the National Museum's survival as community survival—one that can only be understood in "terms of profit rather than in terms of human need."[12] Throughout the night, the convergences among history, profit, and community through "success" recur in different moments that are as violent as they are problematic.

Another way the dinner utilizes "success" is to talk about the National Museum itself as a legitimate educational institution that attendees should want to support. This can only allow for certain responses and emotions to emerge in the celebration of the National Museum. For example, throughout the night and the program, congratulations were made to the museum for being awarded the 2010 National Medal for Museum and Library Services. An image of the president of the National Museum standing with First Lady Michelle Obama with the award in hand constantly circulated throughout the night, as it appeared both in the program and on the reception room's viewing screen. To be recognized for such an award, to be recognized as third in the line for the presidency (Inouye), to be recognized as "successful" by the state—all these place the gala dinner within liberal multicultural narratives of progress sustained by Obama's presidency. In other words, the gala dinner finds itself operating in and benefitting from "a sweeping political sentimentality and popular cultural narrative of progress, hope, change, and racially marked nationalist optimism."[13] The temporality of "look how far we've come" is legitimized by

Obama's Blackness, which marks his presidency as evidence of a "post-racial" society. This "liberal valorization" also mobilizes Japanese American memory to sustain antiblackness by disavowing it. The celebration of the museum's professional success is intimately tied to the success of the post-racial nation. These successes show longtime and potential supporters that the work of the museum is not only vital to the community but to the nation as well and thus is worthy of money. Donors even made financial contributions by placing advertisements in the program that were dedicated to the museum's National Medal.

The gala dinner is meant to celebrate the National Museum's successes, but celebrations within liberal multicultural narratives of progress are violent processes. This celebration informs the audience how far Japanese Americans have come from their incarcerated pasts. It shows the audience that where they are now is because of their (economic) successes and that it can continue that way if they donate money. Celebrating this inherently ignores how racialized violence operates by capitalizing on minoritized success as evidence of minorized failure. The dichotomy of minoritized success and failure is represented as individualized rather than systemic and can prevent Japanese American community spaces from remembering or seeing their history as bound up with other racialized groups. The gala dinner guides its audience through performance after performance of celebration and ceremony; breaking down how it does this allows for an examination of how carceral logics are sustained.

Continuing Family Stories: The Language of Lineage and Legacy

As previously mentioned, the National Museum emerged from a fear of the "permanent loss" of Japanese American history, where founding members directed the "focus to the preservation and documentation of the Issei and Nisei generations."[14] For the Japanese American community, the National Museum became a way not only to address their literal absence from mainstream histories and archives but to legitimize that history within a discourse of diversity. Throughout the dinner, attendees were constantly reminded of the National Museum's successes in preserving such a history and instantly propelled into a "new" phase of our story. This desire to expand history was purposely about articulating a Japanese American identity that did not revolve around incarceration. In addition, while the Japanese American community has always been concerned with preserving living histories in the face of looming death, it is this physical loss of the Nisei that prompts the National Museum to rethink their relationship to the past. It is "the inevitable passing of the generations [that] has brought into question the ability of [the] Nikkei community to maintain its vitality."[15] Fearing and seeing their own disappearance intertwined with that of the Nisei, the National Museum is forced to relegitimate and revitalize their mission. As a result, the National Museum identifies the post–World War II era and subsequently "the Sansei and Yonsei generations and the arrival of a new group of immigrants from Japan beginning in the 1950s" as its new subjects of inquiry.[16]

These "new" immigrants, in particular, otherwise known as Shin-Issei and Shin-Nisei, have been a "major topic of conversation among activist Americans of Japanese ancestry."[17] While the existence of Shin-Issei is recognized, Japanese Americans grappling with these new immigrants have prompted questions about what it means to be Nikkei, asking, first, "is it blood, kinship, descent, self-identification, or affiliation?"[18] And therefore, "What are the ways and possibilities new immigrants might be integrated into a larger reconfigured Nikkei identity?"[19] And yet, as Tritia Toyota finds in her 2012 essay, "The New Nikkei: Transpacific Shin Issei and Shifting Borders of Community in Southern California," the "changing demography of the U.S. Nikkei community" is often articulated as one of disconnect where "the difficulties surrounding the lack of shared language and equally important a common history" have resulted in the "elusive[ness]" of "building ethnic ties between" the two groups.[20] "Shin" translates to "new" and "refers to all Japanese who are post–World War II arrivals in order to distinguish them from the initial nineteenth century diaspora."[21] In many ways, the disconnect is shaped by World War II, not only because of the postwar immigration policy shifts but because it was a significant marker of shared trauma and history. If shared history, reproduced by generations, is what constitutes American Nikkei group identity, then how does one bridge that disconnect?

At the 2011 Gala Dinner, the National Museum attempted to do that by utilizing a language of lineage and legacy to incorporate this "new" history into the Japanese American experience. The National Museum articulated "this new group's history [as] reach[ing] back 50 years or more with family stories reminiscent of the original immigrants and their descendants."[22] Throughout the program and dinner, they reiterated that they will "work diligently to find and document the family stories that have been accumulating during" this neglected era.[23] This continuation of family stories eases the National Museum's anxiety about having to establish a "new" past that authorizes this "new" present they are envisioning. This expansion of history desires not only to move away from World War II but to make visible the connections between Japanese Americans and Japan. It can imagine this history as always having been there, merely overshadowed by World War II incarceration and redress, and thus can situate these stories as belonging to a Japanese American historiography. This language also serves to naturalize a progression of Japanese American history within a linear temporality of progress that can only ever situate Japanese American experiences as "successful." The honoring of successful Japanese businesspeople as transnational cultural ambassadors and their incorporation into Japanese American history as always having been there is meant to firmly establish a common history.

This common history allows for Japanese American history to progress and expand beyond World War II and is articulated as being "healthy for all involved."[24] Here, the Japanese American community is revitalized, or brought back from the brink of death, disappearance, and irrelevancy. Relating to the past in this familial and thus heteropatriarchal way reifies the National Museum itself while mobilizing the family as a proper subject of study—one that is worthy of historical recognition and deserving of state visibility. The title of the gala dinner itself, "Continuing Family Stories: The Expanding Nikkei Community," demonstrates how the metaphor of "family" is used to incorporate histories and narratives that were once outside cultural nationalist boundaries of what constituted Japanese American community and history. Here, "family" is used to bring these narratives into the generational narratives that constitute Japanese American history. "Family" and generationality work hand in hand to legitimate history. Consequently, the family as a unifying narrative institutes a language of obligation and debt to the community to reproduce itself and unintentionally disciplines subjects who remain outside cultural nationalist rememberings of the past.[25]

Three Honorees: Cultural Ambassadors as the New Subjects of History

The dinner sought to honor three individuals, representative of the National Museum's desire to acknowledge previously ignored histories. These honorees are not just emblematic of different immigration patterns, but their contributions to the community are constituted through art, beauty, and food. At the same time, this focus on the preservation of Japanese culture revolves around these individuals' ability to operate within a global economy. Honored with the Cultural Ambassador Award, Stan Sakai, a commercial artist and illustrator best known as the creator of the samurai rabbit character Usagi Yojimbo (1984), a samurai rabbit, was recognized because of his work's ability to share Japanese culture and history with the rest of the world. Similarly, Jane Aiko Yamano, honored with the Creative Visionary Award for her ability to modernize the traditional Japanese kimono and entice young people around the world to wear it, was recognized as having revitalized an important part of Japanese culture indicative of the postwar era.[26] And recipient of the Lifetime Achievement Award, Noritoshi Kanai, the Japanese executive of the food importer business Mutual Trading Company, was recognized for his desire to provide the United States with access to quality Japanese food and preserve Japanese food culture around the world. Within this rhetoric of culture and the global economy, the National Museum identifies these individuals as successful, culturally and financially. In this postwar era, the ideal citizen-subject is no longer confined to the nation-state but is someone who can operate within this global economy that is necessitated on the commodification of difference. Making Japanese culture available for consumption ensures its vitality but also intimately links Japanese Americans to Japan in very particular ways.[27]

Through the honorees, the National Museum is narrativizing the postwar era as a moment when the Sansei are coming of age and when the "exchange and sharing of culture across the Pacific has become more prevalent than ever."[28] In our dinner programs, the National Museum provides historical background to understand this major shift within the Japanese American community. Because of the Immigration Act of 1924, "immigration was reduced to a trickle," and most of the growth in the community came from the births of the Sansei generation.[29] However, with "the passage of the 1965 Immigration Act, which abolished the discriminatory national origins quotas, immigration from Japan and Asia suddenly was placed on equal footing with Europe."[30] The National Museum identifies this influx of Japanese immigrants as crucial to the Japanese American community and the United States. It is this articulation of these new immigrants as cultural ambassadors that allows the Japanese American community not only to make and see connections to Japan but also to narrativize itself within a discourse of economic and cultural exchange that ultimately validates the United States as a geopolitical power of benevolence. This situating of Japanese American historiography and community as beneficiaries of United States benevolence is not a new narrative, but it is one whose recurrence needs to be problematized.

For example, the visibility of the heroic Nisei soldier could simultaneously prove Japanese American loyalty via the ultimate sacrifice of death and provide evidence that the United States was not racist and indeed fighting for democracy and freedom unlike axis powers. Symbolically the Nisei soldier served to disavow racism within the United States even as the Japanese American community remained incarcerated behind barbed wire.

Similarly, the way the struggle for redress is remembered relies upon a redemption of the state that positions Japanese Americans as worthy of an apology and compensation. As Victor Bascara argues, by highlighting the ways Japanese Americans achieved "success" despite racial hardships and incarceration, the United States could demonstrate "how the system [could] correct itself without the need for radical change."[31]

Showing the ways Japanese American history and imaginings of community identity converge with those of the state, I want to consider how the National Museum also aligns its "new" historiography with the United States' imagining of itself in the postwar era and within this contemporary global terrain and economy. The Immigration Act of 1965, in opposition to the 1924 Immigration Act, is characterized as life affirming and, more specifically, a legislation that reinvigorates the Japanese American community with a diversity of peoples and experiences. Unlike the previous era, power now operates as a "potentially productive rather than exclusively negative force."[32] In this way, Japanese American historiography colludes with state power and is unable to critically think about the ways this new mode of power, or the Immigration Act of 1965 itself, creates the conditions for even more exacerbated forms of death. In this way, the global citizen and ideal citizen-subject are "accorded forms of 'pastoral' care" that other citizens are not.[33] Within this same logic of being cultural ambassadors, the National Museum forces our attention to the recent natural disasters in Japan by sharing stories, showing a video montage of footage from Japan, and presenting a musical tribute "to the spirit of the Japanese people."[34] As cultural ambassadors, the National Museum asks that attendees donate money to the Red Cross in the name of the museum. Japanese victims of the 2011 Tōhuku earthquake and tsunami as well as the Fukushima Daiichi nuclear disaster are seen as worthy of aid and care, which establishes them firmly within this global economy of benevolence. Looking at the directions money flows at the dinner via donations demonstrates how transnational connections are being solidified within this familial narrative.

Rethinking Generation: Rupture and Reification

In addition to this rhetoric of the cultural ambassador, the National Museum made sure to highlight the ways these individual honorees did not and could not fit into a Japanese historiography previously invested in categories of "generation," such as Issei and Nisei, as a way to signify that their production of knowledge was progressing. Of the three honorees, Kanai immigrated in 1964, representing a newer generation of immigrants, while Yamano was born in the United States but returned to Japan to fulfill her role as the heir to her grandmother's beauty business and Sakai is the son of a Nisei father and Japanese-born mother. While none of these honorees can fit themselves into the already existing frameworks for understanding Japanese American history, the National Museum narrativizes the Sansei generation through a discourse of "progress" that relies upon the very categories it seeks to distance itself from. Alongside the different immigration pattern of Japanese in the postwar era, many Sansei were attending colleges and being moved by "social causes" such as redress and became involved in fighting to "pursue change within their communities and within their country."[35] They are characterized as the generation that pushed their "grandparents and parents to share their experiences during the war years so it would not be lost to history."[36] In this way, the National Museum is unable to decentralize incarceration entirely from its production of knowledge. Or more precisely, the National Museum is unable to articulate why incarceration (its violences and traumas) may persist in the generations that did not directly experience it.[37] But what marks this generation as unique is that they had many more opportunities available to them than the Nisei and Issei. According to the National Museum, the Sansei had "more choices and greater acceptance into mainstream society," but that ultimately "means that [they] are not always connected to their cultural heritage or their ethnic communities."[38] In this way, the National Museum utilizes the narrative of Sansei "progress" in relation to their parents and grandparents, inadvertently marking the "progress" of the United States. With the civil rights and liberation movements of the 1960s and 1970s making visible the ideological and necropolitical formations constituted through white supremacy, power is forced to shift to accommodate the demands being made by these nationalisms. Even as the National Museum narrates the Sansei as an integral part of those movements and struggles, it simultaneously situates them within a model minority discourse, serving as "proof" that communities of color can materially and economically "succeed." Japanese American racialization through the language of the model minority that is at first imposed on them by the state for a particular agenda is later taken up by National Museum via Japanese American historiography as a means of understanding and celebrating ourselves. And more importantly, the progressive narrative positions the Sansei generation as the museum's prime target to solicit donations from.

As favors for attending the dinner and supporting the museum, attendees were given tins of the National Museum's own brand of Generation Teas, created by the Los Angeles tea retailer Chado.[39] These teas are available in the following flavors, Issei, Nisei, Sansei, Yonsei, and Gosei, which start "with a Japanese tea as the base which is [then] combined with unexpected flavors from new cultures."[40] Each tea honors a different generation, starting with the Issei, who are honored for their immigration and becoming "their family's first generation of Americans," and the Nisei, who are noted for embracing American values while "they honored their parent's Japanese values of *gaman* (perseverance) and *ganbatte* (doing the best they can)."[41] The younger generations are noted for their "imaginative twists" on traditions, rich cultural mixtures, or "youthfulness" and "fresh new perspectives."[42] Each flavored tea is supposed to be representative of those qualities. But despite their differences, they are ultimately marketed within a discourse of family, as "a five-generation family of teas, dressed in colorful labels, snuggling tin-to-tin on the shelf they call home."[43] In addition, the teas are about marketing and pleasurably consuming a way of thinking about history that is reliant upon narratives of "progress" and assimilation as well as our own investments in them. Produced for the knowing post-redress Japanese American consumer, the National Museum commodifies generation in a way that constructs identities you can now purchase. As the museum's public relations officer explains the dinner favors to attendees, he jokingly says that we "do not have to be Issei to drink Issei tea" but that we "just have to *feel* like an Issei."[44] Throughout his explanation and his humor, the audience laughs, signaling the ways they understand the categories of generation as having particular qualities, narratives, and ways of feeling. But the laughter as also about acknowledging the ridiculousness of being able to buy a tea based on Japanese American categories of generation as much as it is about belonging to community. Reading this moment in the dinner exposes disruptions as well as continued investments in what defines a generation.

Conversing with the Senator: Education and Bidding for the Future

The dinner comes to a close with Professor Mitch Maki's enthusiastic and booming voice encouraging the audience to donate money to the Bid for Education Fund, which provides bus transportation for school field trips that were threatened by state budget cuts.[45] The audience expecting Mitch Maki to come to the stage instead finds his eleven-year-old daughter, Lane Maki, standing in the spotlight. What ensues is a staged conversation between Lane and Senator Daniel Inouye, who not so subtly discuss with each other the importance of funding this museum initiative. Lane begins by asking, "You talk a lot about World War II and how it was a really bad time for our nation, and I know it wasn't a good time for you either, so why hold on to those memories? Isn't it easier just to forget about them?"[46] Inouye replies with his own particular history, talking about the ugliness of war; the death of his friend, who is "just a memory now"; his visit to Rohwer, Arkansas, and seeing his "fellow Japanese Americans behind barbed wire"; and witnessing and experiencing segregation in the army.⁴⁷ He situates this earlier part of his history as belonging to an earlier moment of national history, identifying the various ways power manifests itself through white supremacy and the way democracy failed him. But his narration also marks redress as a moment of national redemption in which "great democracy apologized" and Japanese Americans flourished.⁴⁸ Inouye ends with his greatest concern, that the next generations will forget a past that they should be aware of. He tells Lane, "And I hope you won't forget."⁴⁹ To which she replies, "Senator, I won't forget, I promise. And I won't forget you either. Thank you for everything you've done."⁵⁰

Forgetting is not an option because of the way it invalidates the museum's purpose and existence to preserve stories of the past. The National Museum as a community archive has a very important function—it serves to legitimate a marginalized voice, and thus life, in the face of impending physical death and erasure. In other words, the National Museum functions as a way of banishing death—to save marginalized peoples from historical erasure and thus give them a life beyond physical death. In responding to the way the state treats their bodies and lives as disposable and unworthy of historical inclusion, community strategies of memory expel death, but this expelling constructs a very particular kind of narrative and way of remembering itself. These strategies of community remembering remain inherently tied up in the biopolitical logic of life and death.⁵¹ In his article "The Will to Institutionality," Roderick Ferguson argues that the "differences that were once articulated as critiques of the presumed benevolence of political and economic institutions (like incarceration) become absorbed within an administrative ethos that recast those differences as testaments to the progress of the university"—or, in this case, the museum.⁵² Lane's promise to Inouye ensures that he will live on in the memories, actions, and lives of the younger generation—fixing him into a community archive guarantees that his voice (and those like him) will be heard and that he will not have died only to disappear entirely. Inouye's testimony (and the genre itself) functions as a method of truth telling that is most concerned with objectivity and legitimacy. As a result, truth is always on the side of life, while death can only mean something when brought back to life. The intimate connection among truth, life, and remembering is made visible in the way this performance produces a kind of knowledge production that all Japanese Americans should be invested in. This enforces a particular relationship to life and death, where forgetting can only be seen as death and therefore the negation of life that ultimately forecloses other possibilities of narrativizing.

After Lane's promise to Inouye, he promptly leaves the stage, having served his purpose in guiding the younger generations toward an acceptable future. Lane continues to preach to us about the lessons of the past, and she argues that her generation needs "to make sure that we learn about the bad things that have happened so they are not repeated."[53] The audience is told to never forget about incarceration or the sacrifices of Japanese American veterans and how Japanese Americans struggled for redress and "we won!"[54] To "honor the strength and courage of our Issei and Nisei" is "what community is all about."[55] Lane situates herself as a symbol of survival and futurity—she is representative of the generation that needs to be guided and educated about the past in order to move into an "acceptable" and "successful" future.

This anxiety about younger generations' ambivalent relationship to the past and therefore the museum itself is a constant presence. Not only is the National Museum concerned about getting these generations to participate in this kind of remembering, but it is also trying to sustain the Japanese American community through them. As the identifiable future, the museum sees these generations as future investors in its programs. The National Museum has sought to attract a younger audience by holding youth-related events such as the *Giant Robot Exhibition* (2009–2010) and Mike Shinoda's exhibit *Glorious Excess* (2008). In addition, after the dinner, an after-party was hosted by the Japanese American National Museum's Young Professionals Network so young professionals (over the age of twenty-one) could mingle, have fun, and create community together by being convinced to join the organization and support the museum's work. The Young Professionals Network, established in 2010, describes itself as representing "the next generation of leaders and supporters of the Museum."[56] The emphasis on the "young professional" is about who can legitimately be a true museum supporter—that person is someone who can provide monetary support in the years to come, who has and will continue to have a certain economic stability and ability.[57] Participating in community means not just "appreciating the past" but financially investing in and building a particular future.[58] Lane, as this symbol of our future, exposes the intimate connections and collusions between economic success and a poetry from the past that our vitality is said to depend upon.[59]

Identifying a future and a past within the parameters of "success" as the only way of understanding and relating to Nikkei community is dangerous in the way it affirms the state and violently moralizes the deaths of other racialized groups of color. Before Daniel Inouye comes to the stage, he is introduced by his wife, Irene Hirano, a past president of the National Museum. Introducing him means that she must list all his accomplishments and his continued investment in the museum that forces us to honor him as well. And of course, she cannot help but include how Inouye is third in line for the presidency as she proudly jokes that this is the reason why there are Secret Service agents running around. And after Inouye narrates his life story that should never be forgotten (as he tells Lane), he begins discussing "how far Japanese Americans have come" by relating statistical information to the audience about our law-abiding nature, our low crime rates, our high intellectual rates, and that we are among the "three ethnic groups with the highest per capita income."[60] He then goes on to incorporate his own life into this "success" narrative, saying, "Today I stand before you, Lane, when I was first declared an enemy alien on December the seventh and today I am president pro tempore, third in line for the presidency."[61] And then he looks affectionately at the crowd and states, "That's not too bad," to which the audience enthusiastically applaud him.[62]

By incorporating the audience into this logic of "success," Inouye situates Japanese Americans as exceptional citizens who are worthy of state recognition and thus affirmation. Nikkei futurity rests on the generational reproduction of its history through minoritized success. As I have mapped out in this chapter, success is narrated as historical triumph as Japanese Americans are lauded for their ability to overcome racial violence and trauma or their transnational successes (with Shin immigrants). The gala dinner is a celebration of this—and, by extension, Nikkei economic prosperity, as Inouye reminds the audience—which allows for donations to be made to sustain the museum and its mission of education. Although Blackness is never mentioned, Inouye's statistics rest on racialized conceptions of failure that associate Blackness with crime, poverty, and low economic rates. Here, one's distance from Blackness is inadvertently celebrated, located within neoliberal logics of disavowal; Japanese Americans unintentionally invest in antiblackness as a means of obtaining state visibility and recognition. Disguised as success, which relies on meritocracy and model minority discourses to operate, these logics are dangerous as they seep into the reproduction of Japanese American history. This logic of celebratory success institutionalizes affects within Nikkei memory that allow for and teach us to abandon people.[63] This success narrative as a strategy for survival allows Japanese Americans to hold on to the very things that protect the community from state violence but allow for the death of others.[64] This is the way the state can mobilize Japanese Americanness to do "its repressive work and its policing of civil society" and ourselves.[65] By utilizing this notion of "success," Inouye strategically distances Japanese Americans from Blackness that legitimates state violence, but four years later, I find myself at another community event with an entirely different intention. Instead of creating distance between these two racialized groups, this Day of Remembrance event sought to connect Japanese Americans and African Americans by focusing on relationships that developed out of geographic proximity. However, as I argue further, this narration of closeness ends up replicating the lessons Inouye was trying to teach rather than fostering forms of ethical cross-racial solidarity.

Day of Remembrance 2015: A Starting Point in Carceral Connections

Every year, Japanese American communities across the nation hold Day of Remembrance (DOR) events during the month of February to "commemorate the Issei and Nisei who suffered tremendously, including the loss of property, businesses, dignity, freedom and due process of law" when President Franklin Roosevelt signed Executive Order 9066 on February 19, 1942.[66] In Little Tokyo (Los Angeles), the event is put on by four main organizations: the JACL, the National Museum, the Manzanar Committee, and Nikkei for Civil Rights and Redress (NCRR). On February 18, 2015, the 2015 DOR event titled "EO 9066 and the [In]justice System Today" was held at the National Museum and highlighted the urgency of recognizing that the U.S. "justice system continues to imperil communities of color with police violence, profiling, and mass incarceration."[67] This year's speakers were Povi-Tamu Bryant, Rey Fukuda, and Mike Murase, and the event was meant to provide "an opportunity for the two communities to dialogue."[68] Because of the

> recent and ongoing protests sparked by the deaths of unarmed Black Americans, including Michael Brown, Eric Garner, and Ezell Ford, through police use of lethal force, and the lack of related indictments, the nation's attention is turned to the growing concerns of anti-black racism, state violence and the failure of political leadership toward African Americans.[69]

Recognizing police brutality, antiblack racism, and mass incarceration as contemporary forms of state violence, DOR 2015 sought to place the deaths of Black men by police within the context of Japanese American history. In other words, speaking to "the importance of remembering the Japanese American struggle during World War II" means that "we seize today's opportunity to begin a conversation in our community about the interrelated yet distinct injustices other communities face."[70] In this section, I explore how the visibility of Black death via police brutality shifted Japanese American narratives from that of distance to proximity. I argue that while making connections to Blackness via space, these narratives ultimately perform the same ideological work as the gala dinner because of the limitations of familial and generational narratives of belonging that make up Japanese American historical and community identity.

The program began with a somber roll call that asked former incarcerees to stand, followed by an annual remembrance ceremony where each person in the audience was given a tag on their chair "similar to the ones worn by Japanese Americans as they boarded buses and trains to 'assembly centers' and then to the concentration camps."[71] Each tag had a different concentration camp name on it, including the Justice Department detention centers and Citizen Isolation camps—the audience members were asked to stand when the name on their tag was called. Once every person in the audience was standing, there was a moment of silence to pay our respects to those who were affected by Executive Order 9066 as well as those who were no longer with us but "left a tremendous legacy about the Japanese American experience and fighting for justice."[72]

Following this traditional ritual of remembrance, the emcees, Helen Ota (of the Japanese American Cultural and Community Center) and Dr. Curtiss Takada Rooks (professor of Asian Pacific American studies at Loyola Marymount University), began a multimedia presentation that historicized Japanese American and African American collaboration within a familiar narrative of Japanese American history from incarceration to redress and reparations. For the DOR committee, it was important to "show how our two communities have come together during important parts of history," exploring "notable intersections we should not forget."[73] The emcees begin with a history of incarceration, from Executive Order 9066 to the horse stalls used at "assembly" centers that 120,000 Japanese Americans were herded into and the construction of the ten concentration camps, while reminding us that "no person of Japanese descent was ever found guilty of sabotage or espionage."[74] From here, they discuss non-Japanese who believed that Executive Order 9066 was a violation of civil liberties, citing Hugh MacBeth, an African American attorney in Los Angeles who helped defend Ernest and Toki Wakayama (inmates at Santa Anita Assembly Center) by arguing that there was no military necessity for removal.

After the war, "reintegrating into their former neighborhoods proved to be a daunting task for Japanese Americans" as they "like other people of color were met with housing covenants, restricted them from homes in white neighborhoods."[75] In Los Angeles, Japanese Americans were able to find housing in "industrial areas, low rent areas for migrant workers, settling in Boyle Heights and the Eastside, as well as Central Avenue, Little Tokyo and South Los Angeles."[76] In particular, after the war, Rooks states that the Crenshaw district was where "Blacks and Japanese Americans made progress in integrating the Westside with Crenshaw as its central focus."[77] They then identify examples of community spaces where integration thrived, including the Holiday Bowl, a "popular multiethnic bowling alley and coffee shop that served grits, udon, chow mein, and hamburgers."[78] Not only did Black and Japanese Americans have fun together, but they also went to the same schools and churches. Showing a class photo from the Thirty-Ninth Street Elementary School in 1958, the emcees argue that this Crenshaw district school demonstrated that Black and Japanese Americans "were at the forefront of the movement to bring down color barriers."[79] In another photo, the emcees point to the All People's Christian Church in South Central Los Angeles, where "Japanese and Black children as well as that of other ethnicities grew up, learned, and played next to each other in the church's nursery class." By placing Japanese Americans in these Black geographic spaces, the DOR attempts to renarrate Japanese American history and thus identity within a multicultural discourse that demonstrates proximity as solidarity.

While the emcees do try to acknowledge that these moments of interaction are not always successful, they simply state that "many Nisei mirrored the prejudices against Blacks held by the white majority" and that many Nisei and Sansei remember their parents not wanting them to date Black people. Glossing over these not-so-rosy moments of antiblack racism that permeated these shared spaces, the emcees then transition to those who were "ready for the influence of the civil rights movement and the ethnic power movements."[80] In this section of their presentation, the emcees identify Hisaye Yamamoto, Yuri Kochiyama, and the Yellow Brotherhood as key examples of where Black and Japanese American experiences continued to intersect in the 1960s and 1970s. Drawing on the life and work of Nisei writer Yamamoto, the emcees discuss her work for the *Los Angeles Tribune*, an African American newspaper, and her memoir, "A Fire in Fontana," to show another form of solidarity via proximity in the workplace. In summarizing "A Fire in Fontana," the emcees recount the memoir, which centers upon a Black man who came into the newspaper office seeking help after receiving death threats because he and his family had recently moved into an all-white neighborhood. Soon after, the house went up in flames, killing the entire family, with the "police conclud[ing] that the man had set the fire himself and closed the case."[81] The emcees argue that it is through this "essay" and her work with the *Los Angeles Tribune* and the Black community that a transformation took place within Yamamoto. And somewhat similarly, through Kochiyama's experiences with the Black Power movement and most notably her friendship with Malcom X, including the iconic photograph of her holding him as he lay dying, the emcees utilize her relationship to the Black community as a "powerful example of the spirit of collaboration for justice."[82] In addition, they mark that relationship by the proximity of her home within historically Black neighborhoods, citing that she lived in a housing project in New York after the war and later moved to Harlem, where she was further politicized in the struggle for total liberation rather than integration. By drawing on the life narrative of a respected activist in both communities, the presentation tries to show how these moments of proximity and eventual politicization were able to mobilize a form of solidarity between two racial groups.

And finally, before ending their renarration of Japanese American history through examples of Black and Japanese American interaction, proximity, and support, the presentation moves into a discussion of redress and reparations, with the emcees declaring that the "success" of the redress movement "would not have been possible without the support from non-Japanese allies."[83] For example, in 1982, Congressman Mervin Dymally, "who represented the thirty-first district that included Gardena and Compton," worked with the organization NCRR to help "write legislation for monetary reparations" while also offering staff support and the use of his offices.[84] The emcees state that he "will always be remembered as a staunch supporter of redress and a true friend to the community." They also point out Congressman Ron Dellums, who gave an "impassioned speech" on the floor of the House of Representatives before a key vote, "sharing with his congressional colleagues his memories as a young boy seeing his Japanese American friend and neighbor being taken away from his home through no apparent reason other than the color of his skin and the legacy of his ancestry."[85] Concluding this portion of the presentation, the emcees tell us that "these are examples of the exceptional work of Black and Japanese American community leaders committed to fight for each other through struggles of racism" in order to urge us to continue this kind of collaborative work for justice.[86]

A Discourse of Proximity as Shared History: Multiculturalism and Solidarity

In this renarration of Japanese American history that focuses on Black and Japanese American mutual support, interaction, and shared spaces, we can see how a connection to Black lives and communities is being made through a discourse of multiculturalism. Forged through a linear historical narrative from World War II incarceration to its resolution in Japanese American redress and reparations, many of the examples utilized sought to legitimize Black and Japanese American relationships by literally placing Japanese Americans in "Black" spaces (a newspaper office, Harlem, etc.). Constructing this narrative of sharing space (both at work and at home) becomes one of the only "valid" ways these two groups could develop meaningful relationships with each other. As

I outlined earlier, this dominant imaginary for imagining interracial solidarity, which pervades not only spaces of community but also Afro-Asian American scholarship as well, nostalgically remembers moments of connection as only being fruitful ones. While this renarration is powerful, it is ultimately the moments of disconnect, highlighting exactly where our histories diverge and our connections are missed or broken, that reveal much more about state violence and the possibility for solidarity.

For example, in their use of Yamamoto's "A Fire in Fontana" as a narrative of multicultural solidarity, this theme takes precedence over what exactly Yamamoto is struggling with throughout the narrative. The presentation fails to acknowledge what Grace Kyungwon Hong argues is Yamamoto's "contradictory location" as a Japanese American woman. The first is Yamamoto's own critique of her journalistic work, which was an "unbiased" report about the man who moved into a segregated neighborhood, and she wrote a "calm, impartial story about the threats [he] described."[87] Her objective writing of the story did not incite a sense of urgency within readers; it was a type of writing that inadvertently supports and legitimates the state in its denial of property rights and life to African Americans. Her memoir is a rewriting of this event, one that seeks to counter the erasure of this family—that she once unknowingly participated in. This reading of Yamamoto's memoir calls attention to Japanese American participation in the continued denial of property rights for some and, importantly, shows the contradictory location of Japanese Americans. In her article "'Something Forgotten Which Should Have Been Remembered': Private Property and Cross Racial Solidarity in the Work of Hisaye Yamamoto," Hong argues that "to say that African Americans and Japanese Americans have a common history is false" but that "cross racial solidarity based on the critique of property system is possible" by recognizing "the differences between their very uneven and discrepant histories."[88] Here, sharing space is not the focus of cross-racial solidarity; instead, the "relationship between these two groups is defined by differences," which is visible in Yamamoto's linking of segregation and Japanese American incarceration with the difference between herself and the man who comes into the *Tribune*.[89] Furthermore, Hong draws on the juxtaposition of Yamamoto, a housewife, "sitting safely in her house which was located on a street where panic would be the order of the day if a Black family should happen to move in" as Yamamoto watched the Watts Riots on her television, noting her "contradictory location."[90] While she is the viewer and someone who is "benefiting materially from suburbanization," she "cannot participate completely" because of her "memory of the ways in which citizenship and property rights have been denied to Japanese Americans."[91]

In addition to their multicultural reading of "A Fire in Fontana," the DOR presentation concludes by saying that redress would not have been successful without the help of non-Japanese American friends and allies. While this may be true, it is also important to note the way Japanese American redress is inherently predicated on the devaluation of other groups of color. For example, the 1983 report of the Commission on Wartime Internment and Relocation of Civilians recommended reparations but limited eligibility to "living victims" to help "alleviate concern" that "redress could set a precedent for the descendants of slaves, American Indians forced onto reservations, Mexicans who lost land, and other historical victims of racism."[92] Therefore, in response to African American campaigns for slavery reparations, President Bill Clinton replied that "it's been too long and we're so many generations removed."[93] Opponents of African American reparations stated that Japanese Americans as "the victims themselves were compensated for *quantifiable, provable* suffering at the hands of an *identifiable perpetrator.*"[94] Underlying these oppositions was the direct contrasting of African Americans and Japanese Americans with terms like "living victims" and "later generations," coupled with notions of "deserving" and "undeserving" that constituted what a legitimate victim of racial discrimination could and *should* be.[95] In addition, as I argued earlier, redress coupled with the model minority discourse justified the dismantling of social welfare programs where Japanese Americans were seen as having achieved "success" despite racial hardships that included their unjust incarceration. It could then be argued that other groups of color were "undeserving" of social welfare programs because of their own "failures." In this way, the presentation's identification of Black congresspeople's support for the "success" of redress fails to consider the way Japanese American "success" hinged upon the state's abandonment of Black communities.

While intimate connections between Black and Japanese Americans are important to identify, they cannot simply be narrated as merely where the two share space and thus histories. To do this would be to continue participating in the denial of property rights via incarceration that devalues Black lives and subjects them to even more brutal forms of punishment and death. Going beyond a discourse of proximity is very much about interrogating how the state utilizes Japanese Americans to devalue other groups of color. In other words, the presentation fails to consider the ways Japanese Americans are utilized by the state to legitimate forms of racialized violence. My questions then are as follows: How does acknowledging our contradictory location inform Japanese American relationships to other communities? What does it mean to make Japanese American privilege visible when narrating experiences of incarceration and racialized violence?

A Different Set of Statistics

Transitioning from their historical retelling of Black and Japanese American interaction to their panel discussion, the emcees provide the audience with a handful of statistics that expose the way Black lives are devalued today. Rooks tells the audience these statistics:

> Every twenty-eight hours a Black man, woman, or child is murdered by the police or vigilante law enforcement. An estimated 25.1 percent of Black women live in poverty, this is higher than any other ethnic group. The average life expectancy for trans Black/transgendered women is just thirty-five years.[96]

Unlike the statistics that Inouye presents in his Bid for Education speech that are about "how far we've come," these statistics show the ways state violence persists in our present. And in some ways, the presentation identifies the ways "how far we've come" is actually part of the problem. Rooks then states his concern about these statistics within an urgent discourse on Nikkei youth that asks, "What is the impact on our children growing up [in the] absence of these integrated environments, absence of friendships, absence of coalition for action, absence from the shared struggle in the vision for justice?"[97] Similar to Inouye, Rooks draws on youth within a language of family and lineage that intimately ties together remembering the past with generational responsibilities that privilege heteronormative family formations. This heteronormative transfer of memory (in this case, public memory) is pervasive in the Japanese American community and often problematically privileges masculinist and cultural nationalist narratives of belonging that violently erase not just other experiences but other ways of remembering. The presentation is concerned about what happens when "we no longer honor our connectedness as people of color."[98] And so they conclude by asking, "How do Black lives matter to Japanese Americans? Where are the connections today?"[99]

Queering the Conversation: The Panelists Speak

Following the media presentation, the event transitioned into a discussion that featured Povi-Tamu Bryant of Black Lives Matter, Rey Fukuda of the East LA Community Corporation's Real Estate Department, and Mike Murase of the Little Tokyo Service Center, with Rooks moderating the panel. Unlike the media presentation, which explicitly drew out Black and Japanese American connections throughout history, I argue that the panel disrupted this narrative by queering the conversation and forcing a discomfort with cultural nationalist and masculinist retellings of Japanese American history. More specifically, Bryant's and Fukuda's life experiences as a Black queer womyn and a biracial transgender and queer person, respectively, highlight how narratives of Japanese American history violently erase and marginalize them. Queering the conversation not only allowed a rethinking of what it means to be an ally but also forced the audience into an uncomfortable space that required them to think about their privilege as Japanese Americans and within Japanese American memory making. In doing so, the panelists challenged Japanese American community members (and also scholars) who continue to rely on heteronormative narratives of family and generation to understand Nikkei past, present, and future.

Both Bryant and Fukuda situate their life experiences as not only integral to their different forms of activism but also to how they approach solidarity work that disrupts Japanese American historical narratives. Fukuda, who works on equitable transit development in East Los Angeles, "grew up in six different cities including Tokyo (Japan), Santo Domingo (Dominican Republic) and Oslo (Norway)" and self-identifies as an immigrant and a biracial transgender and queer person.[100] In discussing how he got involved in community work, Fukuda stresses the importance of his personal story. Before getting into the specifics of his experience, Fukuda carefully defines what he means by "transgender," telling the audience that "you don't necessarily identify with the sex you were assigned at birth" and "when you are transgendered you grow up not necessarily identifying with those identities."[101] He explains that he was "born female at birth, but identif[ies] as male and also gender fluid because [he is] not 100 percent male, if that exists" at all.[102] Then Fukuda goes on to share how coming out to his parents informed the kind of work he does and how he does it. When he came out, he also had a Black partner, and he realized that his parents, his mom in particular, "had a lot of issues with me being queer and transgender but also a lot of her issues came from me deciding to be with a girl who is Black."[103] Realizing how intertwined his mother's homophobia was with her antiblackness "really shined a light on my understanding of how perpetual and pervasive antiblackness is," which is the reason Fukuda positions the abolition of prisons as a main part of his activism.[104] In thinking about where we go from here, Fukuda tells the audience that he thinks about incarceration, total liberation, and reparation "interconnectedly," which shows us that "we still have a lot of work to do" because "there are still millions of people incarcerated and a lot of them are Black."[105] For Fukuda, the trajectory of his experiences as a transgender queer person, where the violence of coming out to family is intertwined with antiblackness, has informed the kind of abolitionist work he does.

Positioning the family as a site of violence, Fukuda disrupts generational and thus heteronormative transmissions of memory that are inherently embedded in Issei, Nisei, and Sansei narratives of family that not only make up Japanese American communities but inform Japanese American knowledge production. As I discussed with the National Museum's gala dinner, these generations construct very particular identities and memories that naturalize a particular lineage where incarceration is often at the center. Fukuda himself cannot take part in this because of his identity as a transnational biracial transgender and queer person. But I also want to focus on how the community is constituted by the disavowal of the queering of the Japanese American experience.

Incarceration is a contradictory and regulatory space itself. In her article "Looking for Jiro Onuma," Tina Takemoto argues that incarceration's "familial and co-gendered organization" replicated a "heterosexual environment" as a means of "normalizi[ng]" the "confinement of Japanese Americans under the euphemistic rhetoric of 'evacuation' and 'relocation.'"[106] When looking for "same-sex intimacy and queer sexuality" during incarceration, she states that the "cramped barrack spaces, military surveillance, and lack of privacy made all sexual activities conspicuous—especially between same-gendered individuals."[107] At the same time, incarceration is also a space where heteronormative family formations and thus proper gender roles break down and are made impossible by the very carceral structure. For example, some scholars discuss how the traditional roles of men and women were switched because of incarceration. Issei men were no longer the breadwinners or the family's main source of income because children and wives were allowed to work.[108] They also argue that the change in roles was affected by the equal pay that both women and men received that allowed women to have more independence because they no longer had to rely on men for their livelihood.[109] In addition, some scholars have drawn attention to the fact that children no longer sat with their parents during meals at the mess halls—disrupting important family time and parental control over their children. My own great-grandfather decided to take sugar beet contracts in Colorado because of his concern over his daughters' behaviors. In an interview with my grandmother's sister, she remembers her father saying that "we are going to go; if we stay here [in camp] you girls are going to be *bad*."[110] Although there is a problematic way scholarship often talks about women and girls who gain independence while incarcerated,[111] it is important to think about how carcerality at times challenged heteronormative family formations and made them very messy. Taking "bad" subjects seriously illuminates the ways they were made "good" again. By providing racialized labor for the state, they are transformed into "good" daughters but are also taken from enemy aliens to proper citizen-subjects. The inability of Fukuda to narrate himself within Japanese American community and historical narratives not only points to a disjuncture between the DOR's historical retelling of Black and Japanese American relationships but also highlights the violence of it. Fukuda refuses to narrate his personal life story as one of proximity and thus solidarity; instead, he makes it a point to discuss a moment where queerness and Blackness are both rejected within the site of the heteronormative family.[112] Fukuda's use of this personal story refuses to play into cultural nationalist and masculinist narrative logics, and instead, he forces the audience to reckon with the dangers of the heteronormative family. As I discuss later, this is something that the audience does not wish to hear and ultimately ends up dismissing.

On the other hand, Bryant, who was born in Chicago, Illinois, and moved to Los Angeles as a child, talks about what it meant to grow up as the only Black person in her neighborhood or classroom. This meant that, "always for her own safety," she had to think about how to work in solidarity with others, which pushed her to "learn about other people's experiences and learn about other communities to build [a] connection."[113] But she also stresses that doing so meant she was also constantly "challenging people to learn about [her] own experiences [and] the legacy of antiblackness in the U.S."[114] Like Fukuda, Bryant defines exactly what she means by antiblackness, telling the audience that "all of those statistics that we heard, and there are so many more, are representative of the disproportionate ways that Black folks experience harm and violence in the U.S."[115] After clarifying, she begins by discussing her own family as having a diversity of experiences: her brothers, her straight sisters, and she herself as a woman who plays with gender, all experience antiblackness in different ways. Branching off from this discourse around family, Bryant connects queerness to her own understanding of how all Black lives matter. She pushes the audience to think about

> Black queer lives, and what Black queer folks are going through, and how they have to navigate the world differently than Black straight folks, understanding Black women and their narratives, Black trans folk and how being trans informs their experiences of antiblack racism, and included in that is Black mixed-race folks.[116]

In thinking about where to go from here, Bryant (quoting Soya Jung) explicitly states that there needs to be "a model minority critique" where we think about how "we [can] fight for our rights and struggle against our own oppression but not at the expense of or without consideration to the other types of oppression and marginalization that folks are facing."[117] Unlike the media presentation that assumed solidarity via proximity, Bryant is careful to highlight that this kind of narrative is not enough to bridge Japanese American and Black communities together. She ends with practices of being an ally, the first of which is self-awareness, meaning "really understanding yourself and your relationship to the world." In other words, it means to think about all the "identities that I have, all of the ways that I walk through the world, how . . . those things afford me privileges," and how they affect the way one also experiences oppression.[118] In acknowledging a contradictory location of simultaneous oppression and privilege, Bryant skillfully disrupts the entire DOR program by not so subtly calling the audience to action by assessing their privilege, *not* just their oppression. In addition, Bryant lists self-education as an important practice of being an ally where it is important to understand other people's experiences of privilege and oppression. This is exactly what Fukuda and Bryant do throughout the panel: they present no explicit relationship between Black and Japanese Americans for the audience but instead strongly emphasize the sharing of personal stories, not just sharing their own but listening to others as well. In fact, their entire discussion revolves around how their experiences as a "Black queer womyn" and a "biracial transgender and queer person" not only show how antiblackness has been a part of their lives but also how they have come to activism and how they approach solidarity work. Unlike the media presentation, which provided us with a well-crafted historical narrative full of examples of interracial solidarity, the panel refuses to operate within a discourse of multiculturalism. Instead, Fukuda and Bryant force the audience to listen to their life experiences and understand their positionality. In doing so, they strategically push the audience to consider how Japanese American historical narratives have silenced their personal stories.

The third panelist, Mike Murase,[119] a well-known activist in the Los Angeles Japanese American community, narrates his activist beginnings in a familiar Sansei (third-generation) story centering around coming of age in the 1960s and 1970s. He shares that as a student at UCLA, he was influenced and politicized by the Black Power movement, in particular the assassination of Malcom X and Eldridge Cleaver's visit to the school. And although the 1960s and 1970s were often focused on Black/white issues, it was also an era where the Sansei thought about who they were as Asian Americans and as young people. Because Fukuda's and Bryant's identities locate them firmly outside the Japanese American community, their discussion of their personal identities serves to familiarize the mostly Los Angeles Japanese American audience with their activist work. Invited as panelists for their outside location as a hopeful gesture of solidarity building and learning, it is their outsiderness that disrupts a connection between generational narratives of belonging and Japanese American community identity. Murase's iconic upbringing in the 1960s and 1970s relocates the audience back to a familiar story. Challenging the focus on personal identity, Murase discusses the importance of collective identity to think about the question, "What do we do about the conditions that exist?"[120] And what does it mean to act "as a group and not as individuals to address these questions"?[121] Bringing the panel back to the Japanese American community is meant to push the audience to think about their own responsibility to challenge antiblack racism. Murase then discusses his own work in South Africa and his remembering of how it felt when Nelson Mandela was released from prison. He tells the audience that there are other days of remembrance. He goes through a list of murdered Black men from Emmett Till to Martin Luther King Jr. to Eric Garner and Michael Brown, saying that these are "not just [the] killing [of] random individuals but they are significant" because "they represent a continuation of racism, hysteria, and the failure of political leadership."[122] After he says this, the audience loudly applauds him. This is the only time the audience claps during the panel until it is finished. Utilizing this familiar phrase from the Commission on Wartime Relocation and Internment of Civilians, Murase collectively guides the audience to a place of comfortable collective comparison. However, the reemergence of the collective to the panel assumes a monolithic generational and community experience that the centering of queer identity disrupted. The collective is reestablished, as evidenced by audience approval via applause, where Japanese American incarceration and Black death are understood as systemic state violence that can be resolved by redress and reparations. Black lives only seem to matter when Japanese Americans can validate their history through this similar connection to state violence that dismisses the complex difference in how Black life is devalued historically and contemporarily. The queer narratives of Fukuda and Bryant reveal that intimate connections produced by state violence cannot be conflated through similarity or proximity but rather need to be generated by a complex understanding of how privilege and oppression operate via familial, communal, and state narratives.

"The Kids Were the Best Part": Nikkei Futurity

One of the comments circulating about DOR 2015 was that the panel "got off track" or off topic and that the "kids were the best part, can you believe she is only fifteen?" In a call to action that ended the entire program, the event had nineteen-year-old Gosei (fifth-generation) college student Alex Kanegawa and fifteen-year-old African American–Japanese American Mariko Fujimoto Rooks (the daughter of Dr. Curtiss Takada Rooks) give a speech about what they see as the next course of action as Nikkei youth. In doing this call to action, Kanegawa says that he was asked to answer the following question: "Why should this matter to me, and why should others care?"[123] His call to action was to "everywhere here to invest in people," to "invest in justice," to "to converse and express joy, sadness, and be unapologetically angry when it stirs within us," and to urge for a "radical kind of love that is courageous, challenging and sometimes difficult but absolutely critically necessary."[124] Interestingly, Kanegawa's brief call to action asks us not to learn a particular kind of history or narrative but rather to change our investments—ones that are not necessarily about legitimacy but about connecting affect with social justice and movements for change. However, despite the shift he makes, it is Rooks who captures the focus and hearts of the audience. In her speech, she rebuilds the narratives that were broken down by the panel that preceded it.

Rooks centers her speech on her position "as a mixed-race Japanese, African American youth" and questions "how do I fit into the Japanese American community?"[125] To answer this question, she discusses her experience, following Ferguson,[126] that forced her to think about what youth need to do to stand in solidarity with other communities. She eloquently tells us that even after Ferguson, many people did not realize that we "still do live in a racist culture and a racist society, because they are not on the receiving end of this." But she states the following:

> Being part Black, I am. And often the people who don't realize this, are the people perpetrating, not on purpose, but still do perpetrate this sort of racist society because the same people who are tagging photos with #Blacklivesmatter are the ones who also say that people are so ratchet and that they are ghetto or they don't take into account social and political class when they judge other people without knowing who they are. And when I hear that this music is Black and this music is ratchet and I remind them that I too am Black, I'm told you're Black but you're not one of them. To which I say, I am one of them when my father's tailed at department stores, I am one of them when my father is asked if he is the security guard, I am one of them when I am seen as a threat, when I am seen as a threat, as competition for being successful at anything as a woman of color in general. [Clapping.][127]

Here, Rooks is doing something similar to Fukuda and Bryant by discussing how her positionality as a mixed-race Japanese and African American young woman has impacted the way she sees opportunities for interracial solidarity in the future.[128] She is also critical about the ways antiblack racism persists in our daily lives, and she expands on the definition given by Bryant by linking racialized violence to popular discourse about class and Black culture. Antiblack racism looks like Ferguson, but it also looks like youth calling things "ratchet" or "ghetto." In addition, Rooks also thinks about our privilege as Asian Americans, asking how those with "class privilege [or] economic privilege" stop "this less obvious racism."[129] But in asking these questions that address Asian American privilege, Rooks (unlike Fukuda and Bryant) couches her discussion within a generational narrative of family and education. She wonders, "How do we raise awareness as young people?" and "How do we pass this to others?" while also asking the "older generation," "How do we educate young people as to what's happened in America in the past, and how do we stop it in the future?"[130]

Unlike Fukuda and Bryant, who queer the conversation away from family responsibility that is passed down through the generations, Rooks is adamant about the future of solidarity being within this framework. She also sees solidarity with other communities occurring because the "Japanese American community has already experienced and has already fought for *recognition*" and that "we have redress and reparations for EO 9066."[131] Here, Rooks reaffirms the Japanese American experience and positions the Japanese American community as an example to follow in order to achieve recognition whereas Fukuda and Bryant address privilege in order to call out Japanese American narratives that participate in antiblack racism. Rooks identifies recognition and thus visibility as the ideal solution when, in fact, Fukuda and Bryant see Japanese American recognition as part of what justifies and allows for the devaluation of Black bodies that allows for brutal forms of punishment (death, incarceration, etc.). The audience's overwhelming response to Rooks's speech demonstrates how familial narratives of responsibility where Japanese Americans are the leading example of how to deal with racialized state violence are how Japanese Americans have come to know themselves. Fukuda's and Bryant's inability to narrate themselves or their strategies for coalition building within these familial narratives as well as the audience's discomfort with the panel expose how our understanding of interracial connections and solidarity remains problematically within the confines of heteronormativity—a narrative that consequently allows Japanese Americans to be continually narrated as "successful," as "models," and as "deserving of life." In this narrative structure, queerness and queer sexuality drop out of view and become harder and harder to see. As Tina Takemoto laments in her project, to recuperate "same-sex intimacy and queer sexuality," the searching or the ability to look for, becomes complicated by the "the desire to preserve a certain version of historical memory that would maintain the gravity of incarceration as well as the normalcy and morality of innocent Japanese Americans unjustly imprisoned by the federal government."[132] For Takemoto, it is not that queer sexuality and histories did not exist but rather that heteronormativity and family became the narrative vehicles to establish World War II incarceration as wrong. These familial and generational narratives secured Japanese Americans not only redress and monetary reparations but also national visibility and legibility. In order to hold the state accountable, Japanese Americans had to articulate themselves as proper citizen-subjects with nuclear family units. These narratives obscure Jiro Onuma from view in the same way that Bryant's and Fukuda's critiques are overshadowed by the promise of Nikkei futurity: the younger generation. Heteronormativity within generational promise signals to the inability to really hear the queer critiques of family within Japanese American collective memory that are made on the panel. Paying attention to those critiques allows for a different kind of relationality, one that does not rest on mere proximity but exposes the contradictory nature of incarceration narratives and their reproduction.

I argue that queer disruption to generational narratives of World War II incarceration exposes the contradictory location of Japanese Americans in contemporary race relations. By disrupting familial and familiar narratives, queer subjectivity and storytelling wrench the story of incarceration from Japanese American identity. Rather than proximity as solidarity, Bryant and Fukuda articulate an intersectional approach to comparatively understanding carceral experiences. They underscore that one's location in the carceral landscape must lead individuals to grapple with contradiction (simultaneous privilege and oppression of Japanese Americans) in order to truly be an ally against antiblack racism. A new narrative then emerges: Japanese American World War II incarceration is not an exceptional moment in history but is in fact quite ordinary to how the United States manages populations deemed dangerous for their racial, sexual, or gendered deviancy at different historical moments. Queer disruption, then, cannot see Japanese American redress and reparations as a solution to the carceral. Instead, Fukuda and Bryant argue that abolishing prisons be central to Japanese American allyship to Black communities.

And yet, at the end of the program, the audience was asked to sign their names and emails on a large piece of paper hanging in the National Museum's donor hall. The event was supposed to inspire the audience to want to seriously invest in interracial solidarity, and those who put their names on the paper would be put on the Black Lives Matter email list. At the end of the program, there were only four names listed.[133]

Drawing on these two important events within the Japanese American community, I wanted to show the varied ways that Japanese Americans remember incarceration, sometimes highlighting our "success" by creating distance from Blackness and at other times looking for intimate connections by way of our proximity to each other. However, as different as these events may have been, they ultimately perform the same kind of work—one that legitimizes Japanese American history and positions Japanese Americans as worthy of inclusion, visibility, and thus life. In the next chapter, I explore the Densho digital archive as community archive to think about how the digital preservation of memory is motivated by generational disappearance. Interrogating the legacy of linking gendered visibility and legibility with racial worth, the digital archive can open up conversations about preservation, education, and the carceral.

2

The Intimate Connection among Truth, Memory, and Life

Refusal in the Densho Digital Archive

Densho: The Japanese American Legacy Project is a nonprofit organization started in 1996 and based out of Seattle, Washington, that uses digital technology to preserve and make accessible primary source materials on the incarceration of Japanese Americans. Their digital archive contains about 908 interviews as well as historic photographs, documents, and newspapers but also includes an encyclopedia and lesson plans for educators to teach Japanese American history with an emphasis on their World War II incarceration. In Densho's *2018 Annual Report,* Executive Director Tom Ikeda wrote that "more than any other time in our history, Densho is being called upon to bring the story of World War II incarceration to a national stage," where Densho is now a "go-to resource without walls or boundaries" and Japanese Americans can now tell our story to the "widest possible audience."[1] Unlike the Japanese American National Museum, where one has to be physically present in Los Angeles to have access to Japanese American history via its exhibits and events,[2] Densho's use of the digital has made this history more accessible and thus easy to learn and know about. In the space where memory meets technology, the digitization of oral history videos allows for Japanese American incarceration history to be "readily viewed and replayed on demand," breathing life into narratives that always seem to be on the verge of disappearing. Premised on this generational narrative of reproduction in the face of looming death, Densho as a digital archive not only provides insight into how memory practices are currently shifting but offers carefully constructed lesson plans that demonstrate what Japanese American incarceration can teach us in the present. As a result, Densho not only has become an important and vocal community organization but is a key site of Japanese American memory work.

While I mostly document the impact that winning redress and reparations had on Japanese American oral history and archival practices in this chapter, oral history has had a longer trajectory within Japanese American academic and community spaces. According to historian Art Hansen, "some oral history activity" began in the 1960s, and he cites some notable projects.[3] The first is the Japanese American Research Project at UCLA between 1964 and 1969 by Joe Grant Masaoka and members of the JACL. In the 1970s, the Japanese American Project through California State University, Fullerton, conducted interviews that were transcribed, archived, and made accessible to researchers, although Hansen notes that this project privileged Nisei over Issei because "it depended on non-Japanese speaking interviewers."[4] In 1969, under the guidance of California State University, Sacramento, and the direction of Japanese-speaking pastor Rev. Heihachiro Takarabe, the Issei Oral History Project documented over 180 interviews.

Hansen laments that before the 1980s, "only a little oral history work had been done" on World War II incarceration, "as a result of individual repression and social amnesia," which resulted in a "small body of work [that] suffered from the absence of methodological or archival sophistication."[5] However, he documents that by the 1980s and well into the 1990s, "hardly a month goes by without an announcement of the inauguration, advancement, or completion of an oral history project covering a specific Japanese American community."[6] He notes that by the mid-1990s, Japanese American incarceration was "becoming one of the best-documented events in American history via oral history interviews, the main reason was indisputably the campaign for redress."[7] Because of the impact redress and reparations have had on the Japanese American community, this chapter examines how narratives, truth telling, and remembering continue to impact Japanese American oral history projects. With a focus on the technological advances of archiving and accessibility, Densho represents the digital era where the impacts of redress and reparations on telling the story of incarceration linger and sometimes shift.

I explore Densho as a digital archive to deconstruct when and how strategies of community memory function within the boundaries of the state's management of racialized populations. I begin with a brief historical tracing of the biopolitical management of life and death in WRA policies and agendas to consider how Japanese American World War II incarceration becomes the site where these two modes of control determine valued and devalued Japanese American life. Connecting this history is an important way to flesh out how death constantly haunts the Japanese American archive. Densho's mission is to "preserve the testimonies of Japanese Americans who were unjustly incarcerated . . . before their memories are extinguished" by offering "these irreplaceable firsthand accounts coupled with historical images and teacher resources to explore principles of democracy and promote equal justice for all."[8] Death and loss give birth to the archive and its continuing mission to record and circulate this often-overlooked history. Drawing on generational anxieties about the loss of the Nisei generation, Densho articulates itself as "preserving stories of the past for generations of tomorrow."[9] Even its name, Densho, translates as "to pass on to the next generation or to leave a legacy," which is an "American story with ongoing relevance" that "during World War II, the United States government incarcerated innocent people solely because of their ancestry."[10] As I have argued, generational death produces anxiety about and concern for a loss of history where the reproduction of this history is meant to be preserved in the archive before it is gone forever. Additionally, racialized histories are marginalized and thus always on the cusp of disappearing from national narratives. Densho's reiteration of Japanese American World War II history as an "American story" is not just disappearing with the Nisei but is also always fighting for national visibility and "relevance." The digital archive banishes or at the very least circumvents erasure to ensure that Nisei history lives on even after physical death. Examining the reproduction of the archive reveals how the logics of state violence—in particular, the management of life and death—seep into memory practices. In the following section, I explore how death and visibility become intimately connected within incarceration policies and how the precarity of racialized Japanese American bodies continues to exist, whether being marked for death or managed for life.

The Erasure and Disappearance of Japanese Americans for Racialized Belonging: WRA Historical Narratives and Their Impact

Japanese American incarceration was justified and articulated within a language of national security: it was a response to the nation's wartime hysteria as a preventative measure against an envisioned invasion and also was seen as a means of protecting Japanese Americans against the possibility of violent crimes and riots in reaction to Pearl Harbor. The WRA, the federal agency created in 1942 to handle the forced removal, was responsible for the construction and operation of the network of incarceration sites, public relations, the loyalty questionnaire, segregation, and resettlement.[11] Drawing on Foucault's conceptualization of biopower, I argue that the WRA's administration over Japanese American life existed simultaneously with the WRA's right to let some Japanese Americans physically die (Nisei soldiers, those who resisted), culturally die (Issei, Kibei Nisei), or languish (crowded and terrible living conditions).

Despite the WRA's charge to forcibly remove, incarcerate, and continually displace Japanese Americans, it conceptualized incarceration as an Americanizing project and sought to establish "planned communities" where they thought they could "speed the assimilation of Japanese Americans through democratic self-government, schooling, work, and other rehabilitative activities."[12] Not only could the state see itself as protecting Japanese Americans, but it could also position their project as "anti-racist" in its benevolence to help Japanese Americans assimilate. In order to articulate their project in this way, the WRA conflated culture with loyalty and thus disloyalty, which allowed the administration to categorize Japanese Americans as always in need of democratic tutelage. In this racial paternalistic discourse, the WRA identified language, kinship structures of leadership, and generational distinctions as markers of "alleged cultural backwardness."[13] For example, those who were seen as particularly prone to practicing "traditional" Japanese culture were notably the Kibei Nisei, the second-generation Japanese Americans who were educated in Japan and thus the most susceptible to disloyalty. Using the figure of the potentially disloyal Japanese American not only interpellates the Japanese American as not a citizen but also implies that they would still be outside the rights of citizenship without the intervention of the government.

This discourse of democratic tutelage, assimilation, and protection reveals the ways citizenship was spectralized. Japanese Americans must encounter a sort of death (erasure of the racial/cultural "other") in order to become legitimate citizens. Within the logic of the WRA, a citizen is imagined as always innately performing "Americanness," which can only be embodied in the effacement of specific markers of Japanese "culture." Japanese Americans are forced into this violent encounter with themselves (as the identifiable "other") as a means of proving to the state that they are loyal and therefore worthy of citizenship, which, as Mae Ngai argues, has been nullified due to incarceration. Not only does the WRA mandate appropriate activities for incarcerees, but Japanese Americans are under constant surveillance and punished when they refuse or are unable to become the "citizen." Even prior to their forced removal, Japanese Americans prepared for FBI raids and interrogations by literally destroying photographs, documents, and other objects that would link them to Japan. In essence, they were forced to destroy a part of their histories and thus themselves. During incarceration, "loyal" Japanese Americans were selectively relocated to the Midwest or East Coast by the WRA as a means of ensuring their continued "Americanness." Here, their Americanness was ensured by their geographic dislocation from racialized spaces of home and community, creating a Japanese American incarceration diaspora.

As I discussed in the introduction, by looking at the questionnaire issued by the WRA as a technology to determine the loyalty or disloyalty of Japanese Americans, we can see where erasure intersects with the physical death and further deprivation of protection of Japanese Americans. These questions asked incarcerees if they would be willing serve in the U.S. army and would forswear allegiance to the Japanese emperor by swearing qualified allegiance to the United States.[14] By answering yes to the first question, Nisei men (of eligible draft age) opened themselves up to the possibility of dying as the ultimate proof of their loyalty. For Issei, who were not eligible for citizenship, answering yes to the second question rendered them stateless. If incarcerees answered no to either of the questions, they were classified as disloyal, segregated from those who were deemed loyal, and transferred to Tule Lake. As I argued in the Introduction, the War Relocation Authority's Loyalty Questionnaire forced Japanese Americans to make decisions that further made their bodies vulnerable to death, dying, punishment, and statelessness (without protection). The legacies of such violent encounters linger in the Japanese American community and are embedded in strategies of memorializing that often mimic this spectral quality of belonging and worthiness in the face of historical erasure. In the next section, I examine how visibility to the state relies upon gendered performances of masculinity and femininity to narrate incarceration within the fabric of American exceptionalism. I explore how incarceration continues to be articulated as a space of transformation, liberation, and freedom when Japanese Americans remain disposable behind and beyond barbed wire.

Nisei Gender Roles and State Visibility: Heroic Men and Liberated Women

As I argued in the Introduction, Nisei soldiers, death, and visibility are intimately connected in national narratives of disavowal and Japanese American community narratives of worth. The United States' use of the segregated Nisei units and the publicization of their exploits put American democracy and disavowal of racism on display to the rest of the world. For the Japanese American community, the ultimate sacrifice of Nisei life was evidence of their unwavering loyalty to the United States and thus made Japanese Americans worthy of recognition and thus redress and reparations. As a result, male Japanese American narratives are highlighted often at the expense of women's experiences. However, as I explore in the next section, women also achieved visibility through problematic narratives of gender, loyalty, and worth.

If Japanese American men's visibility relied upon their patriotic death narrated as the ultimate masculine sacrifice, then women's narratives often remained peripheral because they did not experience death in the same way. Sacrifice for the nation is gendered and an inherent part of national narratives of loyalty and patriotism. Because women are limited in their ability to prove their loyalty to the United States, their bodies cannot always be recuperated within the logic of the nation. For example, in April 1943, Nisei women were allowed to enter the Women's Army Corps (WAC), but unlike Nisei men, they were integrated into the WAC. Some Nisei women were "trained as linguists," but "most however received training in clerical, medical, supply, and other military support positions."[15] In her book *Serving Our Country*, Brenda Moore states that the Japanese American press articulated Nisei women's military service as advantageous because it provided "training and work experience" and "preference for employment after the war" and enabled these women to be "free to move about anywhere in the United States."[16] However, due to the small numbers of Nisei WACs, the voluntary nature of service, their integration, and the limitation to the domestic sphere, Nisei women's military service did not garner the same kind of visibility that Nisei men's did.

However, women do become visible in connection with the Nisei soldier as mothers whose poignant stories are told to emphasize the sacrifice made by Japanese Americans. The mother is often portrayed as overly emotional because she has made the ultimate sacrifice—her son. For example, in a letter to Ernest Besig, the executive director of the Northern California affiliate of the American Civil Liberties Union during World War II, a mother whose son had died as a soldier while she and the rest of her family renounced citizenship asked for his assistance. In seeking advice on how to restore their citizenship, she writes, "Words [could] not express the agony, the anguish, the utter desolation of my heart" as she struggled to deal with the death of her son (from the war) and her husband (who died while incarcerated).[17] In a WRA promotional still, titled *Another Inmate Gold Star Mother* (1945), a colonel is pictured presenting a mother with a Distinguished Service Cross for the death of her son.[18] The mother is solemnly staring at the medal being transferred into her hands, her quiet grief emanating from the photograph. Death (the absence of her son) and grief make her legible within a narrative of masculine loyalty, but only as an appendage of her dead son and what he means for the nation.

Another avenue of gendered sacrifice had to do with relocation efforts. In her article "Japanese American Women and the Student Relocation Movement, 1942–1945," Leslie A. Ito argues that women, similar to men in the military, were used as "ambassadors to the community" to help break the negative image of Japanese Americans in preparation for the closing of the incarceration sites.[19] However, rather than battling enemies on a battlefield, female students were envisioned as having the real possibility of transforming Japanese Americans from enemy aliens to incorporated citizens. In response to the poor quality of education being offered in the camps, the National Japanese American Student Relocation Council was formed as a means to foster students' success and ensure that they would portray a positive image to the rest of America "within a controlled environment."[20] The colleges that were specifically designated for Japanese Americans were located in the Midwest and on the East Coast because the government hoped that many of the families would "eventually follow their children" once official relocation of all incarcerees began.[21] As a result, students were chosen based on their ability to assimilate into American college life, and consequently a higher percentage of female over male students were selected because "women [were considered] to attract less suspicion of espionage and wartime paranoia."[22] Even while they were at college campuses, these female students were required to give speeches about their incarceration experiences that stressed their loyalty and Americanism. In order to justify early relocation efforts, the use of the male narrative of heroism, patriotism, and loyalty was utilized to make these women legible through gendered sacrifice. This narrative transforms the enemy alien to model citizen whose proper gendered behavior can be useful for the nation while ensuring the nation's continued safety. This narrative of Japanese American women remains within the boundaries of nationalist histories of assimilation.

Because the scholarship on Japanese American incarceration has privileged gendered performances of patriotic masculinity, women's stories and lives are often overshadowed. In order to emerge from these shadows, scholars unintentionally utilize the narratives of gendered liberation to make visible women's experiences that problematically justify incarceration. Scholars also discuss how the traditional roles of men and women were switched because of incarcerated living.[23] Women's independence during incarceration is articulated as a result of Issei men no longer being the family's main source of income.[24] However, arguing for cultural patterns that produce gender-specific roles inadvertently works to justify the need for incarceration. This discussion of incarceration as a vehicle for improved women's rights implies that Japanese American women would still be subject to "patriarchal Japanese culture" without the intervention of the government. It is in this moment that the production of the Japanese American woman becomes essential to the construction of incarceration as benevolent and necessary for their insertion into modernity and their worthiness of reinstated citizenship. Gendered liberation within incarceration is mobilized as providing Japanese Americans with a better life, where death, destruction, and disposability can conveniently be ignored for benevolence.[25] To remember incarceration as the site of "transformation" of gendered roles, behavior, and family life exposes how gendered performances are integral to one's visibility. These performances of proper femininity and masculinity are also performances of American citizen subjectivity. By becoming soldiers, grieving mothers, student ambassadors, and liberated women, Japanese Americans could not only be welcomed back into American society but were seen as worthy of this inclusion. As rehabilitated subjects, transformed from enemy aliens to properly assimilated citizen-subjects, Japanese Americans had to remember incarceration not only as a "military necessity" but as a necessity to their survival. In the next section, I explore how the legacies of visibility during World War II impacted the strategies for state recognition, apology, and monetary compensation used in the struggle for redress and reparations.

Dying to Be Worthy: Japanese American Redress and the Limits of Gendered Normative Visibility

This discourse of death and the gendered performances of proper citizenship is intimately linked to visibility and recognition and is then appropriated by the Japanese American community and figures prominently in the community's narrative of loss in the struggle for redress and reparations. In order to prove that the state committed a wrong against the Japanese American community *and* that they are worthy of an apology and monetary compensation, the movement for redress and reparations capitalized on the gendered normative performances described in the previous section. Loss can only be calculated, understood, and mourned within the hearings *if and only if* Japanese Americans can clearly articulate themselves as rehabilitated and innocent subjects. The testimonies of innocence are predicated on performances of gendered behavior and sacrifice as good American subjects.

Between July and December 1981, the Commission on Wartime Relocation and Internment of Civilians held hearings and took testimony from more than 750 witnesses. The hearings were a space for Japanese Americans to narrate loss (death and economic) to prove that the state harmed them during World War II. It was the first national opportunity to hold the state accountable for incarceration, let alone be listened to, and testimonies serve as evidence of state violence. In the hearings, Japanese Americans developed these ways of speaking about and remembering incarceration that deeply impact how Japanese Americans continue to talk about World War II on both a communal and national level. After twenty days of public hearings and eighteen months of investigation, the commission published a 467-page report on their findings. The published report devotes an entire section to Japanese American men's participation in the military. The report narrates that despite the continued detainment of their families and their own incarceration, Japanese American men were expected to volunteer for the army. Some of these men were used for intelligence services that required them to interrogate enemy Japanese prisoners, persuade enemy soldiers to surrender, and take part in combat.[26] This particular narrative emphasizes and tallies the heavy casualties suffered by the 100th Infantry Battalion and the 442nd Regimental Combat Team (segregated Japanese American units), who still to this day are the most decorated troop, having been awarded 3,600 Purple Hearts, a medal given to those injured or killed while serving.[27] Emphasizing both the casualties and the awarded honors is an important strategy for the Japanese American community because this narrative demonstrated how this ultimate loss of human life made them worthy of redress. As Takashi Fujitani argues, by literally sacrificing their bodies, militarism "transported the Japanese American male from the outside to the inside of the American population" and gave them a direct avenue to show their patriotism.[28] Redress resurrects the Nisei soldier, whose death functions to gain recognition of the Nisei as Americans who deserve an apology for being treated otherwise.

Yet this narrative of injury and death is problematic for the way it allows the state its great moment of national redemption. The remembering of patriotic racialized masculinity during the 1980s is significant because it also plays into a national discourse on welfare. As Victor Bascara observes, although Japanese Americans were able to obtain an official apology and reparations, this attempt to remedy a wrong committed by the nation coupled with the model minority discourse justified, among other moves, the dismantling of social welfare programs, which had reached a fever pitch in the 1980s at the exact moment of the redress movement. By highlighting the ways Japanese Americans achieved "success" despite their racial hardships and incarceration, the United States could demonstrate "how the system [could] correct itself without the need for radical change."[29] Bascara argues that the "failures of a curiously successful redress movement" reveal the ways the United States' interests converged with the Japanese American community's desires. As I argued in the introduction, national conversations and policies concerning welfare dependency racialized and gendered certain groups of color as deviant through a discourse of heteronormativity that criminalizes and punishes them for being poor. Consequently, redress inadvertently gives life to the state at the expense of the welfare of other groups of color. Patriotic Japanese American masculinity not only proves that Japanese Americans were wrongly incarcerated but also proves that despite racial hardships, Japanese Americans were and continue to be "successful." Racial trauma gets written out of the narrative even as it acknowledges it (Nisei death). In this moment, Japanese Americans are allowed to live while others are made to die by being racialized as unworthy of life (or resources that sustain life).[30]

This is not to say that the commission hearings only operated in this way. They did not. They were a space for Japanese Americans to voice how the state had harmed them during World War II and continued to do so by not acknowledging or remembering what had happened to them. At every turn, trauma seeped into testimony after testimony and was often uncontained by the parameters of the hearings themselves. Although memories of dislocation, property losses, and racial discrimination could now be publicly articulated and acknowledged, the struggle for redress and reparations itself constructed a very specific way of remembering incarceration that continues to structure community strategies against historical erasure.

The Specter of Death and the Archive: Densho and the Legacy of Redress

In the second half of this chapter, I extend my analysis of the biopolitical administration over life and death during incarceration to demonstrate how this deeply impacted Japanese American ways of remembering and knowing themselves and their history. These carceral logics of devaluation and thus valuation structured redress testimonials that then continued to impact the oral history projects that boomed redress's aftermath. Here, I explore the relationship among death, life, and archive by analyzing Densho's materials to understand how Japanese American oral history projects gain momentum, legitimacy, and urgency. Densho incorporated its archival material into lesson plans and promotional materials, and I examine this content to better understand not only Densho's mission and significance but how it imagines the archive should be used. Drawing again from Foucault's concept of biopower, I explore what I call the biopolitical logic of the archive, where the management of disappearing memory through archiving seeks to circumvent the physical death and historical erasure of Japanese Americans. To preserve memory, the archive must banish forgetting and refusal of memory and remembering, which then become vehicles for sustaining a neoliberal racial order. In other words, the archive constructs narratives of visibility and worth that must be remembered, unintentionally supporting narratives that allow for the death and dying of other minoritized groups. To be archivable, or worthy of remembering (communal and national), the biopolitical logic asks memory to be in the service of existing national narratives and racial hierarchies. However, this chapter also theorizes an alternative reading of the archive (against its own mission and the biopolitical logics of archiving) to construct a more precarious lesson on Japanese American incarceration. I read the archive for moments of refusal: where interviewees cannot or will not remember their incarcerated pasts to understand forgetting as an important strategy of survival that resists archival attempts to establish the living witness or when the curriculum is unable to center Japanese American incarceration and instead establishes the United States as a carceral state. The complexities of the archive show us the limits and possibilities of Japanese American memory practices. In this next section, I explore the mission of Densho and the narratives produced within promotional material found on their YouTube channel.

About Densho: Combating Memory Loss

Because of the way Japanese Americans had to make their experiences of racialized violence legible to the state via a discourse of death, testimony as a genre of speaking became a popular form and strategy for addressing their literal absence from mainstream histories and archives. Oral history projects allowed Japanese Americans to give voice to a variety of experiences and have remained an integral part of the community's formation of its past, present, and future. For marginalized groups, there is a sense of urgency in their concern about the memories of the next generations that illuminates the very real fear of disappearance. As I have been arguing, because the nation will not remember, if the next generation forgets, then it would be as if they never existed; death is an integral part of marginalized communities via the passing down of memories and customs. That is, the telling of life stories is always wrapped up with death. As Ann Cvetkovich notes in relation to lesbian public cultures in *The Archive of Feeling*, "The specter of literal death serves as a pointed reminder of the social death of losing one's history."[31] As I have laid out in this chapter, this relationship between life and death in the process of remembering is one that is simultaneously necessary and problematic for marginalized groups, and in this section, I show this dialectic in relation to Densho and Japanese American incarceration history to interrogate how death has become such an integral part of Japanese American memories, narrations, and the archive. Death as the motivating factor for archiving relies upon memory practices that are wrapped up in establishing the living witness as proof where remembering is reliant on state recognition and visibility through state redemption (a vestige from redress and reparations). The Japanese American community's relationship and vulnerability to death as a racialized group have shifted them from the outside (incarceration) to the inside (as protectable life). Interrogating this is important because it reveals how Japanese American community memory practices are unintentionally susceptible to neoliberal logics that sustain racial hierarchies of worth. A more thorough analysis of Densho's mission reveals how life and death operate in the digital archive.

In a nine-and-a-half-minute "About Densho" video located adjacent to the archive on Densho's YouTube page, the Densho Project articulates its mission, history, and significance to show the impact a Japanese American digital archive has on the world. The video begins by framing Densho as a historical education project where these "thousands of voices" in the archive "can teach us about a dark chapter in America's past."[32] As a result, it is the Densho Project's mission to "preserve these memories before they fade away."[33] This "fading away," like many of the forms of public memory within this book, is what fuels and legitimizes the museums, pilgrimages, plays, and, in the late 1990s, the emerging digital archive. Ikeda tells us that in the beginning there were two forces shaping Densho:

> The first one was that our elders in our community were dying. These were people who lived through World War II, and we need to get their story, so there's a sense of urgency. The second force was the emergence of high technology. Here we had digital video, the internet, and multimedia computers to preserve these stories for the future.[34]

The feelings of urgency to address the death of community elders combined with this new technology enabled Densho to capture the voices of those who witnessed and experienced historical trauma via racialized state violence. And yet, Ikeda goes on to claim that the biggest hurdle to overcome when the project started was to convince these community elders to share their stories. He states that many of them said that "the stories were too painful."[35] In an interview with Rainmakers TV, Ikeda also admits that the project met with some ambivalence, with potential interviewees arguing that "we know the story, why should we tell people?"[36] However, in the end, Densho convinced Japanese American elders to share their stories by telling them that "the stories weren't for them, or really for my [the Sansei] generation, they were for future generations."[37] In other words, it was important for interviewees that their "grandchildren and great grandchildren hear about the stories, and that is how Densho got started."[38] The traumatic memories of incarceration are what make many Nisei hesitant to share and preserve their stories, and it is only when Densho utilized a discourse of generational responsibility to the family that they began to agree. Drawing on a language of familial guilt to share racialized trauma is meant to "capture these stories so that people *know* what happened."[39] Transgenerational haunting "suggests [that] an unspeakable trauma does not die out with the person who first experienced it," but "rather it takes on a life of its own, emerging from the spaces where secrets are concealed."[40] Taking the trauma from the "spaces where secrets are concealed" to the public archive makes the trauma legible. Generational responsibility to the familial transforms the trauma from unspeakable to recordable. As recordable, the trauma is now legible to the state; it is redressable and becomes co-opted by the state to articulate that racism is officially over. The archive fixes the racialized trauma within the historical past. The replaying of that trauma and its accessibility as well as its fixity within the digital archive ensure that even in the face of looming death, Japanese Americans' World War II experiences remain. Furthermore, the use of digital video within the archive allows for the resurrection not just of memories but of that person—their life history, image, gestures, and voice.

Within this promotional video, Densho also narrates a brief but linear and generational Japanese American history that supports and grounds the archive's mission. This history begins with Issei immigration to the United States; "by 1940" they were "more or less settled into American society," which was quickly transformed by December 7, 1941, "when suddenly [Japanese Americans] looked like the enemy."[41] From the archive, Densho pulls a collage of interview videos where Nisei men and women talk about how December 7 changed their families, their lives, and how they imagined themselves. While there are three interviewees speaking about their separate experiences, Densho places them right after each other, constructing a cohesive narrative in which time can be marked as before and after Pearl Harbor:

> And before my mother got home, the FBI showed up, and it must have been shortly after lunch.
>
> They came for my dad that night, early in the morning of December 8.
>
> One of the teachers said, "You people bombed Pearl Harbor." And I'm going, "My people? All of a sudden, my Japanese-ness became very aware to me.
> I was seen as a 'Jap,' just the same as the enemy."[42]

The transition for these children is remembered as "sudden." They go from students and children to enemies in a matter of a day, which is seen in the examples of the FBI's appearance in exchange for family disappearances and the accusations of the teacher. This "suddenness" of racialization is felt immediately, and Densho highlights this shift from "more or less settled" to "just the same as the enemy" to demonstrate the lived consequences of a post–December 7 world for Japanese Americans. While we can dispute the "more or less settled" narrative Densho succinctly narrates for pre–Pearl Harbor Japanese American life, the shift is meant to illuminate the centrality of World War II incarceration to Japanese American historiography. It is also meant to make the viewer realize the importance of Densho's work. Inserting these videos from the Densho archive (which they point out in text as the interviewees speak) works to support the historical narrative being constructed within the promotional video that is legitimized via the living witness. The oral histories prove that these experiences need to be learned.

After the collage of interviews, the narrator returns to discuss how "the surprise attack on Pearl Harbor made America angry and afraid," which led to "most Americans" thinking it was "perfectly reasonable to take action against their Japanese American neighbors here at home" as images of Executive Order 9066 and incarceration appear on the screen.[43] However, what is striking for the narrator is that even today, "many Americans still don't know that more than 120,000 Japanese Americans, two-thirds of them U.S. citizens, were forced from their homes and put behind barbed wire because of their race."[44] Lamenting how forty years had passed before the United States created a congressional commission that "would uncover evidence from the war years proving there had been no military necessity for the mass incarceration of Japanese Americans," Densho's mission, then, is not only to preserve but to teach.

In an interview, Ikeda articulates the archive as being for "the rest of America," which he identifies as having the ability to be "much more powerful."[45] Initially, Densho focused solely on the collection of oral histories because they were a "small nonprofit with limited resources" that was unable to "launch [a] large marketing campaign."[46] However, with their continued growth, Densho has been able to focus on creating "curriculum, videos, and other materials so that we can" now "outreach to the rest of the country."[47] In the promotional video, while Ikeda expresses his excitement about how many people visit Densho's website (over eighty thousand every year), there is footage shown simultaneously of three students looking at Densho's website in their school library. For Ikeda, the fact that the majority of these visitors are students is important because Densho's mission is to educate, as they are not "just about preserving the past" but about "inspiring the future also."[48]

To show the kind of impact Densho has on the future via students, the video gathers testimonials from students and teachers who attest to the significance of the archive. Many of the testimonials attribute the oral history video as having the most impact on them. For example, a college student states, "When I see them talking about their experiences it hits me much harder. And I really *feel* their presence and their experience."[49] A high school student then tells us that "the most important thing is to have firsthand experience," which is something you cannot get in a "textbook, no matter how hard you try."[50] For this student, "to have someone actually tell you what happened, that's priceless."[51] Here, the students' affective responses are produced by the ability of digital technology to reproduce the witness, and it is this connection that seems to enhance student learning about Japanese American incarceration. However, the centrality of the reproduction of the witness mimics the use of testimony as evidence of racialized violence in the congressional hearings about incarceration that eventually led to redress and reparations. The video makes that connection itself by jumping back into its historical narration, and we find ourselves at the signing of the Civil Liberties Act of 1988, which "mandated monetary payments and formal apologies to all survivors of the incarceration."[52] In this way, Densho argues that "for anyone who didn't live through World War II, the idea that the American government would put its own citizens inside barbed wire camps might seem *beyond belief, not possible*."[53] Testimony makes it possible to believe. The affective responses of students and teachers to using the archive in their classroom, like redress and reparations, rely on biopolitical logics like "witness," "truth," and "what really happened" to legitimate Japanese American incarceration. In order to protect life from impending death/disappearance, Japanese American oral history projects rely on a kind of management of memories where truth and remembering must always be in the service of the United States as a liberal democracy. The students believe it happened, and the teachers can easily teach that it happened because these witnesses relive their experiences of trauma right there on video. To have these stories is to make trauma legible to the law, education, and other state institutions.

In this way, Densho argues that they are teaching about Japanese American incarceration and the valuable lesson that comes with it: "Anytime we single out a group because of how they look, or what God they pray to, we undermine America's democracy. That happened during World War II, and it's happening again today."[54] This narration occurs while newspaper headings and footage of 9/11 destruction play on the screen, drawing a direct connection between 12/7 and 9/11. Ikeda, then, states that "during World War II, our country made a terrible mistake," and that "we want people to understand this."[55] However, Densho does this "not because we want to dwell on the past, but [because] we want people to make better, more informed decisions."[56] The promotional video then ends with another collage of interviews from a high school student, a professor, a former incarceree, and a justice, who all reiterate this message of taking what Densho has or will teach about the "mistakes of history" so that one may determine for oneself that "in our lifetime it will never happen again."[57] As former incarceree Gene Akutsu states, "Don't hesitate, but get out and speak up [about] your feelings and let them know that you want justice."[58] Densho resurrects the dead and the dying to ensure a particular kind of future that draws on the temporality of "never again." This temporality must identify Japanese American incarceration as an exceptional moment in history that can help us speak out against and prevent future injustices. "Never again" is always invoked within Japanese American historical accounts of incarceration, and in a post–9/11 world, "never again" becomes a mantra repeated in community spaces that aim for solidarity with Arab and Muslim Americans. This slogan works to legitimate the importance of World War II incarceration to the present moment, and it states that an injustice like this should never happen again *even* as it happens over and over. The connection between Japanese Americans and Muslim and Arab Americans is often the only one that is identifiable to Japanese Americans (although in a post-Trump era of white supremacist and anti-immigrant rhetoric this is drastically shifting once again) in public spaces of memory.[59]

Densho is where the residues of Japanese American redress linger, the growing anxiety about Nisei death and disappearance takes formation, and "never again" takes shape through education. All these discourses, narratives, and histories converge within the digital archive; this is how it gains legitimacy and funding and how it continues to grow. The digital manifestation of all these discourses in the archive demonstrates how intimately twined testimony, proof, and death are and how central they are to Japanese American public memories. In the next section, I explore how Nisei death is producing generational anxieties around the imagined ability of Japanese American communities to effectively tell their histories of incarceration.

Dying to Be Archived: Recuperating Life in the Densho Archive

Death is a prominent feature of Densho and their websites.[60] And yet, despite this prominence, the organization cannot think about death in any other way than that of life. For example, in their archive, when a visitor clicks on a particular person's name, a summary of that individual along with their picture is featured in the main frame of the web page. This blurb summarizes the person's life history and always includes whether the person has already passed away. This notification of death seems to point not so much to the fact that these people are no longer here but that they continue to live in this very archive despite their physical absence. In addition, when a significant community member passes away, Densho often posts a notice of that person's death with a link to their obituary and oral history video. For example, when Hisaye Yamamoto passed away in 2011, Densho wrote, "Influential writer Hisaye Yamamoto passed away on January 30th. The Densho Digital Archive contains a life history interview with Ms. Yamamoto conducted by Emiko and Chizuko Omori for their 1999 documentary *Rabbit in the Moon*."[61] These announcements of death are sorrowful in their language of loss, but they also simultaneously bring that person back to life. By watching the interview, the deceased is resurrected even in the moment one has become aware that they have died. As Densho promises, even when memories begin to fade and people grow old and die, the interview remains.[62] Their fixity in the archive guarantees that their voices will be heard and that they have not died only to disappear entirely. In this way, the archive replaces physical life with oral history, and in doing so, it situates itself as a repository of life.

Because oral history projects began to emerge in the aftermath of redress, and, as Ikeda laments, "most of the Issei generation had [already] passed on, the stories we have of them come secondhand through Nisei memories."[63] In this way, the Issei pose a problem for organizations that seek to recuperate life because they are no longer physically alive to give voice to the variety of their experiences. The death of the Issei is the kind of death that Densho so desperately seeks to prevent. In the face of this erasure and disappearance, Densho instead must stress that it is through these family stories that we can learn about "how hard [the] parents [of Nisei] worked and how they instilled in their children the values of integrity, tradition, and family honor."[64] *Densho* is the Japanese word meaning "to pass on to the future," and it is within this mentality of legacy and lineage that the Issei live through the memories of their children. For example, children reminisce about what it was like for their parents as immigrants laboring in a racially hostile environment as well as their very different but devastating struggles after the attack on Pearl Harbor. In these stories, we catch glimpses of the Issei being remembered by their children, who attempt to make sense of their parents' reactions, actions, and lives. Densho circumvents death by strategically narrating the Issei into legitimate history that is vividly and respectfully told by their children.[65] Issei life is resurrected by the nuclear family where children honor the memories of their mothers and fathers. Densho never really seems to consider the Issei in any other way—they can only make sense of them if they are brought back to life. In considering what Densho refuses to do, I am interested in what it would mean if the Issei were to remain elusive. What would it mean to acknowledge the gaps within these kinds of projects? If we so easily dismiss what we can never really know for the knowable, then how does this foreclose other ways of knowing (such as forgetting) that do not rely upon the factual/truthful? Forgetting, refusal, silence, and gaps in memory tell a story too. But the archive is always about preserving life (memory) beyond death (absence). The resurrection of the dead and the dying by Densho makes visible the way that community strategies utilize and enforce a particular relationship to life and death that fails to interrogate the biopolitical logic of archiving, knowledge production, and memory.[66]

However, Densho's archive is not the only part of its website that intimately addresses death. On its "Giving to Densho" section, they offer several suggestions and reasons for donation that range from pledging a donation to donating stock or volunteering.[67] According to Densho, making a tribute gift "offers you a thoughtful way to celebrate and honor a special person or occasion while contributing to Densho's mission."[68] In addition to the impetus to archive and record living histories on the verge of dying/disappearance, one has the option to donate money because someone has already died. In other words, that person via monetary contribution can "live on" by ensuring the archive will continue to exist. Densho also suggests "including Densho in your estate plan" so that "you can leave a legacy of your own."[69] This generous donation will "support our work to educate all Americans and inspire them to act in defense of liberty and the highest values of our country."[70] As an organization that relies upon the support of donors and donations, this section of the website is vital to its continued existence. Despite the death of a loved one or even one's own death, one's money can productively preserve Japanese American histories. The donation exceeds death by extending the life of Densho, which in turn prolongs the living histories of the dead and dying for future generations. Here, the combining of the biopolitical logic of archiving and discourses of generational reproduction with a desire for capital work to legitimate memory in ways that market the archive as survival—a way of living beyond death. In doing so, Densho unintentionally reifies the relationship between visibility and death, a relationship that was once set up by the very structure of incarceration that was then carried over into Japanese American redress and reparation testimonies. In this way, death is capitalized upon as motive for archiving and for sustaining the archive itself.

Teaching Japanese American Incarceration: The Limits of Constitutional Value, Civil Liberties, Individuals, and the Common Good

Densho's curriculum development ranges from elementary school to high school and provides a window into what lessons from incarceration are important to teach the next generation. The curriculum draws on a variety of primary source material on Japanese American incarceration while featuring oral history interviews from the archive as an important resource to understand what happened during World War II. In the previous sections, I laid out how Densho's mission sustains a biopolitical relationship among archive, memory, and life that banishes death and forgetting. I continue this interrogation in their lesson plans by analyzing what stories are worthy of investigation and knowledge by high school students. I begin by exploring the framing question and goals of the curriculum to interrogate what narratives are produced, how they are produced, and the consequences of teaching World War II incarceration this way. To be clear, I am less interested in the pedagogical and learning outcomes of the curriculum, and I do acknowledge and understand the limits of K–12 education. I am more interested in when and how these lessons either reproduce or challenge carceral narratives of exceptionalism and state redemption. To interrogate the larger narratives provides insight into how archival spaces can provide new ways of knowing and surviving.

I look specifically at Densho's "Constitutional Issues: Civil Liberties, Individuals, and the Common Good," a three-week unit designed for high school students that includes activities, resources, and assignments in a seventy-nine-page curriculum guide.[71] This lesson plan was created by Densho in collaboration with the National Park Service's Minidoka National Historic Site (in Idaho) in 2009. This particular unit is designed to fit the "Idaho state standards in social studies and language arts, specifically in geography, U.S. history, and writing."[72] The essential question this curriculum asks is: "How can the United States balance the rights of individuals with the common good?"[73] This guiding question is meant to provoke student thinking about "their own value and beliefs" and how they might feel when their individual rights are taken away for the "common good." To get students to think about how they would feel is a methodology of relationality that is meant to place students in a similar situation. The interrogating question of "how would you feel?" is meant to establish an empathetic curiosity that will enable students to imagine what life was like for Japanese Americans during World War II. However, this framing of incarceration as an attack on the "rights of the individual" is often how the state, via redress, frames incarceration. It allows the state to renarrate incarceration on the level of the individual in a way that then absolves the state of its racist past. This unit is interested in establishing what are the "democratic ideals" and "constitutional principles that form the backbone of the U.S. government" that then get disrupted by Japanese American incarceration. Within the confines of high school curriculum requirements, Densho must position incarceration within the realm of the "individual" as a strategy of enacting high school critical thinking about democracy while the "common good" is used to question if the government is always pursuing the democratic ideas and values it purports. Problematically, the curriculum never quite pushes high school students to intentionally understand the "common good" systemically or as a tool of white supremacy.

Densho goes on to state that at the end of the course, students should not only be able to "develop and carry out a research plan" and have gained other academic skills but should be able to

> demonstrate knowledge of the Constitution and laws of the United States. Relate underlying values to actions taken by individuals and by governments. Identify the tensions between individual rights and the common good. Identify issues of racism and injustice in the United States and connect them with relevant court cases and the Constitution. Understand the gap between constitutional ideals and actual practice and identify ways the Constitution has been changed to narrow that gap. Explore how change has taken place in our history, and how we can act to bring about change. Move from research to action.[74]

The "gap between constitutional ideals and actual practice" is where Japanese American World War II incarceration lies, and in the assessment of "underlying values" and "actions taken by individuals and governments," the curriculum situates incarceration as an exception to American democracy rather than an inherent part of it. Students are supposed to learn that sometimes individuals or governments make "bad" choices concerning "good" people for the "common good." Japanese Americans and their oral history interviews serve as evidence of that. However, in the next sections, I examine places in both the archive and the lesson plans themselves where this overarching question fails. In other words, sometimes the assignments and oral history examples veer from the curriculum's overarching goals. Reading these moments reveals a more nuanced lesson from the archive: that Japanese American incarceration is not an aberration of American democracy but rather a condition of it. The biopolitical management of memory cannot contain this or wholly teach "civil liberties" to future generations, just as it cannot neatly contain the trauma of incarceration and all its forms into neatly edited and consumable video clips.

Lessons from the Archive, Part I: The Failure of Memory in the Archive

Densho's "Constitutional Issues: Civil Liberties, Individuals, and the Common Good" begins by establishing what are the "democratic ideals" and "constitutional principles that form the backbone of the U.S. government." However, it is during the second week of the curriculum that the lesson shifts to focus on and situate Japanese American World War II incarceration. The curriculum makes this transition by asking students: "What happens to our democracy when there is a crisis such as war? How does this affect our relationship to the Constitution, to constitutional principles, and to our democratic ideals?"[75] The lesson uses the example of incarceration as raising "serious constitutional questions regarding the rights of individuals living within a larger society perceived to be under threat."[76] Incarceration as a contradiction to "democratic ideals" and "constitutional principles" inherently situates World War II as an exception that is important to study so that this may not happen in our future. Within this framework, week two of the curriculum draws on oral history videos for the first time. Densho only utilizes four oral history interviews in this unit, which can be accessed on their YouTube page so that students do not even have to enter the archive itself.

But first, Densho must introduce oral history as a primary source. In a critique of history, Densho states that "our knowledge of a historical time period is limited to major events" that gloss over the "everyday experiences or feelings of individuals."[77] Oral history allows for such an opportunity. However, Densho warns the students that "because of the *subjective* nature of an oral history interview it should not be used as a substitute for analysis of historical materials like official documents, diaries, letters, newspapers, and books."[78] Oral history testimony, then, "can help illuminate by placing an individual's experience within a historical period."[79] Densho situates oral history as "evidence" of what happened to Japanese Americans during World War II, and yet it cautions students about its validity as a source because it is an "individual's experience." In the biopolitical management of memory, the individual experience is valued and valid because in death that experience would be lost. Loss of the individual would mean a loss of history and thus the inability to teach this history to future generations (generational reproduction). In their lesson plans, Densho positions oral history as less valid than other historical documents. Rather than stressing that oral testimony can tell us "what really happened," this lesson cautiously identifies these voices as "subjective." Although it problematically situates oral history in opposition to "official documents," and thus one as subjective and the other as objective, I argue that the shift from "truth" to the subjective allows for the trauma of carceral violence to be heard and thus made visible. The oral history videos register the complexity of "truth" telling that "official" documents supposedly provide us with.

The biopolitical management of memory (Densho's mission) and the teaching of oral history are contradictory and demonstrate the limits of traditional historical analysis. The use of the words "individual," "feelings," and "subjective" all point to the affective nature of the archive, all things that are not "evidence," "factual," or entirely the "truth." Even as the interview makes the audience feel personally connected to that individual's experience, it is simultaneously scrutinized as a partial truth that needs more evidence to substantiate it. Furthermore, what happens when affective registers and responses such as silence, discomfort, refusal, or forgetting make their way into the archive? These responses are not as useful to Densho or historical analysis because they cannot be used to construct a narrative of World War II incarceration history. What happens when the biopolitical management of memory fails to capture life and subsequently truth? What happens when we pay attention to these moments instead of glossing over them as not useful?

Drawing on Jack Halberstam's conceptualization of forgetfulness, I argue that forgetting is a form of knowing, "one that resists the positivism of memory projects" and refuses the heteronormative and generational transfer of memory.[80] There is no story to pass on that produces discontent as the archive fails to capture memory. In these failures, forgetting not only tells us information about racial trauma but also disrupts linear historical narratives that place racial violence distinctly in the past. In the next part of this section, I read the lesson plan for these failures and contradictions to find possibility in what the archive tries to erase and ignore.

Forgetting: Surviving Carceral Trauma

While the selected interviews provide us with examples of how four different Japanese Americans experienced their incarceration to supplement historical materials in the unit, I provide an alternative reading for trauma in the archive to illuminate the ways these subjects resist biopolitical logics of archiving and memory. The interview clips are all under five minutes, and each have been carefully selected for the students, who are also provided with transcripts. These easily digestible clips are meant to show students what this time period was like for Japanese Americans. In a short excerpt, Frank Yamasaki, a Nisei draft resister born in Seattle, Washington, is asked to talk about how he felt when he "was moving from 'Camp Harmony' to Minidoka." Yamasaki responds by telling the interviewer, "That's the area, that's the area I kind of blanked out. I don't recall at all. I'm sure there must have been some apprehension there. I try to recall several times, but I don't know why." Despite the interviewers' awareness of this "blank" period in Yamasaki's memories, they still try to ask him about the transition, but he is unable to answer them, so they must move on to their next question. While the clip does not make space for the blank period, Masao Watanabe narrates his memories of Puyallup as being "a real traumatic type of living" where he intentionally "forgot a lot of 'Camp Harmony.'"[81] He tells the interviewer that he "hate[s] to use the word 'harmony'" because "it was just not a good experience."[82] These interview excerpts do provide viewers with the ability to learn about different facets of daily life for incarcerees, including what it was like to eat sand with one's food because of the dustiness of incarceration and the degradation of having to live in former pig and cow stalls. And yet, these blank periods and forgetting are small interruptions to an interview full of memories. The mission of biopolitical management of memory is to remember for the sake of living (in the archive) beyond death, and these interruptions disrupt the ability to tell the story of incarceration. In these moments, interviewers push for a memory even when there is not one (that is their job and the point of the archive). However, I argue that these blank periods and forgetting are in fact a form of storytelling and cannot be negated. Here, forgetting is a strategy for survival racial trauma. It cannot be recuperated because the memory would be harmful to their survival. To forget the past to ensure the future means that this memory cannot be archived.

Even when they are being asked to remember, some former incarcerees are unable to narrate anything other than their forgetting. In an interview with George Morihiro, born in Tacoma, Washington, he narrates how he went from his high school graduation to Puyallup Assembly Center to Minidoka before being drafted into the army in 1944. When prompted to describe his reaction to arriving at Puyallup, Morihiro starts by saying, "That's hard to say because we forget a lot of things," but then he quickly transitions to the trauma of that moment:

> There are some things in your heart that you can't forget and that is the day you walked through that gate, you know you lost something.

> Up to that point, it was news or something like that. But when you walk through that gate, you know you lost something. 'Cause, you know, the gate's got guards and barbed wire fence and everything, and you're walking from a free life into a confined life. And I know one thing, it was hard to explain to somebody what was it like in camp, because we never tell them the truth, what it was like in camp. It was horrible.[83]

For Morihiro, forgetting, remembering, and trauma are intimately tied up in narrations of carceral violence. In these excerpts about incarcerated living, we see how forgetting is a necessary means for survival. Even though Densho, as an archive and as an educational tool, is premised on preventing the forgetting of Japanese American World War II incarceration by pushing both incarcerees to remember and students to learn so that they will never forget, forgetting and forgetfulness make their way into the archive. Densho's reliance upon truth and remembering carceral violence for future generations means that it forecloses the possibility of engaging with other ways of narrating and knowing the past. These moments of memory loss expose how the trauma of carceral violence (one that Densho dismisses often for its mission) is an integral part of Nisei experiences. George Morihiro describes this as unexplainable and something that he never told the truth about. His repetition of the phrase "we lost something" demonstrates his narration of loss, as well as a simultaneous inability to even name what he has lost. Judith Butler articulates this as the "loss of loss itself," where "somewhere, sometime, something was lost, but no story could be told about it" and "no memory could retrieve it."[84] This "loss of loss" and his articulation that "we never tell the truth" imply not only an inability but an unwillingness to speak the trauma. Its horribleness exceeds narration, and it is at once something one forgets and cannot forget. The messiness of Nisei memory retrieval is that, for some, remembering is wrapped up in a kind of forgetfulness. It cannot be recuperated within a language of family that produces guilt to incite memory (Densho's mission). Instead, all we are left with are silence, gaps, and what we may never know. Grappling with these absences forces us to think of different ways to relate to the past. These moments in Densho's carefully crafted lesson plans expose something contradictory in the archive—in particular, the ways the biopolitical management of memory fails and forgetting and silence seep into the archive. The messiness of Nisei memory retrieval disrupts the archive where the trauma of incarceration cannot be neatly contained to gendered narratives of worth that students must learn. Instead, what emerges is racial trauma and violence that cannot be contained to the historical period of World War II (or even just to the past). Emerging out of carefully crafted lesson plans about this exceptional moment in history is a different way of understanding how the carceral functions.

Lessons from the Archive, Part II: Comparative Historical Methodology within the Confines of Democratic Ideals

A central component of Densho's education initiative is to make Japanese American World War II incarceration relevant, something that students should learn and know. In order to do so, the final and third week of the curriculum does a shift and focuses on comparative historical analysis beginning with slavery and moving to 9/11. I argue that this relevancy through education allows for a meaningful comparative analysis to emerge where students are given the opportunity to critically think about other "issues of injustice." This last unit places Japanese American incarceration within a much longer history of carcerality and racialized violence. Here, the contradictions between democratic ideals and practices are unraveled as students are asked to research their own topics of "ongoing injustice" and are pushed to think about actions that bring about meaningful change.

Assigned a reading of "The Meaning of July Fourth for the Negro," the section on Frederick Douglass is meant to have students continue their critiques of the Declaration of Independence and the Constitution within the "tensions between the real and ideal" to introduce the "Ongoing Injustice" assignment due at the end of the unit. Here, the curriculum suggests that

> these issues of injustice, unlike those we looked at the past two days, cannot be simply blamed on a reaction to a crisis. Our study of history leads us to view the incarceration of Japanese Americans as an aberration, an exception to the more typically democratic and fair manner in which we operate our democracy. For many groups within our society, unequal or anti-democratic treatment is more the rule than the exception, at least as it pertains to them. What does that mean?[85]

This lesson simultaneously positions Japanese American incarceration as an aberration while acknowledging that these injustices exist and continue to do so for other marginalized groups. In this way, Japanese American incarceration is exceptional and yet displaced as the exception within a longer history of this critique of democratic ideals. Placing Douglass within the unit is meant to focus on the ways the Declaration of Independence and the Constitution are "deeply flawed" and slavery cannot necessarily be "blamed on a reaction to a crisis."[86] However, I argue that the placement of slavery, Douglass, and abolition within the unit opens up the possibility of assessing Japanese American incarceration outside of aberration and within an analysis of what Clyde Wood theorizes as "racialized social-spatial enclosures," or the space that is used to "establish stable control over specific territories and their populations' which are maintained by a system of militarized regulation, physical boundaries and social, political, and economic traps."[87] Even though the curriculum never makes an explicit comparison between slavery and Japanese American incarceration, there is a subtle shift away from a discourse of "never again." As I have previously argued, the "never again" discourse of Japanese American memory politics establishes a temporality where World War II incarceration is an exception that has happened in the past, is not a part of our present, and can "never happen again" in the future. It mobilizes Japanese Americans into action but often ignores or cannot see that imprisonment as racialized punishment happens to many other groups of color. This subtle shift away from a discourse of "never again" forces students to place Japanese American incarceration within this longer lineage of carcerality. "Never again" is actually *has always been* and *continues to be*. But the lesson also focuses on Douglass's abolition work and demonstrates how movements over time have "struggled to bring us closer to the ideals of equality," which are often led by "oppressed people."[88] Citing Lani Guanier's "canaries in the mine," Densho reminds students that often those "most vulnerable to the injustices of the system, who are sensitive to that which poisons all of us," are the ones "addressing those toxins of injustice" and "are actually working for the health of us all."[89]

Before the final project is due, students do one last lesson and classroom activity called the "Town Meeting." The town meeting is articulated as a role-playing exercise in democratic practice where students are put into groups and assigned one of the following roles: the Bush administration, the American Civil Liberties Union, a U.S. soldier who is a patriotic nationalist, a second U.S. soldier from a working-class/poor background who is ambivalent about the war on terror, a Japanese American former incarceree, the Exxon Mobil corporation, an Arab immigrant, a victim of 9/11, local law enforcement, an "ordinary man or woman on the street," a member of a veteran group, an antiwar activist, a student from Iraq, a professional from the Middle East working in the United States, and a Holocaust survivor.[90] They are given the following hypothetical scenario, months after September 11:

> The specific proposal under consideration today would grant the President the power to detain indefinitely, without a hearing, any individ-

ual the administration suspects of aiding terrorist organizations, even if there is no hard evidence to support the suspicion.[91]

At the end of the town meeting, students are asked to vote on this hypothetical proposal. According to the guidelines, this assignment is intended to "stimulate dialogue to help students realize the complexities of decisions that individuals, families, local governments, and national governments have to make."[92] In other words, the guidelines share that the lesson is not the "vote that takes place at the conclusion of the meeting, but the critical thinking and communication that happen along the way" as a means of helping students "better understand the complexity of constitutional questions that require balancing freedom, security, and the many varied rights and interests of those who make up this country."[93] While none of the lessons in the unit really interrogate notions of "security" or explicitly address who gets to be secure and who does not, this particular assignment draws parallels between December 7, 1941, and September 11, 2001. Pedagogically, these assignments in this last lesson are meant to uphold democratic ideals and practices even as we question them, but the placing of slavery with Japanese American incarceration and the war on terror highlight the banality of carcerality. Beneath the surface of the lessons' objectives, students begin to glimpse the transformation of racialized spatial enclosures at different historical moments. Forms of security are achieved and maintained when racialized populations are imprisoned and that imprisonment is justified by democratic ideals.

This comparative methodology continues in the final project of the unit. The "Ongoing Injustice" assignment requires students to produce a five-minute presentation and a five-page paper that asks them to look at the following: the history, who has been affected, different viewpoints, tensions, relevant laws or court cases, the current state of the issue, and how have people in the past brought about change or taken action, and what can be done now.[94] The assignment also provides students with some starting point suggestions for picking their topics and links to websites to conduct more research on the following: unequal pay, broken treaties with Native Americans, struggles over water rights and usage, unequal allocation of resources, religious discrimination, discrimination on the basis of sexual preference, the death penalty, and incarceration rates. It further suggests that students draw on their own experiences of injustice. The purpose of the assignment is to "not have a moan and groan session" but to "sort out the gap between the real and ideal" and "between what we say about our democracy and how it functions."[95] Despite the assignment's efforts to assert that it is really about investigating the reality of American democracy, it also makes visible how racialized social-spatial enclosures are a part of that reality. In this way, this assignment uses Japanese American incarceration to open up the possibility of seeing how integral carceral landscapes have been to U.S. formation and democracy.

Within this comparative methodology, the temporality of "ongoing" means that students not only investigate how their chosen topics are happening in the current political moment but must interrogate their longer history. In other words, the temporality of "ongoing" makes visible carcerality and other forms of racialized and sexualized violence as part of the fabric of this American "democracy" *and* as something that needs action against. The lesson inadvertently identifies Japanese American incarceration as "over" in contrast to the way that these other instances of injustice are "ongoing." The beginning (Pearl Harbor) and ending (redress) of Japanese American incarceration commonly is what allows for its legibility as a "wrong." Its linear narrative and temporality as distinctly "over" allows the United States to take ownership over this democratic "failure." As a result, state violence like the prison industrial complex can be denied because it is ongoing and confronts the state with racialized violence in the present versus a past. However, as the archive has shown us, redress has not resolved Japanese American experiences of incarceration. The traumas of racial violence continue to linger in the present. In fact, the trauma is most present in the archive itself as interviewees first struggled to *want* to tell their stories and later as they retold their stories for the camera. Their stories, memories, refusals, and forgetting do not produce neatly packaged stories to be later consumed by students who must learn about this moment in history. The carcerally produced trauma cannot be contained by the celebratory logics of redress that only absolves the state of its guilt by proclaiming Japanese American innocence. Assigning students to partake in researching and writing about something that is "ongoing" forces a rethinking of how racial logics transform over time. Slavery, Japanese American incarceration, colonialism, prisons, and other forms of racialized social-spatial enclosures are juxtaposed in this part of the unit. Rather than exceptionalizing Japanese American experiences, a historical trajectory of these racialized social-spatial enclosures is compiled from past to present, challenging linear conceptions of the carceral. The "ongoing" part of the project is meant to engage students with contemporary examples of racial and sexual violence that exist in the moment of "right now," but ironically instead the assignment opens up the possibility of understanding Japanese American incarceration history as only one of the many ways the state deals with racialized and sexualized deviancy. Students then research these other methods of dealing with deviancy in the present moment that have historical legacies wrapped up in each other. Despite the limits of its own learning outcomes of "democratic ideals" and "constitutional values," the assignment perhaps unintentionally produces a carceral genealogy that reveals the inherent unfreedom and injustice of U.S. democracy.

Conclusion

The legacies of Japanese American redress and reparations as well as the importance of testimony have made Japanese Americans archivable. Coming out of this legacy, Densho preserves memory in the face of the physical death of the Nisei and their disappearance from national memory. The biopolitical management of memory relies upon an intimate connection among truth, memory, and life that seeks to banish other ways of knowing, such as forgetting and refusal. It also requires a centering of Japanese American incarceration in order to establish its historical significance to the nation and creates opportunities for younger generations to learn it, remember it, and pass it on. The archive's biopolitical management of memory fuels Densho's mission where generational reproduction needs former incarcerees to willingly share their stories. In the archive, their memories can be extracted, contained, replayed, and translated into teachable units. However, death, trauma, and forgetting are unable to be completely banished from the archive, and they manage to seep into interviewees' narrations. In addition, Densho's centering of Japanese American incarceration is disrupted in its lessons to compare World War II with other moments of racialized violence. This decentering offers the possibility of seeing and hearing different narratives that reveal a longer history of the carceral to punish racialized deviancy. Reading the archive from its contradictory location within a U.S. carceral landscape allows for an understanding of how memory can serve an abolitionist future—a future that narrates carcerality as inherently a part of U.S. democracy and not an exception. As we see in the next chapter by examining a Japanese American grassroots community organization, the same contradictory location of Japanese Americans emerges as Japanese American activists engage with Indigenous communities to fight a long-standing enemy.

3

The Colonial and the Carceral

Building Relationships between Japanese Americans and Indigenous Groups in the Owens Valley

> What if things changed to obscure what truly happened here so many years ago? What if the injustices perpetrated upon our people cannot fully be understood? Would this not be disrespectful? To us? To our family? To our community? And disrespectful to our country? Would this not be tragic? Today, there is a *danger* that this might happen.
> —Bruce Embrey, cochair of the Manzanar Committee, 2014 Annual Manzanar Pilgrimage

The danger referenced by Bruce Embrey, cochair of the Manzanar Committee, was the proposed LADWP construction of the Southern Owens Valley Solar Ranch, a 1,200-acre solar energy generating station just east of Manzanar that can be seen from any point at the site.* The Owens Valley is located east of the Sierra Nevada and is about two hundred miles north of Los Angeles, California. The proposed solar ranch would be situated on what is already LADWP-owned land in between the cities of Independence and Lone Pine and about four miles from U.S. Highway 395 off of Manzanar Reward Road, the same exit for the Manzanar National Historic Site. The Owens Valley is home to the Big Pine Paiute Tribe, the Bishop Paiute Tribe, the Fort Independence Indian Community of Paiute Indians, and the Lone Pine Paiute-

---

* This chapter previously appeared as Wendi Yamashita, "The Colonial and the Carceral: Building Relationships Between Japanese Americans and Indigenous Groups in the Owens Valley," *Amerasia Journal*, 42:1, 121–138, DOI: 10.17953/aj.42.1.121. © 2016 The Regents of the University of California, reprinted by permission of Taylor & Francis Ltd, http://www.tandfonline.com on behalf of The Regents of the University of California.

Shoshone Tribe. In this chapter, I argue that while the logic of the Manzanar pilgrimage often overlaps with U.S. nationalist memorializations of Japanese American incarceration that narrate racialized state violence as a thing of the past and can replicate settler colonial erasures of contemporary Native dispossession, the fight over the Southern Owens Valley Solar Ranch provided an opportunity for the Manzanar Committee to contest these erasures. Through fieldwork, as a member of the Manzanar Committee since 2014, I explore how new relationships were formed fighting the LADWP that ultimately have had a long-lasting impact on the Manzanar Committee's work.

The Manzanar Committee is a nonprofit educational organization that currently consists of approximately twenty-one volunteer members who meet monthly throughout the year to plan the day program at the Manzanar pilgrimage. The members are dedicated to educating and raising public awareness about the incarceration of Japanese Americans during World War II as well as continuing to fight when other people's constitutional rights are endangered. As a result, the preservation of Manzanar's carceral landscape is integral to the preservation of Japanese American history. The disruption to Manzanar's viewshed by the proposed solar ranch project would have taken away this ability to teach about the fact that Manzanar was chosen as a location for Japanese American incarceration as part of "a carefully calculated plan by the U.S. government to instill a feeling of isolation, desolation, and despair in the minds of those incarcerated as a means to control them."[1] Were the view to be disrupted by large-scale industrial renewable energy facilities, the Manzanar Committee believes it would no longer be able to teach Manzanar's story of what it was "truly" like to be "locked up behind the barbed wire at Manzanar, with nothing but open space and mountains all around the camp."[2] If the solar ranch were to be built, that feeling would be lost and visitors would not be able to experience it as part of learning about what happened to Japanese Americans at Manzanar, which, according to the committee, would be "absolutely criminal."[3]

Examining this danger to the Manzanar National Historic Site reveals not only a budding relationship between Manzanar stakeholders and the Indigenous groups of the Owens Valley but also a recognition of colonial and carceral violences as distinct but intimately intertwined. This danger has pushed Japanese Americans to stand together with the Big Pine Paiute Tribe, the Bishop Tribe, the Fort Independence Community of Paiute Indians, the Lone Pine Paiute-Shoshone Tribe, the Owens Valley Committee, and the residents of Inyo County to stop the continued destruction of the valley by the LADWP.

Manzanar National Historic Site: Preserving the Japanese American Experience

Going back to the place where Japanese Americans were once incarcerated is a political act of remembering what the state had chosen to forget and now chooses to remember in very particular ways as redeemed from its racist past. The Manzanar National Historic Site and the Manzanar Committee (and all those who support its continued existence) provide participants with the opportunity to physically engage with Japanese American history. However, remembering Japanese American incarceration by going back to Manzanar and claiming ownership over it inadvertently must involve forgetting histories of colonial violences that occupy the same land. In particular, after redress and reparations, Japanese Americans can remember their incarceration because it also serves the interests of the state.[4] By celebrating Japanese American loyalty and acknowledging state violence via their wrongful incarceration—and resolution through redress—the United States was able to declare racism officially over. Consequently, redress and reparations make other claims of state violence illegitimate within this logic. Native American claims of dispossession via colonial and settler colonial violences cannot garner legibility or visibility within this structure of remembering because these violences continue into the present. They cannot be narrated solely as part of the past. Manzanar and its pilgrimages thus occupy a contradictory location where memories of Japanese American dispossession and incarceration remember state violences committed against a racialized enemy alien who, in turn, unintentionally gains from colonial legacies and settler colonial desires.[5]

Looking at a brief history of the Manzanar pilgrimages and their current manifestation, we can see this contradictory position emerge through the ownership of land via the National Park Service and remembering incarceration. The preservation of Manzanar began with student interest at UCLA in 1969 and was propelled by a number of key figures, such as Sue Kunitomi Embrey and Warren Furutani, who created the Manzanar Project (later named the Manzanar Committee) as an organization dedicated to educating the public about Executive Order 9066 and earning California State Historic Landmark status for the site.[6] This was how the first pilgrimage began, with a group of 150 (mostly Japanese American) people who drove by car and bus to locate Manzanar.[7] In 1972, Manzanar was designated California State Historic Landmark #850, and in 1992, it was designated as a National Historic Site by the National Park Service, a bureau of the Department of the Interior. Throughout this period, the Manzanar Committee joined in the struggle for redress and reparations and collaborated with the National Council for Japanese American Redress, the Little Tokyo People's Rights Organization, and the National Coalition for Redress/Reparations; the committee also participated in these efforts by giving testimony before the Commission on Wartime Relocation and Internment of Civilians, which provided evidence that Japanese Americans were in fact incarcerated during World War II.[8] When the Civil Liberties Act of 1988 passed, including an official apology from the state and monetary redress of $20,000 to every living incarceree, the work to establish Manzanar as a historic site intensified, leading Congress to pass HR 543, the bill that designated Manzanar as a National Historic Site.[9] Although there were initial protests and death threats about the construction of a possible "Jap Museum," the creation of an advisory commission that met with local residents helped build support and understanding about the benefits that the Manzanar National Historic Site would bring to the Owens Valley.[10] However, the Manzanar Committee has always struggled with the LADWP, and it was not until 1995 that the LADWP finally transferred the land (though they still own the water rights) to the National Park Service. It was not until 2002 that the Manzanar Committee was able to obtain the funds to begin construction on the site.

Currently, the Manzanar pilgrimage consists of two components, a day program and an evening program, sponsored by the Manzanar Committee. The pilgrimage program is thoughtfully produced by the Manzanar Committee and not only seeks to educate the public about Japanese American experiences through personal stories and memories but also hopes to entertain the audience with the end goal that we remember so this may never happen again. Hinged upon a discourse of personal responsibility, remembering incarceration is about claiming that state violence did happen to us but is intimately connected to narratives of Japanese American loyalty via our wrongful and unjust imprisonment. These kinds of narratives and ways of remembering ultimately end up establishing Japanese American innocence, which disallows discussions about those who have experienced or are currently experiencing containment in similar ways. This does not mean that these narratives are not important or do not serve a valuable purpose. However, these narratives do have unintentional consequences.

A typical day begins at noon with various welcomes from different Manzanar stakeholders that include the Manzanar Committee, the National Park Service, and—for the first time in 2014—representation from one of the Indigenous groups in the Owens Valley. After welcoming the audience, the program includes awards that honor various people for their work in the Japanese American community, cultural performances (including poetry, *taiko*, and sing-alongs), and speeches that address what is currently happening in the community as well as the importance of remembering incarceration. Before and after the program, visitors are encouraged to explore the site. The visit to Manzanar consists of an auto tour on which one can see the remains of the site, including orchards, gardens, building foundations, the camp cemetery, and the Interpretive Center, which incorporates audiovisual presentations, artifacts, oral histories, and photographs.[11] The Interpretive Center houses a bookstore and gift shop where visitors can continue to educate themselves about Japanese American incarceration long after they have left the site. Adjacent to the Interpretive Center are two newly reconstructed barracks, including a block manager's office that contains exhibits as well as audio and video stations inside each building. These barracks show what it was like to live in these crowded spaces and visually provide visitors with a glimpse of the experience of those incarcerated at Manzanar.

The pilgrimage then transitions to its evening program, held in recent years at Lone Pine High School. This transition from day to evening is about passing along that discourse of personal responsibility from the Manzanar Committee (which consists mainly of second- and third-generation Japanese Americans) to the younger generations (Yonsei, or fourth generation, and beyond). Manzanar at Dusk is cosponsored by the Nikkei Student Unions (NSUs) at California State Polytechnic University, Pomona (CPP); California State University, Long Beach (CSULB); UCLA; and the University of California, San Diego (UCSD).[12] Through a creative presentation, small group discussions, and an open mic session in which participants share what they have learned, Manzanar at Dusk seeks to provide participants with the opportunity to listen to and share stories and personal experiences with a former incarceree who encourages everyone to talk about the relevance of the Japanese American incarceration experience to contemporary issues.[13] By providing the students with facilities and some guidance and consultation with the program, Manzanar at Dusk is meant to empower young people to get involved with Manzanar and the preservation of Japanese American history. Generating a sense of personal responsibility in Nikkei youth via the transmission of personal stories and experiences that places them in leadership roles aims to create a new generation of community activists and leaders. Journeying on these annual pilgrimages to various incarceration sites provides Japanese Americans with a means to remember the past as well as to make younger generations feel connected to a past that they did not experience themselves.

Before exploring how the Manzanar Committee began to forge relationships with the Indigenous groups of the Owens Valley, it is important to theorize about the intimate connections between the colonial and carceral violences that do not equate the two. To begin such an analysis, I turn to *Asian Settler Colonialism*, in which Candace Fujikane and Jonathan Y. Okamura refute multicultural narratives of Asian economic and political successes in Hawaii by highlighting Asians as settlers to expose the colonial processes that made Asian settlement possible in the first place.[14] To situate the Asian (and, in this case, the Japanese American) as a settler who benefits from U.S. settler colonialism is to look, as Alyosha Goldstein suggests, at these "complex reciprocities, seemingly opaque disjunctures, and tense entanglements" that offer us "new insights for anticolonial struggle."[15] In other words, to identify Japanese Americans as settlers via their remembrance of the carceral is an attempt to interrogate not only how the carceral and the colonial often sustain each other but how to engage in ethical and anticolonial struggle. Furthermore, I draw on Sherene H. Razack and Mona Oikawa's methodology of unmapping, which denaturalizes how a space came to be and the worldviews that rest on it by historicizing what has been rendered invisible. I argue that one needs to place the sites of Japanese American incarceration within a larger history of expulsion and containment in the United States.[16] To find a cartography of Japanese American incarceration means acknowledging that another map has been rendered invisible—that of the Indigenous nations from which the United States was founded.[17] To uncover this map would be to uncover the Asian settler. In doing so, I argue that Manzanar as a case study shows us how the carceral and the colonial often sustain each other and, in turn, reveals how to break down these intimacies of power.

Prior to World War II, Japanese immigrants were subject to anti-Asian legislation: they were both barred from immigrating with the passage of the Immigration Act of 1924 and denied naturalization and access to citizenship based on their racial ineligibility. In addition, their increased presence on the West Coast—and, in particular, as farmers—made them appear as threats to white economic security. In 1913, the first Alien Land Law was passed, making the ownership of agricultural land by "aliens ineligible for citizenship" illegal; in addition, they could not lease land for more than three years, thereby "producing a socioeconomic condition that unilaterally favored white landlords," as Eichiro Azuma explains.[18] Some of the Issei found loopholes and bought land in the name of their Nisei children or were able to find citizens willing to be owners of the land on paper only. Historicizing this formal denial of citizenship and property rights demonstrates how Japanese American incarceration was not an anomaly, but rather a function of the racial state. Incarcerating Japanese Americans under the guise of national security was about punishing those on the outside of white national belonging or citizenry.

The carceral targets a racialized "enemy" for punishment, while the colonial seeks to eliminate Indigeneity through containment, frontier homicide, and blood quantum logics.[19] The colonial is about punishment as well as elimination. As Patrick Wolfe explains, the increase of Indigenous people obstructed settler access to land that could then be turned into private property, a cornerstone of liberal democracy.[20] The primary motivation to justify eliminating Indigenous peoples is not about race, but settler access to territory.[21] Elimination via settler colonial logics persists into the present, as Native Americans are denied rights to their land and access to resources that sustain life. Here, we can see how property functions within the racial state. The state's violent emptying of the land of Indigenous peoples allows for that land to become private property. As a result of this violent process, anti-Asian legislation and Japanese American incarceration function as a means to deny access to property for Japanese or Japanese Americans. Furthermore, the denial of property rights to Japanese Americans is contingent upon Native dispossession. Seeing how the racial state intimately relies upon the colonial and the carceral to maintain itself allows us to see the parallels between the two. In fact, containment—which in its many forms includes incarceration and reservations—is how the racial state dispossesses different groups of people of color.[22] There is an intimate connection between containment and dispossession, by which the racial state is maintained in order to ultimately sustain and legitimate white supremacy.

But it is also important to think about the ways Japanese Americans are in fact settlers themselves, those who can preserve Manzanar on land that settlers took from Indigenous groups in the Owens Valley. Acknowledging that Japanese Americans sometimes unwillingly participate in the maintenance of a U.S. settler state is an important part of thinking about the relationship between the colonial and the carceral because it shows us how they are intertwined and can sustain one another. Breaking down the relationship between the two will provide Japanese Americans with ethical ways of remembering their histories. As I argue in the following, it is this recognition and reckoning with colonial violence made visible by the continued destruction brought on by the LADWP that can shift how stakeholders in the Owens Valley relate to one another.

Stakeholders in the Owens Valley: Recognizing Colonial Violences

While it is clear that the Manzanar Committee and those invested in the preservation of Japanese American history are in fact interested in securing the vitality and legitimacy of their historical narratives, I want to focus on what emerged from the dangers posed by the solar ranch construction. This fight against the LADWP has pushed Manzanar stakeholders to acknowledge the struggles and histories of other people residing in the Owens Valley.[23] During his closing remarks at the 2014 pilgrimage, Embrey states this conclusion:

> And this is why we, the Manzanar Committee, and many organizations within the Japanese American community, as well as our friends and allies here in the Owens Valley, including the Big Pine Paiute Tribe, the Lone Pine Paiute Shoshone Tribe, the Bishop Paiute Tribe, and four independent tribes along with friends in the Owens Valley Committee . . . all demand that the DWP withdraw this massive industrial solar facility and not build it. We demand that the DWP finally respect our history and not just our people, but the people of the Owens Valley. [Clapping.][24]

It is clear that standing in solidarity with other stakeholders in the Owens Valley means Embrey must acknowledge a much longer history of violence—of which Japanese Americans are only a part. He goes on to say that in asking the audience to join the fight against the LADWP, we must remember that

> there are hundreds, if not thousands, of sacred sites in this valley of the Paiute Shoshone people who have walked this valley for thousands of years. We cannot allow this to happen. We cannot allow America to forget. We must not stand by and watch our past or the past of other peoples of the Owens Valley be erased.[25]

Although they are using a language of responsibility that serves to legitimize Japanese American history, there is a way the Manzanar Committee is acknowledging how colonial violences in the Owens Valley are an integral part of its history—and, significantly, one that persists in the present.

Japanese American incarceration can be nationally acknowledged as a "wrong" committed by the nation precisely because it ideologically and materially serves to position other groups of color as "deserving" of punishment or continued state violence. Furthermore, Japanese American incarceration via redress and reparations can be marked as historically "over" by the state, whereas colonial and settler colonial violences expose how state violence continues to persist. Although it is not precisely within the Manzanar Committee's mission to imagine the relationship between the colonial and the carceral, this fight against the LADWP has opened up a space to begin talking about what that conversation might look like and how to put solidarity into action.

Sponsored by the Seventh Generation Fund for Indigenous Peoples and Graven Image Films, *Saving Payahüüpüü: The Owens Valley Solar Story* is a film produced by Angela Mooney D'arcy and those invested in the Owens Valley to ask those of us living in Los Angeles to question the construction of the solar ranch and the irreparable harm this site will produce.[26] It does this by exploring "the land, people, history, and future of the Owens Valley as its community members work to build broad-based grassroots support at home and in Los Angeles to protect the natural, historic, and cultural resources of their valley."[27] The film begins by describing the solar ranch and debunking its environmental claims, even calling it "the dirty green project."[28] Many in the film argue that there are more efficient ways to bring energy sustainability, including utilizing rooftop solar energy as the City of Santa Monica does. Historicizing the construction of the solar ranch within a larger history of resource extraction, the film exposes how the LADWP destroyed the Owens Valley by first taking water.

The film also makes connections between the different stakeholder groups as well as across different historical moments. In the film, Gann Matsuda, as one of the representatives of the Manzanar Committee, is featured exposing the solar ranch as a settler colonial project, although he never names it as such. He states that it is another "example of desecrating Native lands," where "whenever someone wanted something, usually natural resources, in this case [the] sun—it's like oh, you can move—you don't matter."[29] He then asks, "When is it going to stop?"[30] Connections are also made by other stakeholders: Harry Williams, a Bishop Paiute elder and environmental activist, talks about Manzanar as a place where "Japanese people that lived in LA and around the country" were incarcerated and put "on reservations, hidden away."[31] He goes on to say that "it was no good to steal all their property and take them out of their homes, take their property and put them in captivity and just stole their lives like they did the tribes."[32] In contrast to Matsuda, Williams explicitly goes on to name this violence as colonialism; in reference to the construction that would have to take place, he states that the LADWP will "ruin it. Just kill it. Like colonialism does. It destroys your history. It rewrites it. And if they destroy it, then you were never there because there's no proof of you ever being there."[33] Here, Williams makes a connection between Japanese Americans and Indigenous experiences by misnaming incarceration as "reservations" in an effort to think through how Indigenous and racialized dispossession occurs. He also makes visible the ways the U.S. acquisition of Indigenous lands and the taking of Japanese American properties are linked to a destruction of history that leads to physical death and erasure. This physical death and historical disappearance are about erasing Indigenous claims to land as well as invalidating Japanese American political acts of memory. The LADWP's continued destruction of the Owens Valley is very much tied up in maintaining a settler state that denies that the colonial and the carceral continue to persist.

The arguments that Matsuda and Williams present to the audience are very important conversations that both acknowledge their own respective histories as well as each other's histories of dispossession and violence. And what they both acknowledge is a much longer history of the LADWP and the Owens Valley. By turning to a discussion of water, many of the film's interviewees identify the connection among resources, land, life, colonialism, and the LADWP, beginning with claims to water rights. As Matsuda says, "So they got their water and now they want their sun too? And they want to cover pristine open space with solar panels? 1,200 acres or more? Enough is enough."[34] Similarly, Alan Bacock, the Big Pine Paiute Tribe water coordinator, notes that "water was there and then all of a sudden it was not there."[35]

In other words, the construction of the solar ranch can be situated within a much longer history of colonial violence that manifests itself in settler ownership of land and the destruction of the Owens Valley for the benefit of the settler. Prior to the LADWP, the Paiute called the Owens Valley *Piyahu-Nadu*, or the "place where water flows," because it was a place where water was once plentiful and central to Paiute creation stories and ways of living. However, the Owens Valley Paiutes' relationship to water began to change drastically in 1859 with the permanent settlement of mainly Anglo-American stockmen in the Owens Valley.[36] Conflicts erupted between the Owens Valley Paiute and the white settlers, whose grazing sheep and cattle polluted water being diverted to Paiute irrigation systems. Settler ownership of both water and land made it extremely difficult for the Owens Valley Paiute to have access to clean water and to find sources of food. As Williams states, "We were known as the 'Indian problem'" because the settlers "can't make money with [us] in [the] way."[37] Because the conflicts between the Owens Valley Paiute and the white settlers only increased due to a harsh winter and a scarcity of food between 1861 and 1862, the California Volunteers forcibly and temporarily removed the Owens Valley Paiute to the El Tejon Reservation.[38] The state also removed the Owens Valley Paiute to Fort Tejon. The removal of the Owens Valley Paiute from the valley was, according to Chantal Walker, meant to "separate them from settlers, who then would have free control over the land and water."[39] Upon their return, white settler ownership and social structures forcefully integrated the Owens Valley Paiute into the labor sector for survival.

Here, we can see how the very existence of "the Native" obstructs the settler's access to land and ownership of it, justifying removal. By 1905, the City of Los Angeles began purchasing land in the Owens Valley in order to gain access to water rights due to the city's own shortage because of its population growth. The exportation of water from the Owens River through the Los Angeles Aqueduct in 1913 was rationalized as a "public service" where the water of the Owens Valley would be put to better use in Los Angeles. The Owens Valley Paiute no longer had access to their land or water, with the City of Los Angeles owning 85 percent of all private property in the valley.[40] Roberta Hunter, the secretary of the Big Pine Paiute Tribal Council, states that the LADWP considers "all the resources to be plentiful without realizing what they are taking away from other people." *Saving Payahüüpüü* exposes the intimate connection among land, water, life resources, and how, in particular, Indigenous groups in the Owens Valley were made to let die in order for the settlers of the Owens Valley and then the City of Los Angeles to flourish and grow. The settler state can be broken down in discrete entities that often overlap and clash or collude with each other: the white ranchers, who use ancient Paiute irrigation systems for their own economic prosperity; the LADWP, as a municipal utility agency whose ownership of land and water rights in the Owens Valley violently prevents the Owens Valley Paiute from Indigenous ways of living; and, finally, Japanese American settlers, whose racialized deviancy marked them for incarceration in the Owens Valley and whose return, in cooperation with the National Park Service, continues to play a role in the continued dispossession of the Indigenous people of the valley.

Reexamining "Isolation" and "Desolation" in the Owens Valley: Settler Colonial Desires and Manzanar

While the Manzanar Committee, in its 2014 program, highlighted some of the intimate connections between Japanese Americans and Native Americans in the Owens Valley, what was presented was indeed fleeting and for the purpose of garnering support for petitions to send to Mayor Eric Garcetti. A letter drafted by the Manzanar Committee and stuffed into the pilgrimage programs tells a story of Japanese American incarceration that highlights how our civil and constitutional rights were "discarded without due process, freedom of religion or other basic rights afforded to all Americans."[41] With the signing of Executive Order 9066, Japanese Americans were then "exiled to remote, desolate, and harsh environments." With the signing of Executive Order 9066, Japanese Americans were then "exiled to remote, desolate, and harsh environments" where they were "forced to endure unforgiving environments." These conditions are an "essential part of the story."[42] It goes on to state that the Manzanar National Historic Site and its surrounding environment tell this story, in large part because the region remains largely *untouched*. Visitors to this site can easily appreciate the *isolation* and *despair* the families felt upon arriving to Manzanar.[43]

It is interesting to note that the Manzanar Committee identifies "isolation" and "despair" as being a key way to teach future generations about what happened to Japanese Americans at Manzanar. And yet, for Indigenous groups in the Owens Valley, this place is their "home." In critically thinking about this contradiction between spaces of desolation and spaces of home, we might be able to get at the relationship between the colonial and the carceral as well as to interrogate Japanese American identity as being hinged on settler colonial logics.

While the Manzanar Committee alludes to colonial violences against Indigenous groups in the Owens Valley, they never explicitly state what those violations are. Going back to their usage of the words "isolation" and "despair," these descriptions of the landscape are the traces of colonial projects that were brought on by settler and later LADWP ownership of land and water rights. The "isolation" and "desolation" were and continue to be created out of colonial violences that deny Indigenous peoples access to land, resources, and thus life. However, if we further interrogate these terms to describe the Owens Valley, we can see how the carceral—the forced removal of Japanese Americans to "isolated" and "desolate" places—also relied upon the colonial to violently create such a place. It purposefully and violently emptied the space of Indigenous peoples, who were contained on reservations to make room for settlers, and it was emptied of water as the population of Los Angeles grew beyond its own supply. It was an "ideal" area to incarcerate Japanese Americans because the state had already made it that way.

It was also already a site of containment that was made invisible by settler logics and could be justified as a location for incarceration. Here, the state's colonial and carceral projects intersect and sustain each other: The colonial created the perfect space for the carceral to exist, and the carceral—with commemorations of its past—continues to allow for settler colonial desires to permeate the future of the Owens Valley. Naming and identifying colonialism means we would have to reassess Manzanar as a National Historic Site and how claims to land are often inadvertently settler colonial in their nature through ownership of territory. In other words, to remember the carceral is inherently predicated on the forgetting of Indigenous relationships to the land. However, as I have been arguing, we can see how the possibility for solidarity can occur in ways that disrupt settler colonial desires.

Lessons from Harry Williams: Centering the Owens Valley

In my interview with Harry Williams, Bishop Paiute tribal member and environmental activist, he furthers this critique of "home" through an articulation of settler colonial dispossession in relationship to capitalism to think about how struggles over water and land need to confront not only colonial violences but Indigenous strategies of resistance. He begins our interview by situating himself within the context of the work he does; he tells me, "I like my valley. I'm willing to get up and fight for it, because LA's like a big bully." He states, "This is my homeland, and it needs to be fought for and taken care of." Throughout the interview, he constantly refers to the Owens Valley as "home" and therefore something that is "his" or "ours." He very strategically highlights Indigenous claims to land that are continually denied in the face of constant dispossession via the settler state. For Williams, this denial materially manifests itself in the dispossession of water—a necessary resource for life. By reasserting his claims to the land and its resources, he very carefully constructs a critique of capitalism. When I ask him what he thinks allows Los Angeles to take the valley's resources, he says,

> I just think it's arrogance, like we're the big city, we have the power, it's the principle of capitalism. They believe they own this entire valley, and they will stick to it, they will really fight for it . . . and the water gets dragged out of here as fast as they can take it.[44]

In a later part of the interview, he theorizes that "capitalism doesn't care, it just uses it up. And when you use it up, what do you have left? You have nothing left."[45] He positions the dangers of capitalism and the ownership of water and land via the LADWP to not only contrast Indigenous worldviews with settler colonial logics but to highlight how these differences mean that they "are still the enemy as a tribal people."[46] He states, "We want to protect Mother Earth, we are always being destroyed."[47] In contrast to Japanese Americans, who are no longer racialized as the enemy in a post-redress era, Williams asserts that Indigenous peoples continue to be the enemy (of settlers, private property, capitalism) and thus subject to death.

Although I intended my interview to be an interrogation of the budding relationship between the Manzanar Committee and Native American activists in the Owens Valley, there were many times throughout the interview where Williams purposefully steered the conversation back to the struggles of his valley. Williams's activist work takes the form of education: he gives talks in different cities and colleges throughout California, takes water rights classes, and participates in films like *Paya*, a documentary about the politics of water. Williams is very clear that the LADWP is the enemy and the one who has "dried and killed the valley," but he also holds local politicians and organizations responsible.[48] Sometimes they fold to LADWP pressures or LADWP infiltrates their committees, and for Williams, this kind of work is "tough." However, what he wants people to think most about (especially those in Los Angeles) is where their water comes from. That process is often a violent one. He sees the Owens Valley as a "microcosm of the rest of the world."[49] The valley is always being watched—studied by those who want to emulate the LADWP's takeover of the water or those who want to know how to fight against the theft of water. Examining Williams's understanding of his home provides further lessons about how to maintain relationships between Japanese Americans and Native Americans, but it also provides insights into the daily activism and work that many do to fight against the destruction caused by colonial and settler colonial violences.

New Beginnings: Coalition Building in the Owens Valley

In a personal interview, Manzanar Committee member Gann Matsuda tells me that what brought together Native Americans who live in the Owens Valley and Japanese Americans was the fight against this solar ranch.[50] Williams states that although he grew up knowing about Japanese American incarceration, the Indigenous groups in the Owens Valley had no relationship with Japanese Americans. His knowledge is made up of fragments: he heard about incarceration from his grandparents, his classmate's mother was an assistant cook at Manzanar, and the Native American basketball team would go play games there. "So we always knew about it," Williams tells me in our interview.[51] And yet prior to the proposal for the solar ranch, the stakeholders of the Owens Valley "were all little separate units," in Williams's words; in particular, the Manzanar Committee did "their own thing" of "really support[ing] the Manzanar Park and got everything going there."[52]

However, after they began to work together against a common enemy, their relationship changed. Williams tells me that "it's become a lot better because when they fought for what they wanted, you know, they really became better, we became friends." He then goes on to identify the Manzanar Committee as "movers and shakers" who "really jumped on the ball" with this fight, and he believes that in the end they had become "allies."[53] Interestingly, for Williams, this sense of "becoming allies" stems from the fact that the Manzanar Committee "really started looking at what we [the Indigenous peoples of the valley] were talking about [and] what we were fighting for," and vice versa.[54] For Williams, Japanese Americans were finally understanding "why [Native Americans] felt the way [they] did."[55] This understanding of each other's particular histories with state violence—the colonial and the carceral—helped forge, then solidify, trust and respect as they collaborated in this fight with LADWP. Matsuda also states that "a byproduct of [the Manzanar Committee's] work had to be building stronger relationships with the locals in the Owens Valley, that included the Native Americans up there."[56]

In 2014, the Manzanar Committee invited Genevieve "Gina" Jones, the tribal chairwoman of the Big Pine Paiute Tribe, to welcome pilgrimage participants to "our land." Matsuda states, "That's why we had her speaking that day, because we had met her, we developed a relationship *finally*, something we'd always wanted to do" but were never able to.[57] This was the first time the Manzanar Committee had invited a tribal representative to welcome pilgrimage participants, and it has continued and will continue in the future. Working in coalition with other stakeholders in the Owens Valley against a common enemy, the LADWP, has provided the Manzanar Committee with the means to develop meaningful relationships with those who call the valley their home. Logistically, the pilgrimage lasts for only one weekend a year. This temporariness of the pilgrimage, and also of Japanese American incarceration (that forced incarcerees to call Manzanar their home for three-and-a-half years), is what prevented a coalition from occurring in the past. Japanese Americans were thus connected to the carceral landscape but not necessarily the community surrounding them, from whom they were closed off by barbed wire.

Not only have stakeholders of Manzanar learned to work collaboratively, but they are learning to support one another. Despite the fact that the LADWP's solar ranch project has been tabled, a tribal representative continues to welcome participants to the land, as well as talk about a few significant issues affecting the Indigenous communities of the Owens Valley. In 2015, the Big Pine Paiute Tribe newsletter makes mention of the annual pilgrimage, urging their readers to attend the weekend events,[58] while the Owens Valley Committee, an organization dedicated to the sustainable management of Owens Valley water and resources, invited Manzanar Committee cochair Bruce Embrey as their guest speaker at their annual fundraiser event. Having begun these conversations about how the colonial and the carceral intersect and even sustain each other has been important to the growth of these budding relationships. As Matsuda contends, "We developed the relationships we needed to develop, so we're hoping that continues for a long, long time."[59]

After conducting my research for the beginning part of this chapter in 2014, I became a member of the Manzanar Committee, codirecting its Manzanar at Dusk program and eventually helping develop a new program. My positionality within this new program situates my analysis that follows, where I am not merely a researcher but also a collaborator. In this final section, I detail how these lessons from the LADWP solar ranch continue to impact the Manzanar Committee, who have since tried to incorporate Indigenous history into their generational educational programs.

Keeping Japanese American Stories Alive: Generational Storytelling and Its Disruptions

In March 2018, the Manzanar Committee launched Katari: Keeping Japanese American Stories Alive in collaboration with the National Park Service at the Manzanar National Historic Site and Southern California NSUs.[60] Due to the shifting dynamics and demographics within the Japanese American community, including a growing recent immigrant population from Japan, and the younger generations, a large group of Japanese Americans are either two or three generations removed from the experiences of those who were forced to endure America's concentration camps or have no connection to this history at all. Recognizing these changes in the Nikkei community, as evidenced by the Manzanar at Dusk NSU representatives, Katari seeks to bridge the generation gap that has made it much more difficult for young Japanese Americans to teach others about incarceration history. Gann Matsuda, director of Katari, states that the Manzanar Committee "wanted to provide these students opportunities to learn this history, keeping the voices of those former Japanese American incarcerees alive," and give them "some of the tools needed to the teach this history to others."[61] To address and solve the issue of generational reproduction in the face of Nisei death and youthful distance,[62] Katari, which means to tell stories, is two days of intensive, experiential, place-based learning about the unjust incarceration of over 120,000 Japanese and Japanese Americans during World War II, held at the Manzanar National Historic Site.

Katari addresses the generational gap by reestablishing generational transmission that has been strained by new generations (Shin immigrants), removed generations (Yonsei, Gosei), and non–Japanese American NSU members. In other words, "young people are continuing the work of their parents, grandparents, and family members in telling their unique stories of life behind barbed wire."[63] Katari allows students to learn about Japanese American history through personal interaction, both with place (the Manzanar National

Historic Site) and with former incarcerees who share their stories. Utilizing storytelling, the program draws on excerpts of oral history interviews and invites former incarcerees to share their personal experiences.[64] Being able to hear about incarceration from the Nisei or Sansei who experienced it or who worked to establish Manzanar as a National Historic Site is identified as much more valuable. In her reflection, Kevin Amemiya of UCSD NSU wrote that Katari allowed him to walk on the same sandy path those who were incarcerated once walked on in their daily lives and eat in the mess hall that some were forced to eat all their meals in, she got to see what was left over of parks that couples strolled through to "get away from the world," and he sat in a replica barrack that "incarcerees slept in for over three years."[65] It is the immersive quality of Katari that moves students the most. And similar to the pilgrimages themselves, it is the physical site of incarceration that pushes the students to engage with this history. For example, Erica Wei, of UCSD NSU and member of the first Katari cohort, states that "by participating in this project, I got to see Manzanar with my own eyes and hear the stories of those who were incarcerated with my own ears."[66] She argues that "it is one thing to see photos and read articles online or through a textbook" but "it is another thing to experience something firsthand." In other words, going "beyond textbook facts and information" makes Katari, like Densho's digital archive, "incredibly unique because it makes history feel tangible and real."[67] For Watanabe (who participated in Katari twice), even an online format, due to COVID-19 safety measures, did not diminish the "intimacy" that Katari provides. She was still able to hear "the voices of the people who can truly attest to what happened at Manzanar," which has allowed her to "understand, empathize, and imagine something" that was difficult before.[68] Students are able to "feel a personal connection to the people who were incarcerated at Manzanar," and it is this intimacy of place and personal experiences that provides students direct access to "the people who lived a part of their lives [at Manzanar]" in a way that they could listen to and see "their memories, emotions, and thoughts."[69] It is the emotional connection to land, story, and Japanese American history that amplified student learning and impacted students in deeply personal ways, but it was not the only history they would learn that weekend.

As I have been arguing, the heteronormative impulses of generational transfers of Japanese American memory also work to bolster that of the nation state, reifying the nuclear family (literally and metaphorically) while failing to question state violence beyond World War II incarceration (positioned as exceptional). The Manzanar Committee, through its educational projects, does ultimately reinforce generational responsibility through familial discourses by charging its students with the task of ensuring that Japanese American World

War II history does not disappear or become insignificant. Katari was born out of this concern for younger generations and exists to guide students to care for this history. Like many of the organizations in this book, Katari was born out of the fear of Nisei death and historical erasure, relying on generational responsibility to continue telling the story of World War II incarceration.[70] Reprosexuality is not absent here, but Katari finds itself having to navigate outside of generational categories of family to include newer Japanese immigrants as well as non-Japanese student members of NSUs, which allows for a comparative approach, analysis, and connection to be developed.

On the other hand, for Indigenous communities, the management of Indigenous gender and sexuality has focused on "Indigenous reproduction and child-rearing (from boarding schools to eugenics to forced sterilization)," where the physical and social reproduction of Indigeneity and thus "regeneration" are important parts of decolonization. Settler colonialism and white patriarchy as structures seek to disrupt Indigenous reproduction in order to make settler claims to land "legitimate."[71] Here, the generational reproduction of Japanese American history and the denial of generational regeneration of Indigeneity often go hand in hand to solidify heteropatriarchy and settler colonial desire. To complicate things further, the significance of place-based learning within Katari is only possible because of Indigenous dispossession in the Owens Valley, with first white settlers, then the LADWP, and through the preservation of Manzanar as a National Historic Site by the National Park Service.

Despite its reliance on generational reproduction, I argue that Katari works to challenge the impulses of settler logics through moments of disruption to how it introduces students to Japanese American history at Manzanar. As a place-based learning opportunity, the land is central to the lessons of Katari. For the pre-COVID cohorts, this connection to Manzanar itself is what students comment the most on. In his reflection, Kevin Amemiya writes of his experience:

> The connection to the land and its history was so great that every single thing I learned was amplified to the point where my emotions would often get the best of me and honestly, I'm glad they did. It only made the experience that much more impactful for me.[72]

Katari establishes a physical intimacy to the land, where Manzanar itself operates as evidence of carceral violence that tells visitors a story through reconstructed buildings, exhibits, left-behind objects, rocks, gardens, and so on. The land itself is a significant part of the storytelling process that is embedded in the Katari project. But the storytelling of Manzanar and the land it stands on would not be complete without recognizing that carceral violences are established on the unceded territory of the Paiute Shoshone. In other words, the land is not romanticized as belonging to Japanese Americans, and the Katari students are charged with engaging in and carrying on Paiute Shoshone history when they tell the story of Manzanar. For example, in its first year, Katari invited the Irene Button family to discuss their relationship to Manzanar. The Button family's history is a part of the Manzanar National Historic Site exhibit (2017) where visitors can learn about the "first inhabitants of the Owens Valley."[73] As a result, students get to hear not only firsthand accounts from Japanese American incarcerees but also from Paiute Shoshone members. Students (some of them for the first time) learn about forced removal in the context of Indigenous experiences where they heard about boarding schools (Stewart Indian school), the forced march to Fort Tejon (1893), and the continued environmental degradation of the Owens Valley. In 2020, the virtual Katari program hosted three Paiute and Shoshone activists, Alan Bacock, Cheyenne Stone, and Topah Spoonhunter, to highlight the ways Paiute Shoshone history and identity impact the work they do today (environmental protection, cultural revitalization, etc.). Learning this layered history through the land itself forces students to grapple with the very things they have been made to forget, "that Manzanar shares land with the Paiute and Shoshone of the Owens Valley," and to consider the "Indigenous people who may have lived there in the past or still live their today."[74] The inclusion of Paiute and Shoshone history and activism through storytelling is a direct result of the relationship building Japanese Americans have done in the Owens Valley since the proposed solar ranch. As a developer of Katari curriculum, I find myself asking if this mere inclusion of Paiute and Shoshone history and activism is enough. Limited by time (the weekend) and students' prior knowledge of the event, it is merely an introduction that barely touches the surface of the complexity of carcerality and its relationship to settler violences. But it is a step in an important direction—one that I hope continues to grow and change and challenge white supremacy with allyship.

Drawing on Manzanar pilgrimages allows for an examination of the relationship between the colonial and the carceral which provided Japanese Americans with the opportunity to rethink Japanese American memory practices. While settler colonial desires are inherently a part of Japanese Americans' relationship to Manzanar and the Owens Valley, these desires can be disrupted. The fight against the LADWP's proposed solar ranch put Japanese Americans and the Indigenous tribes of the Owens Valley in conversation with each other for the first time. In collaborating together, they formed relationships with each other based upon the layers of racialized and colonial violences that were a part of the valley's history. Highlighting the contradictory location of Japanese Americans, the Manzanar Committee's work reveals how the colonial and the carceral often sustain each other. Reexamining the way Japanese Americans remember World War II incarceration in this way forces the committee and the future generations it works with to reckon with those histories and learn how to be ethical allies to Indigenous communities.

4

NSU Cultural Night and Generational Transmissions of Memory

Performative Disruptions and Other Futures

In an article published by the Los Angeles–based Japanese American newspaper, *Rafu Shimpo* in July of 2011, the author's first line asks, "Where are the youth?"[1] It states that those who have ever been involved with the Japanese American community have heard this question before. As I have argued, this anxiety about Nikkei youth involvement in the face of Nisei death not only grows with every passing year but is in fact central to gendered discourses of generational transmission of memory and thus responsibility. This anxiety relies upon and is entrenched in a Japanese American history that is generationally determined by the categories of Issei, Nisei, Sansei, and so on. These histories also produce very particular generational identities that many organizations rely on to engage with and serve the community. The article then goes on to talk about the importance of community engagement within the Japanese American community:

> It was that engagement in community organizations that built up the community and its leadership, history and memories, and created the bonds that hold us together today. Where would we be without our churches, temples, basketball teams, community centers, museums, festivals, and so on?[2]

This anxiety, while not necessarily new, has resulted in the emergence of youth-oriented organizations in the Japanese American community, such as the Japanese American National Museum's Young Professionals Network, the Manzanar Committee's Katari: Keeping Japanese American Stories Alive program, and Kizuna, a Little Tokyo–based organization founded to engage the next generation of community leaders.[3] Including Yonsei (fourth generation) and Gosei (fifth generation) into already existing organizations and the development of these organizations highlight how the future of Nikkei community is being imagined.

Disrupting notions that tie together younger generations with futurity, this chapter breaks down how college-aged Nikkei understand their complicated place in community. In other words, how do they simultaneously accept and challenge the generational responsibility placed upon them? How do they respect those who made their organizations possible while redefining understandings of belonging and community? As I argued in the previous chapters, generational structures of memory limit the possibility of relationality needed to sustain interracial solidarity, and in this chapter, I explore how the NSU at UCLA grapples with these boundaries through the medium of performance.

Returning to Michael Warner's theorizations of reprosexuality, NSUs are the most tangible representation of the "interweaving of heterosexuality, biological reproduction, cultural reproduction, and personal identity."[4] As generational successors, NSUs are tasked with fulfilling a debt that is "structural, a matter of position rather than payment, [that] places the [generation] ever in violation."[5] Drawing on erin Khuê Ninh's conceptualizations of the debt-creditor relation within a community demonstrates how the heteronormative nuclear family mobilizes guilt to ensure that Japanese American history continues to find its "proper temporality" and "fulfillment in generational transmission."[6] If not, younger generations, as indicated by the *Rafu* article, not only become invisible or nowhere to be found but become ungrateful. In other words, NSUs must always remember Japanese American history and the community from which they were born. To remember is to repay those who came before them, the place where existence is tied to both past and future. And yet, this structure of debt (that also structures Japanese American history, community, and knowledge production) is one in which the youth are "trapped" because they "could never suffice in addressing the original sacrifices made."[7]

UCLA's NSU was founded in 1981, and its objectives were to "promote Asian Pacific American awareness in the pursuit of [a] better understanding of the Japanese American identity, to encourage student involvement in the Los Angeles Japanese American community and its issues and also to promote service activities within said community," as well as to "act as a medium for the members social, cultural and political objectives" both on and off campus.[8] As an alternative to the Asian fraternities and sororities of the time, UCLA's

NSU articulates itself as more than just a social organization, recounting its history of development as being in response to the need to address cultural awareness on campus and as intimately connected to the struggles for redress. In fact, it is the redress movement itself that began to increase the presence of NSU in the Japanese American community as they became involved with the National Coalition for Redress and Reparations (now called Nikkei for Civil Rights and Redress) by not only "generating campus and community support" for redress but also through their lobbying efforts, their thousand letters of support, and their organization of educational programs and rallies in support of redress legislation. According to Alan Nishio, founder and co-chair of NCRR, "NSU was a critical factor in the considerable involvement of students in the struggle for redress."[9] Redress was also how the first iteration of Cultural Night was born. NSU's annual Cultural Night originally began as a weeklong, on-campus event called "Week of Remembrance" that served to commemorate the signing of Executive Order 9066 with panels, guest speakers, and presentations.[10] It is this tradition that the current manifestation of Cultural Night strives to maintain through a variety of performances—a play, dance, and *taiko*.

In addition to being involved with the redress movement, in 1986, NSU played a crucial role in the three-year battle of Professor Don Nakanishi's tenure case through organizing walkouts, pickets, and marches to highlight the racism of UCLA's administration. The NSU president even gave a presentation on "Racism and the Glass Ceiling" before the U.S. Senate Committee. In 1987, NSU established a scholarship program for incoming Japanese American high school students that emphasized community involvement over academic achievements. These examples of NSU activities from the 1980s are meant to demonstrate that the organization was founded as a space for Japanese Americans not only to educate others about their particular "ethnic experience" but was also always meant to be a space of political action and organizing. Its history and emergence are intimately intertwined with that of Japanese American redress, and thus its visions of community are often wrapped up in the gendered discourse of post-redress memorializations. Even as NSU organizations across Southern California struggle to interest their members in these kinds of political and community events rather than merely social ones, the Cultural Night has persisted.

Cultural Night is a very important part of a larger tradition of ethnic and minority student organizations on college campuses, in particular Asian American groups.[11] Pilipino Cultural Nights, which began in the 1970s and emerged as a genre in the 1980s, have been widely documented.[12] Many of these works analyze the use of cultural performances to highlight the colonial relationship between the United States and the Philippines as Filipino American youth try to make sense of what it means to be Filipino American. Culture has historically been a marker of difference and "foreignness" for Asian American groups, but it is through these nights of performances that Asian American cultural organizations make claim to "traditional" Asian culture—dances, song, music, and so on—in a celebratory fashion. The Cultural Night is a vehicle for Asian American students to play with "culture" as well as showcase it to the rest of campus.

For UCLA NSU, the Cultural Night ranges from topics such as Japanese Americans' World War II incarceration experiences (*Walking against the Wind*, 1992) and those of the Japanese American segregated army units (*A Hero's Welcome Home*, 1996) to saving Little Tokyo (*Always Welcome, Never for Sale*, 2009) and Issei farmers (*Brothers Miyazaki*, 2010). These plays, written, run, and performed by students, signal what Nikkei youth find important and moving to them. Through an exploration of UCLA Cultural Nights, I demonstrate how Nikkei youth grapple with generational responsibility and guilt through the medium of performance. The heteronormative transfer of memory is not an easy or clean process. On stage, Nikkei youth pay tribute to generations before them where generational reproduction of history often becomes its own genre. The dramatization of heteronormative memory transfers and responsibility preoccupy the concerns of Nikkei youth who struggle with these communal requirements while also trying to come to terms with the shifts within the community and the world around them. They complicatedly replicate generational responsibility and at times challenge it, demonstrating the limits of heteronormative, cultural nationalist history making. The Cultural Nights are an important site of interrogation, where Nikkei youth on a communal stage (literally and figuratively) test the boundaries of generation and history. In the next sections, I analyze three UCLA NSU Cultural Nights where generation is performed, tested, and reconfigured in order to understand what can and "cannot be contained within a generational model of the history" of Japanese Americans.[13]

The Drama of Generational Debt: Youth and Generational History

In 2011, UCLA NSU's Cultural Night entitled *The Last Generation: Every Generation Needs a Regeneration*[14] revolved around NSU's growing concern with "generations" and how, in particular, the Yonsei fit into the larger history of the Japanese American experience and figure into the future. The title, *The Last*

Generation, was stressed as having a double meaning—to remember and understand the generations that have come before while also questioning the construction of "generation" itself. The Cultural Night producers introduced this theme of "generation" by critically musing on the ways they are always asked to "look to the future, to the next generation" by passing on their stories and heritage as a means of preservation. In the program, they then ask the audience a series of questions: "But what about the last generation? The generations that have come before us? What about our generation? How do we define when a generation ends? Or does it?"[15] These provocative questions demonstrate that generations "are by no means neutral entities" because generational definitions are determined along an "axis of power that wields tremendous discursive and psychic force" that exposes who does and does not belong.[16] These questions and the resulting performance dramatize how generational categories have material consequences.[17]

By asking the audience these questions, the producers not only situate their performance within a critical rethinking of knowledge production but also create a dialogue with the audience that asks for their participation as well. These questions prompt the audience to complicate their conceptualizations of "generation" or consider how this category of belonging utilized by the nation and the Japanese American community may no longer be useful (and possibly has never been sufficient to encompass the variety of experiences). These questions illuminate the way each "generation" is categorized within a notion of linear time and progress that differentiates each group as having a particular set of experiences, feelings, and thus narratives. As I explored in previous chapters, recent shifts in immigration and community formation expose the ways these categories are not concrete, stable, or predetermined. This interrogation of the way the Japanese American experience is organized forces the audience to rethink the ways Japanese Americans have come to know themselves before deciding how they will move into the future.[18]

And yet, even as the producers trouble these categories, they also reinforce the very "generations" they seek to destabilize throughout the play. Articulating memory as a means of never forgetting "that [their] privileges today are a result of the sacrifices made by those who came before [them]," NSU constructs a history reliant upon generational categories of difference.[19] "Sacrifice" signals the debt-obligation that the youth must pay back as community members, not always or necessarily through money, but by honoring a particular rendering of Japanese American history as proper subjects of nationhood. In order to be a "good" Yonsei, the youth reproduce this history as grateful subjects of those who metaphorically and literally gave them life. For example, in the 2011 program, there is an entire page devoted to what this history looks like, divided into four sections: Issei, Nisei, Sansei, and Yonsei. The Issei are identified as immigrants and laborers who fought against discriminatory policies (like the Alien Land Law). The Nisei, or second generation, are categorized as being born in the United States, as citizens who are characterized by their experiences of incarceration and whose "perseverance and strength" allowed them to "rebuild their lives."[20] The Sansei, or third generation, are classified as those who pushed and fought for redress and reparations as young college-aged students. And finally, NSU writes that the Yonsei are "well-assimilated into American culture," where "ideas such as overt discrimination and internment are no longer directly linked to their daily existence."[21] As a result, their greatest struggle lies in "maintaining a connection to their cultural heritage."[22] Similar to the *Rafu* article, NSU positions themselves within a generational conflict that can only be resolved through "reproductive legacies of filial transmission."[23] By identifying and featuring these generational struggles prominently in the program as an index and guide of Japanese American history, NSU reestablishes the generational narrative that ultimately determines the way the performance will take form.

The Temporality of Regeneration: Transforming Apathetic Nikkei Youth and Performing the Debt-Obligation

In her book *The Archive and the Repertoire: Performing Cultural Memory in the Americas*, Diana Taylor articulates performances as vital acts of transfer or transmission of social knowledge, memory, and a sense of identity through reiterated or "twice-behaved behavior."[24] Placing performance within this analysis of memory, Taylor forces a consideration of embodied knowledge that challenges traditional conceptualizations of memory and the archivable. I begin with an exploration of the ways Nikkei college students are utilizing the genre of performance as a way of expressing their histories but also as a means of teaching while entertaining their audience (mostly other students) about the particularities of the Japanese American experience.

The Last Generation: Every Generation Needs a Regeneration revolved around the story of Cate Kitamura (a fourth-generation Japanese American) whose life perspective is challenged after the death of her grandmother, Mizuki.[25] The death of a Nisei woman catapults the granddaughter into grief, mourning, and an existential crisis as she seeks to understand all the things she never knew when her grandmother was alive. Nisei death serves a vehicle for the play, where the Nikkei youth's physical connection to the past (in particular an incarcerated past) is dismantled by the physical loss of a Nisei grandparent. But it is more than a devastating personal loss; as Cate recovers family history, she discovers her connection to the Japanese American community. In this way biological reproduction (family) is intimately connected to community (social reproduction). To reproduce family, community, and history is to go back to the past to find resolution in proper temporality and fulfillment in generational transmission (by overcoming youthful apathy).[26]

The play begins with three unidentified cast members' reading of Janice Mirikitani's "Who Is Singing This Song"—where each person takes up different sections of the poem almost in conversation with each other, shouting out lines that are heavy with emotions—anger, concern, hope, and love. In addition, these three cast members move across the stage in many different directions, constellating around each other and working together to create constant movement and formations. Shifting from this prologue, the scene opens to the Kitamura family mourning the loss of Mizuki, with Cate's grandfather presenting her with a box of mementos that include a locket, a diary, a stack of letters, and dog tags. Each object prompts Cate to have a conversation with a different person: her grandmother's friend, her dead great-grandmother through the medium of the diary, her grandfather, and her father. Through each conversation we see a shift in Cate from a disinterested Yonsei (the very Yonsei that the Japanese American community fears) to someone who understands not only her family's history but her community's as well. This transformation through an immersion in her family's incarcerated past changes Cate's mind about her previous decision to not attend a Little Tokyo rally because she believed she could not really make a difference. In the end, she learns that she needs to support her community and discovers how to do so. She becomes the model responsible Japanese American Yonsei. The play ends with a final scene that is another rendition of Mirikitani's poem; this time all the cast members participate in its telling. Like the prologue, the poem is shouted as if everyone is in conversation with each other, but this time there is no movement except for the growing number of people who walk out onstage. This recitation is triumphant in the way that the cast is united and strong in its stance. Cate stands up at the front as if she is leading us all to her own realization that everyone is a part of this community—that all Japanese Americans (including those in the audience) are singing this song.

Generational categories are reiterated throughout the performance, and by tracing Cate's character development, the audience can see the ways each story and each person embodies a different generation's specific struggle. After the recitation of Mirikitani's poem, the play begins with Cate running into her childhood friend Rachel, and they attempt to find a time to reconnect. Rachel suggests that Cate come to a rally with her in Little Tokyo, but this suggestion turns into a heated argument when Rachel angrily raises her voice at Cate's disinterest in community by telling her that she should *care* because it does and will matter. But Cate will not budge, and Rachel, clearly irritated and disappointed, abruptly leaves. Cate is representative of those college students that the Cultural Night articulates as struggling to maintain a connection to their community, and she is also the person these performances seek to reach and speak to.

Visualizing Storytelling: The Gendered Limits of Cultural Nationalist History

As Cate sorts through her grandmother's mementos, she is prompted to have conversations with different family members and friends, and the play provides visual reenactments of the storytelling to which Cate finally becomes a witness to. The right side of the stage features the present, with Cate and her subject of inquiry conversing about the past, while the left half of the stage displays that memory as it is being told. This visuality of memory and the interplay between the reenactment and the storytelling serve multiple functions throughout the performance. First, visuality of memory provides a moment of both humor and a sense of anxiety to know what will happen next. For example, this occurs when Cate's grandfather is recounting his memories of war—this memory plays out on the left side of the stage where two men are talking about their fear of dying as explosions go off all around them. Cate's grandfather is trying to convince his friend to stop hiding and get back into the fight. Just when a grenade lands next to the two men, our attention is abruptly brought back to the right side of the stage, where Cate's grandfather interrupts his story to tell us that he has to use the restroom because he drank too much tea. Because he has stopped narrating his story, the soldiers on the left immediately freeze in midair as they attempt to get away from the soon-to-be-exploding grenade. The audience laughs at this awkward moment and must acknowledge the grandfather's bodily function as they are left waiting in anticipation, wondering what will happen to the two men on the left. When the grandfather comes back to the stage and resumes his story, we discover that his friend rejoins the battle only to die while saving Cate's grandfather's life. But this interaction between the present and the past also comments upon the assumptions of storytelling that are not necessarily about "fulfilling the melodramatic fantasy" that comes when a "trauma survivor finally tells all and receives [the] solace of being heard by a willing and supportive listener."[27] Although this does happen between Cate and those with whom she journeys through the past, this journey is interrupted by the daily business of living. By interrupting the "melodramatic fantasy" of storytelling or witnessing with humor, the performance strategically catches the audience off guard and even demonstrates the way the audience is complicit in this desire for solace and resolution.

In another example, when Cate finally asks her father to tell her about his redress days, he excitedly recounts the day he made a speech at an important rally. On the left side of the stage, a younger version of her father powerfully delivers a speech about the need for justice in their community, and at the end of it, the crowd cheers and picks him up in their excitement. As soon as they pick him up, the left side of the stage freezes as the audience is brought back to the present as Cate comments upon her dad's involvement and investment in the community. And then Cate asks, "Did they really pick you up and carry you off?" and her dad sheepishly replies, "Umm, no." The crowd immediately drops him as another speaker comes to the stage, shifting the audience's attention back to the left side. Once again, the audience laughs at the father's embellishments within his storytelling as we are made aware of the dynamic between the present's constant interaction with the past and the way memory does not simply revolve around truth.

This illumination of storytelling was also a constant concern of the writers and producers of the Cultural Night. When talking to one of the Cultural Night producers about the use of the reenactments, she tells me that part of their desire to have these visuals on stage was to avoid the misinterpretation of those memories. By visually providing the images for the audience, UCLA NSU believed they could accurately portray what they wanted the audience to know. This need for the performance of memory to be accurate exposes the way NSU producers are aware of the ways they are constantly under surveillance for the type of narratives they portray. In particular, she was concerned about discussing the experiences of "No-No" boys, who have a long history of stigmatization within the Japanese American community for their inability to fit within the narrative of redress. In response to such a history, NSU carefully dramatizes the experiences of both the Nisei soldier and the "No-No" boy as courageous men, only doing what they each thought was right. In this way, the "No-No" boy cannot be morphed into someone to be looked down upon.[28] The placement of the dramatization of memory right next to the moment of storytelling guides the audience through a particular narrative of the Japanese American experience. Despite the way it comments upon the relationship between the past and present with the interplay of the performance and audience, NSU's use of this dramaturgy essentially leads us on an all-too-familiar path of remembering.

Another way UCLA NSU seeks to remember is through the death of the grandmother. The first scene opens to the family grieving the loss of Mizuki while gathered in the living room of their home after the funeral. Later that night, Cate's grandfather brings out a box full of mementos that belonged to her grandmother. The box serves as a literal archive of her grandmother's life—each object tells Cate a story about Mizuki that she did not know before. It is only because of the death of her grandmother that Cate begins to understand and appreciate her family history while also connecting that history to her own life *and* the contemporary struggles of Japanese American communities. But what is interesting in this use of death is the fact that it never gives life to the dead grandmother. Instead, her death regenerates the lives of the living and in particular allows for male narratives of patriotism, loyalty, and courage to become visible to Cate. For example, when her grandmother's friend visits to pay her respects, she tells Cate about the photo she has just found in her grandmother's locket. The photo is of her grandfather as a soldier, and it allows her grandmother's friend to remember a conversation she had with Mizuki about the absence of their husbands. While Cate's grandfather is absent because he is a soldier, the friend's husband is gone because he is a draft resister. As previously mentioned, this scene seeks to validate both the soldier and the draft resister as loyal Americans who, as Cate's grandmother argues, are both doing what they think needs to be done for the nation. In addition, when Cate begins to read through letters that her grandmother saved, the audience realizes that these letters are not about Mizuki; instead, they allow her father to reminisce about his days fighting for redress.

Despite the fact that these objects belong to the grandmother, she is resurrected momentarily, but only to bring life to others. Death performs a very particular function—to reiterate a narrative of masculinity and loyalty that is reliant upon the absence of the grandmother. In other words, the vitality of community necessitates not just reproduction of cultural nationalist and masculine history but "relies on patriarchal understanding[s] of history and a linear cause-effect narrative."[29] This narrative of masculinity and loyalty is then taken up by Cate, who is regenerated by the stories she hears in relation to these objects. By immersing herself (and even finding herself) within these stories, Cate is transformed from an unconcerned Yonsei girl to a community member dedicated to the preservation of Nikkei life. Mizuki is excess to the project of generational reproduction of Nikkei community, and so she remains elusive and unknowable to the family and thus the audience throughout the entire performance even if her death is at the center of the script and propels the story. This elusivity illuminates the way knowledge production requires the silencing and death of Mizuki in exchange for Cate's transformation to respectable youth, which rewards her with national and communal belonging. Mizuki herself remains outside generational models of Japanese American community and history; as a Nisei she is mourned by the family but not recoverable. The following year, NSU would take their generational concerns from *Regenerations* further to explore how divisions exist within their own organization.

It's More Than Blood: How the Shin-Nisei Disrupt Generational Narratives

In 2012, the UCLA NSU Cultural Night entitled *Our [I]dentity: It's More Than Blood* made a generational shift and chose to showcase the struggles of the Shin-Nisei, or the "new" second generation, because of the way "the Japanese American community is diversifying with a more mixed and new immigrant population."[30] Identifying the way the Nikkei youth "consists of two different generations—the Yonsei and the Shin Nisei," this play dramatizes the complicated space of Nikkei identity where the Yonsei are unknowingly implicated in the continuing exclusion of Shin-Nisei from the community.[31] Following the lives of college students Mark and Maki as they struggle with their Shin-Nisei identity and grapple with what it means to be Japanese American, the play not only problematizes the heteronormative and familial logics of generations but simultaneously opens up a space for intimately connecting Japanese American histories to those of other marginalized groups. Generational disruption allows for "coalitional intimacies" to be seen and acted upon, no matter how fleeting they are.[32]

The performance begins with four high school boys on the stage discussing the recent revelation that Cameron, a female classmate of theirs, is an undocumented immigrant. Addressing the 2010 Support Our Law Enforcement and Safe Neighborhoods Act (SB 1070), the play dramatizes racial unbelonging where anti-immigrant sentiment, legislation, and the carceral intersect to punish "Latinos and others who may look or sound 'foreign' including many U.S. citizens."[33] SB 1070 made it a state misdemeanor to be found without one's federal registration papers, which allowed the police to "investigate immigration status if they suspect[ed] a person [was] undocumented," and thus they could "arrest individuals without a warrant if they believe[d] they [were] a deportable immigrant."[34] Utilizing this anti-immigrant discourse, the high school boys on stage discuss how they are "glad that Arizona finally passed that bill, SB 1070," because now they can "finally tell the difference between us and them."[35] One even adds that he is "glad we have one less immigrant to worry about. They're just here trying to take our seats in school."³⁶ Cameron and her boyfriend, Mark (the play's main character), walk into this discussion, and Mark's anger erupts at their anti-immigrant rhetoric as he finds himself defending Cameron and himself as "citizens" who were "born here." But suddenly the scene changes and Cameron starts accusing Mark of abandoning her, saying, "You already have your citizenship, so you don't have to worry."³⁷ Mark's peers plus Cameron circle around Mark and begin to close in on him as he shouts "no, no" repeatedly. The scene immediately fades to black, coming to a jarring close, and in the next scene, Mark is asleep on the couch being woken up from a nightmare by his friends.

Unwilling to talk to his roommates about Cameron, it is only when his current girlfriend, Maki, is struggling to understand her Japanese American identity that he opens up about Cameron's deportation. In the retelling of his past, the audience learns that Cameron was deported because of Arizona's SB 1070, which profiles and criminalizes undocumented immigrants. At the time of the play, SB 1070 was being examined by the Supreme Court (*Arizona v. United States*), and it opens the play as an issue important to NSU but also serves as a vehicle to dramatize the differences between Shin immigrants and the Yonsei. Because of his experience with SB 1070, Mark specifically and strategically identifies himself as "American" and emphasizes his citizenship because "looking like an immigrant" is dangerous.³⁸ This is why he cannot understand Maki's insistence on identifying as Japanese when she struggles to deal with how she cannot relate to other Yonsei. The seemingly recurring nightmare that opens the entire play situates Japanese Americans within a history of immigration that acknowledges state violence as ongoing and unresolved. Mark's intimate relationship with Cameron, her deportation, and her haunting absence momentarily force the audience to consider the ways the surveillance and carcerality of World War II incarceration continue to impact other marginalized groups in the present.

Shifting to Maki's story, the play also centers on the way she struggles with not being like the other Japanese American college students around her who play in Japanese American youth basketball leagues, do not speak Japanese, and eat spam *musubi*. Ironically, when she is studying for an Asian American studies class on the Japanese American experience and frustratingly cannot fit herself into canonical Japanese American history, Maki realizes that because she cannot identify with other Japanese Americans, she must identify as Japanese. While the other Japanese Americans have no trouble studying for the exam because this history is "theirs," Maki cannot identify with any of the historical narratives she must learn. As she tries to regurgitate the information she has learned, she hesitantly tries to recap Issei history by discussing the Alien

Land Laws that were put in place to prevent Japanese immigrants from owning land by "*hakujins*," which Mark and another friend quickly correct her by saying "white people."[39] Then Mark humorously recaps the rest of the Japanese American experience by saying, "They were discriminated against, sent to concentration camps, had more children, fought for the injustice of the incarceration, civil rights movement, more children."[40] Maki's uneasiness with learning and remembering this history for her test exposes how this sense of ownership is something Maki does not have, and it continues to frustrate her. While this conceptualization of identity seems simplistic, I argue that her thought process points to a critique of the way Japanese American community and knowledge production collude in her marginalization. Japanese American historical experiences as articulated through generational narratives serve to naturalize a particular lineage with World War II incarceration as its center. Even Mark's humorous repetition of the line "more children," which garners loud laughter from the audience, makes fun of this lineage and its relationship to Japanese American historical memory. The reproduction of history that occurs through the reproduction of compulsory heterosexuality to naturalize a progressive, linear temporality of Japanese American experience (from immigrant to American) produces humor and laughter, demonstrating its centrality, power, and significance.

The Cultural Night plays with generational reproduction as a form of critique. The subtitle of the play, "it's more than just blood," reconsiders the way Japanese American history is problematically narrated within this language of family and legacy. This interrogation of the way the Japanese American experience is organized challenges the audience to rethink the ways Japanese Americans understand themselves before deciding how to move into the future. "Blood" or generational reproduction is exclusionary and cannot contain or encompass Shin immigrant experiences. At the end of the play, Maki realizes that her unbelonging does not necessarily mean she is not Japanese American but rather that "blood" and thus community need to seriously reconsider the way identity is policed.

While the play has these moments where the Japanese American community is forced to reckon with the consequences of their knowledge production, it is limited by the parameters of the Cultural Night itself. The purpose of the Cultural Night is to educate the UCLA community about the Japanese American experience in a celebratory fashion that ultimately must center Japanese American identity. While a coalitional intimacy through generational critique is established at the very beginning of the play, where the carceral logics of the United States linking Japanese American and undocumented immigrants are visible, the play never returns to the character of Cameron. She only momentarily appears in Mark's nightmare as a vehicle to discuss his conceptualization of identity. I argue that her disappearance not only from Mark's life but from the entire play itself exposes the way Japanese American visibility is often relationally reliant upon the unfreedom of others. In other words, generational critique opens up the possibility for coalitional intimacies, establishing a queer genealogy that questions axes of power (familial, communal, national) and makes visible carceral contact zones, but the Cultural Night is limited by its own parameters: a night of education and celebration of Japanese American cultural identity. Despite being limited by the scope of the Cultural Night itself, the producers found a way to make a very important critique of community itself. The way both celebration and critique coexisted in the same space demonstrates the possibility of performance in making legible a critique of community memory, identity, and thus history. Both Mark's and Maki's struggles highlight the very real damages that these generational narratives have done and expose their limitations.

Senbazuru: Nikkei Apocalyptic Futurity

In 2016, NSU performed the play *Senbazuru*, which translates to the tradition of folding one thousand paper cranes to "symbolize wishfulness and longevity" and "acts as a perfect representation of what [NSU] hopes for Japanese American communities such as Little Tokyo."[41] In her welcome to the audience, Cultural Night producer Emiko Kranz tells the audience that "it is with this night of celebration of our culture, talent, and concerns that we hope to inspire the activism necessary for the further prosperity of the Japanese American community."[42] Addressing generational responsibility head on, this play opens to a newswoman standing in front of a wall of caution tape reporting on the demolition of the Japanese Village Plaza, which is "located at the gateway to the Little Tokyo District" in downtown Los Angeles that offers a variety of shopping and restaurants.[43] A tour guide with a group of students comes by commenting on the missing iconic red *yagura* tower, a replica of a Japanese fire tower. Built in 1983, the *yagura* tower serves as a "proud testimony to the Issei, Japanese pioneers who first settled in this area, so it is also a testimony to the opportunity this country offers to all."[44] Mixing fantasy (the destruction of the *yagura*) and reality (the physical structures of Los Angeles's Little Tokyo), the main character, Kevin, comes to the stage and in his opening monologue laments what has happened:

> This all happened because of me. I should have acted, I should have cared. I could have prevented this. Or at least tried. Soon everyone is

going to forget. Or they just won't even care. Why is it that only now do I realize that I should have given back to the people who were always there for me? I was so selfish. And now it's too late. For whatever it's worth, I'm sorry. [Scene fades to black.]⁴⁵

It is a somber opening scene, one that centers on destruction and an apology that the audience does not quite understand yet. However, it is clear that the yellow caution tape along with Kevin's monologue serve as a warning. This warning must be taken seriously, otherwise the Nikkei community might end up in this dystopian future without the Japanese Village Plaza and the *yagura*. The audience is then transported to the past that led us to this future.

The play centers on two friends—Nicole Hashimoto, who is the president of the fictional Japanese American Student Association (JASA) on a college campus, and Kevin, who serves as her vice president. Nicole and Kevin are complete opposites. Nicole is very invested in community, and when she learns that the Japanese Village Plaza is going to be destroyed, she immediately goes into activist organizing mode. Sometimes her enthusiasm is met with resistance or reluctance, especially from Kevin. Nicole sees the possible loss of the plaza for an upscale mall as a devastating loss to the community. In a confrontation with Kevin, she angrily tells him that "Little Tokyo is our home . . . we are losing our home."⁴⁶ On the other hand, Kevin is only involved in JASA because he wanted to meet new people and make friends and stayed because he met Nicole. We also learn that he is vice president because Nicole asked him to be. He has no political or personal investment. As Nicole plans a benefit concert to save the plaza and later a protest, Kevin tells Nicole that "we're just a bunch of kids, why would anyone listen to us? We don't have the power to change anything."⁴⁷

The City of Los Angeles designates Little Tokyo as "67 acres, bordered by Third, Alameda, First, and Los Angeles streets."⁴⁸ Historically, this area in downtown Los Angeles was "first settled by Japanese at the end of the 19th century," offering Japanese immigrants "stability and safety."⁴⁹ It is home to *Rafu Shimpo* and Nisei Week, "a summer festival organized in 1934" to "promote unity, Japanese heritage, and Little Tokyo businesses."⁵⁰ Despite the forced removal of Japanese Americans from the area, which briefly became home (Bronzeville) to African Americans experiencing housing discrimination, Japanese Americans returned to Little Tokyo in 1945. Today, "Little Tokyo remains a symbol for ethnic identity and a link to the past," despite a "postwar flight to the suburbs," as it "continues to unify Southern California's Japanese American community."⁵¹ Nicole's generational responsibility figures Little Tokyo as a cultural and communal "home" where Japanese Americans belong, have ownership, and maintain historical roots. "Home" within the familial logic of generations means that both Nicole and Kevin have certain obligations to care for and maintain the home that is important for Japanese American social reproduction. Evelyn Nakano Glenn argues that social reproduction "refers to the creation and recreation of people as cultural and social, as well as physical, beings," which involves "mental, emotional, and manual labor."[52] Some examples of this kind of reproductive labor include "purchasing household goods, preparing and serving food, laundering and repairing clothing, maintaining furnishings and appliances, socializing children, providing care and emotional support for adults, and maintaining kin and community ties."[53] While Glenn examines the role of race, gender, and domestic service, I use her theorizations to analyze the kind of labor necessary for "maintaining [Japanese Americans] on a daily basis and intergenerationally."[54] First, care is what mobilizes the labor necessary for social reproduction, which, as I have been arguing, is structured through a familial language of debt, sacrifice, and loss. Here, care is not necessarily gendered as male or female labor, as both Kevin and Nicole must partake in the labor of social reproduction as generational successors. Rather, it is the "normative familial relationality" that relies on "patriarchal understanding[s] of history," represented by Kevin's (intergenerational) conflict, that shapes what the youth need to know to properly save their community.[55] In other words, in order to pay back the debt of their elders, they must perform the labor of knowing Japanese American history, preserving that history (even physical spaces), and passing it on. This is what motivates Nicole's activism and belatedly coerces Kevin to care (when all seems to have already been lost), and thus he must apologize in his opening monologue.

Throughout the play, Nicole's optimism and Kevin's pessimism are constantly at odds, and when the plaza is ultimately destroyed, the audience is fearful that Nicole and Kevin will never be friends again. Hurling the audience back to the present for a moment, in another apologetic and reflective monologue, Kevin says, "I didn't show up to the protest and I didn't help Nicole with any plans she had to help save the plaza. Maybe if I did there wouldn't be caution tape all over Little Tokyo by the end of the month."[56] It is only when the plaza has already been destroyed that Kevin has any remorse for his lack of action, and it is only when he feels this remorse that he and Nicole can resolve their friendship. In other words, Kevin must first learn his proper role in the Japanese American community in order for the play to have any resolution.

Kevin is a representation of the youth the Japanese American community is fearful of: apathetic, uncaring, and ignorant about the histories that came before them. On the other hand, Nicole is the youth the Japanese American community desires and hopes for. She is invested in the past as a means to ensure the future. And yet, ironically, Nicole is unable to save the Japanese Village Plaza. Her activism, enthusiastic care work, and generational responsibility ultimately fail. Throughout this book, involved youth have been positioned as the ideal solution to Nisei death and loss, the Japanese American community's singular hope of surviving into the future, but in *Senbazuru*, the future is much more complicated. In the sections that follow, I explore how these two positions (apathetic vs. involved) will not save the Japanese American community even if the overall moral of the story is to learn to care.

The Benefit Concert: Nikkei Youth and the Ties That Bind

At the benefit concert organized by Nicole to garner donations from the community via student performances, a spoken word piece is performed. This performance within a performance is the only serious one in the imaginary benefit concert, and this particular piece contemplates the ways memory, place, and future collide. While the spoken word artist begins by discussing his favorite childhood dessert, red bean mochi (a Japanese sweet rice dessert), he identifies it as something he greedily enjoys. However, this consumption is not just about the dessert itself; rather, mochi serves as a metaphor for the hard work of the previous generations that is now greedily consumed by the youth. The spoken word artist goes on to explore for the audience exactly what those generations have done:

> We don't talk about memories much but when our grandparents pound rice they are giving us an alternative explanation to the world that we live in. They are the museums that showcase our histories to the public. They are the ethnic studies programs that translate experiences into knowledge. They are the political minds that compelled the U.S. government to apologize and pay for its atrocities. They are the human barricades that protected American Muslims during prayer after 9/11, so when our grandparents pound rice [pounding of his fists], I can't help but apologize because we've forgotten why we're here.[57]

In this part of his poem, the character lays out exactly what those previous generations have done through the tradition of pounding rice—a cultural ritual that is laborious as steamed sweet rice is pounded with a wooden mallet into sticky rice that is later cut and shaped into round balls of mochi ready to be consumed. Using the metaphor of pounding rice, he lists the ways the blood, sweat, and tears of a previous generation's struggle are what gave the youth not only these spaces of community but also a history to know, one they are intimately wrapped up in. It is a living history, one that does not stay in the past but continues to struggle for social justice in the present, like his example of Japanese Americans standing up for American Muslims. Generational responsibility is about acknowledging this kind of debt to our living histories that have paved the way for current generations. And then it is about feeling guilt for not caring for and about those living histories.

The poet then moves on to explicitly name the destruction of the plaza as gentrification, telling the audience that these "dessert shops mean nothing if Walmarts destroy our uncles' and aunts' businesses" in reference to the "dynamite of gentrifiers" looming in the future.[58] Using the language of family to establish a kinship with those businesses that will be destroyed affirms a familial responsibility for the plaza. It is no longer about eating mochi but about familial, personal relationships and connections that are established and solidified in these community spaces. As the poem comes to an end, the poet concludes with a countdown of what he has learned:

Very slowly I understand that
5. these reparations can't repair our unfulfilled promises
4. that we as young people must fight for.
3. That we wasted gifts of pounded rice freely.
2. I know I'm not perfect but I should be responsible too.
1. Mom, I just want you to be proud of your son.
0. Time's up. And this mochi doesn't seem so sweet anymore.[59]

To continue his mochi metaphor, the poet reminds the audience that Nikkei youth have "wasted gifts"—gifts that were given to them "freely." In other words, intergenerational conflict occurs when the youth are "bad" at remembering the things that have come before them. In order for the poet to be a son that his mother would be proud of, he must assume his responsibility for the debt and therefore do his part in the maintenance of community livelihood and vitality. He must do what he can to save the plaza as he urges others to do the same through his artful expression. Here, and throughout the poem, the familial is intimately connected to the public memory of Japanese American history and culture. Again, the reprosexuality of Japanese American memory and community finds "its proper temporality and fulfillment in [these] generational transmissions" that guilts Nikkei youth into action as proper subjects who must pay back their debt by remembering that they are inheritors of cultural nationalist rememberings of Japanese American incarceration and redress and thus are responsible for justice.[60] Creating a genealogy through the metaphor of mochi allows the poet to make visible why JASA and, more specifically, Nikkei youth need to take action. Their action is crucial to Japanese American community survival.

The Temporality of "Maybe If I Did"

After the benefit concert, Nicole continues to push JASA to fight the impending destruction of the plaza. While the scene opens with Nicole dreaming of a successful protest, with many JASA members holding signs and chanting about saving Little Tokyo, her daydream is disrupted by another member asking if she thinks more people will show up. The idyllic marching and chanting are then broken up by the reality of the situation. On the stage, there are very few members protesting. And those who pass by the protest remain uninterested and uncaring as JASA members attempt to pass out informational flyers on the destruction. After Nicole decides to give up for the day, the scene transitions to another Kevin monologue, where he tells the audience that not only did he not show up to the protest but he also stopped helping Nicole with anything related to saving the plaza. He ends by saying, "Maybe if I did, there wouldn't be caution tape all over Little Tokyo by the end of the month."[61] His articulation of "maybe if I did" is an important temporality of the play and is expressed most often in Kevin's monologues that are commenting back on the past few months. These temporal disruptions to the linear timeline of before and after the plaza destruction are about expressing a lesson to the audience. Kevin's regretful monologues and his character serve as a warning about what happens when one does not care about history, memory, family, and community. The lesson is that this is a Nikkei almost future. Even if this destruction of the Japanese Village Plaza is merely an imaginary one, Japanese Americans are always on the verge of this possible future. "Maybe if I did" acknowledges the unfulfilled debt-obligation, and this is what the crises of community centers upon. Kevin's interruptions to the scenes that play out in front of the audience serve as a disruptive affective guide meant to make the audience feel a sense of guilt—a feeling that Nikkei youth are all too familiar with.

However, as the play ends, these lessons about "maybe if I did" shift as the play finally catches up with the present and the audience is without Kevin's narrations about the past. The plaza is now officially gone, and both Kevin and Nicole are devastated by the destruction and the seemingly irreparable damage to their friendship. In the final scene of the play, Kevin and Nicole's friends arrange for the two to accidentally run into each other in Little Tokyo, in front of the destroyed plaza, signified by the return of the yellow caution tape. In this scene, Kevin is hopeful, telling her that "we might have lost our space, but we still have our community."[62] On the other hand, Nicole's community/political spirit has been defeated by the loss of the plaza, and she confronts Kevin's new hopeful attitude with his own words about apathetic youth being unable to make changes in the world. But Kevin's change in attitude is not swayed by Nicole's newfound pessimism:

> KEVIN: We might have lost those things [the plaza], but we still have our culture, our traditions, our history. And most importantly we have people like you who treasure it and share it with everyone. As long as we have people like you around, the community never really dies.
> NICOLE: Well, that's oddly thoughtful of you, Kevin. Thanks. I guess it was a little early to give up hope. But what can we do now?
> KEVIN: [Standing up.] Well our work doesn't have to end with JASA. Some do amazing things after they graduate from college. We'll fight and we'll rebuild. We'll get our space back and strengthen our community so they never have to face these problems ever again. So it's not too late.[63]

Offering her a crane he made, symbolizing his hope, wishfulness, and longevity for both their friendship and community, Kevin then offers her his hand and says, "Come on, we got a lot of work to do."[64] She takes his hand and the scene fades to black. While the play does end on a hopeful note and with the same theme of generational responsibility that is stressed throughout, the play does not end in any sort of resolution. Despite Nicole's activism and hard work in supporting the community and Kevin's transition from an ungrateful, apathetic Japanese American youth to his political consciousness, the plaza ultimately still gets destroyed. In an interview, Emiko Kranz, 2016 Cultural Night producer and 2016–2017 UCLA NSU president, stated that the writers and all those involved in the script wanted to have this less "cheesy" ending because they felt like it was more realistic. She muses that Cultural Nights often end with the message that "everything is going to be okay," but recently many in NSU have been feeling that "no, everything is not going to be okay if things continue like this." She says, "You can't expect for it to all magically get better."[65] In this way, the plaza had to be destroyed. It serves both as a warning of what the future will look like—a bleak tomorrow of disappearing racial space—but also functions as a moment of crisis for Japanese American youth. When the

Nisei and Sansei ask, "Where are the youth?" UCLA NSU's 2016 Cultural Night chose to answer with this drama. *Senbazuru* says that the youth are here, but Nikkei community, spaces, identities, and thus futures are changing.

The Continuing Limits of Generational Debt: Carceral Realizations in the Age of Trump

In the interview with Kranz, she stated that as the current NSU president, her overall vision was to bring back a political and historical consciousness to the club.[66] She argues that it is "dangerous" to be a cultural club while lacking this kind of consciousness and being unable to serve your community. As a Nikkei college student with NSU leadership experience and community involvement, Kranz candidly shared what generational responsibility means to her and other college students as well as the limitations of this discourse that is placed upon her.

When asked about generational responsibility, Kranz stated that there is a truth to it, that the accusations are in some ways "valid" even if she is "irked" by them. As a result, she had several critiques about the Japanese American community's expectations of Nikkei youth. The first is the pressures of being a college student who "struggle[s] with, like, these generations telling us to, like, oh study hard become, like, a doctor or lawyer and all that stuff, and it is not very easy, especially at institutions like UCLA that are very highly competitive and people spend a lot of their time just studying."[67] For Kranz, it is difficult to "tear people away from their studies" and "force those priorities onto people," but she believes that as long as one person attends a community event and is "in the know," then they can easily disseminate information to the rest of the group. Reflecting on the pressures of the model minority for Nikkei college students, Kranz demonstrates how generational responsibility feels impossible. Not only do Nikkei youth have to participate in Japanese American community organizations to preserve memory, but they are also expected to be academically successful to obtain economic wealth in their future professions to monetarily give back to the community. Community survival, and thus generational responsibility, is predicated on the intimate connection between economic success and the reproduction of cultural nationalist history. In other words, Nikkei youth must reproduce themselves as model citizen-subjects in order to be worthy of the sacrifices of their elders, a debt they are well aware they can never repay.

While Kranz admits that past Cultural Nights have rarely addressed other groups of color, she says that UCLA NSU does collaborate with other communities both on and off campus. Because NSU was born out of a mother organization, the Asian Pacific Coalition, they do work closely with other Asian American groups on campus by holding general meetings together and attending other Cultural Nights. In 2016, Kranz also created a support group for Cultural Night producers in the Asian Pacific Islander community on campus so they could help one another with questions about staging, advertising, or anything else they needed help with because Cultural Night is "one of the most important events that happen throughout the year." Despite these coalitions, Kranz tells me that they have mostly been "more social" and "not so much programming." Additionally, NSU works closely with the JACCC on two multicultural celebration events: Fiesta Matsuri and FandangObon. Fiesta Matsuri is held in the month of May and combines the Children's Day celebrations of Japan's Kodomo no Hi and Mexico's Día de los Niño. On the other hand, FandangObon is described as an annual festival "that brings together Japanese, Mexican and African American communities into one circle to share participatory music and dance traditions to Celebrate Mother Earth."[68] Kranz articulates these events as sharing space, where "although we are the Japanese American community, we're very much surrounded and in contact with other cultural communities around Los Angeles."[69] She goes on to say that it is really important to have solidarity with these communities, where these events are

> really giving those communities more of a space as well because we're lucky enough that again, America likes Japanese culture pretty much, so we are given these spaces, and our community is also *wealthy* enough we're able to maintain these spaces. So, I think that the JACCC has a certain . . . or they feel a certain *responsibility* for being able to help those communities out as well and also help the Japanese American community why it's important to have cross-cultural programming.[70]

While the Japanese American community often utilizes notions of familial responsibility to produce feelings of guilt within the youth to get them to prove that they care, this care work is often wrapped up in narratives that ignore Japanese American privilege by highlighting their World War II incarceration as an anomaly. Kranz makes this comment about Japanese American privilege again in the interview, saying that one of the proposed scripts for the 2017 Cultural Night was set to look at "the motivations behind Japanese Americans getting involved in the community because we are such a *wealthy* and *complacent* community."[71] The script also asks, "Why [then] do we still feel the need to organize?"[72] For Kranz, Japanese American privilege often means that Nikkei are a politically complacent community, and this complacency she identifies is in relation to other groups of color. She argues that Japanese Americans (because they have privilege) should be responsible to other groups of color. Here, responsibility is not necessarily about Japanese American legitimacy or visibility per se, but instead about how Japanese Americans use what they have gained from redress—the protections of legitimacy and visibility—to care for more vulnerable populations. This kind of care work can then be about abolitionist and decolonial projects wherein Japanese Americans are able to acknowledge both their relationship to incarceration and their privilege within neoliberal race relations. This care work asks a different kind of question: how can Japanese Americans be better allies to vulnerable groups of color? This does not mean that Japanese Americans have not made intimate connections or built solidarity with other groups of color who experience carcerality. Nor does it mean that only youth are considering these comparative histories and moments. For example, in 2010, the JACL joined "as a plaintiff in a lawsuit challenging the constitutionality" of SB 1070 in Arizona, "fear[ing] this will lead to racial profiling."[73] As I have shown in previous chapters, all community organizations and spaces (despite what generation is in leadership) both replicate and challenge the centrality of World War II incarceration.

Although an NSU member initially proposed having a Muslim American parallel script for Cultural Night 2017, NSU was advised to pick a different topic because logistically there would need to be a lot of research done for the script and not enough time. NSU then switched gears and began focusing on another gentrification message. However, after the election of Donald Trump, whose campaign utilized xenophobic, racist language to mobilize bans and walls, Kranz planned to immediately talk to their club's advisor to change the script again. She believes that "the JA (Japanese American) community has a much greater responsibility to say something in these times."[74] Drawing on a Japanese American incarcerated past, she argues that Japanese American people were affected by the outcome of the election because "what is really stopping another internment experience from happening to another community?"[75] Because of this, UCLA NSU feels that they have a responsibility to say something about the election and its consequences. She tells me her conclusions:

> So it would be a lot more focused on, like, the JA experience and understanding, like, perspectives from different marginalized groups currently. And how our experiences relate to theirs. So it's not going to be focused on, like, only the Muslim American experience. I would love for it to happen. But it's just like we need to get approval for it. And be able to pull it off. But I think it's something that we need to do.[76]

Trying to show their Cultural Night audience how the election affected the UCLA community and NSU, Kranz says that that would be "the dream," although she ends by saying, "We'll see what happens."[77] Despite the fact that she did not know if the 2017 Cultural Night would be able to move forward with this idea about comparative carceral experiences, the fact that the idea existed not only shows how some Nikkei youth have been affected by the 2016 presidential election but reveals that their understanding of the future does not necessarily lie in generational reproduction of history and memory. So, while Nikkei youth feel a sense of guilt to the generations that have come before them, they also feel a sense of responsibility to other marginalized communities (even within Japanese Americans themselves). This does not mean they are not invested in Japanese American history and community but rather that they utilize these memories differently. By making generational responsibility hypervisible, they demonstrate the limits of generations as categories of knowing that do not allow for a comparative carceral analytic—an analytic that Kranz pointed out as necessary for the uncertain future brought on by Trump's election.

The 2017 Cultural Night ultimately was unable to address the political climate of Trump or the relationship between Japanese American and Muslim American experiences. Instead, *Chirashi* (2017) addressed a shifting Japanese American community through spatial change as a family-owned restaurant comes into conflict with a contracting firm. Another lesson on generational responsibility, the failures of caring, and the consequences of gentrification.

Conclusion

The Shifting Futures of Japanese American Memory from 9/11 to the COVID-19 Pandemic

The launch of Donald Trump's 2016 campaign for the presidency marked a significant shift in the Japanese American community, inciting new fears and anxiety over Trump's promise "to make American great" through his anti-immigrant, anti-Muslim rhetoric that led to his eventual election. Not only did new organizations, such as Vigilant Love (2015), Nikkei Progressives (2016), and Tsuru for Solidarity (2019), develop in this wake, but different strategies for organizing and mobilizing memories of World War II incarceration emerged alongside the existing framework of "never again." To conclude, I gesture to these shifts in relational organizing that emerged alongside Trump's campaign, election, and presidency to understand how Japanese Americans centered feminist, intergenerational, interracial, artistic notions of healing in their solidarity and allyship work.

Theorizing the urgency of Trump that shifted Japanese American organizing marks his political ascendancy as exceptional. However, as Dylan Rodriguez has argued, Trump has always been here, he is "the persona his predecessors possessed but disguised so well," where "many of those in the throes of liberal-white-people panic *know this deep down* because their revulsion to him is driven by a hatred of the intimate, the familial, and maybe the same."[1] In other words, what is it about "this *particular* abhorrence" that birthed new organizations and new ways of relating to one another that positioned abolition as a solution to carceral logics of white supremacy for the very first time? The first is that the logic of redress visibly crumbles on a national level as Trump gains power, and it becomes clear that gendered respectability does not ensure total safety even for Japanese Americans. For example, in response to the rise in Syrian refugees, 2015 Virginia mayor David Bowers cited Japanese American World War II incarceration as a historical precedent to deny assistance to Syrian refugees because it was "better [to be] safe than sorry."² The second is the terrifying realization epitomized through Trump is how these organizations come to be in the first place, where former strategies of resistance no longer work and entirely new organizations are needed. In the next section, I analyze the "never again" discourse that developed in response to 9/11 national security policies to understand the shifts to this current exceptionally unexceptional moment in history.

12/7 and 9/11: "Never Again" as a Discourse of Relationality

Since September 11, 2001, Japanese Americans have utilized their memories of World War II incarceration to rally against the racial profiling of Muslim Americans and have worked on building relationships between the two groups. The relationship between 9/11 and 12/7, and thus Muslim Americans and Japanese Americans respectively, has been the most nationally visible comparison. Drawing out the parallels between 9/11 and 12/7 has commonly relied upon a discourse of "never again" that often problematically centers Japanese American personal experiences of incarceration as an exceptional moment in history. For example, as the former secretary of transportation during 9/11, Norman Mineta's memories and visibility as a political figure often get mobilized in the service of a neoliberal racial order that *Carceral Entanglements* critiques. In a Densho interview, Mineta recalled what happened the day after 9/11. He states that in a cabinet meeting, a congressman from Michigan said,

> Mr. President, we have a very large Arab American population in Michigan and they're very concerned about what's happening and they're very concerned about what they're hearing on the radio, television, and reading in the paper about some of the security measures that might be taken relating to transportation.³

Former President Bush responded that "we are also concerned about this and we want to make sure, what happened to Norm in 1942, *doesn't happen today*."⁴ In the immediate aftermath of 9/11, Mineta becomes a physical representation of the lessons of incarceration. His body reminds the room about what could happen so that it "doesn't happen today." As I have argued in this book,

Japanese Americans are representative of state redemption. In other words, Bush's reassurance to the congressman is less about Arab and Muslim American safety and more about the state's desire to reassure itself that it is not racist. And yet, from Guantanamo Bay to the National Security Entry-Exit Registration System (NSEERS) and the PATRIOT Act, surveillance, racial profiling, and carceral punishment continued to happen even while being disavowed through the Japanese American experience.

On a community level, 9/11 provided many Japanese Americans with the opportunity to connect their history to the present moment through the rallying cry of "never again." This slogan has its roots in the passage of the Civil Liberties Act of 1988, where the act of giving testimony not only allowed Japanese Americans to voice their racialized violence on a national stage but also allowed for the continued education of this historical moment so that "wartime incarceration based on racial prejudice will not happen again" via the Civil Liberties Public Education Fund.[5] "Never again" establishes a progressive, linear temporality that presumes that state violence is not happening in the current moment but is in fact always on the cusp of occurring. It does not question or even recognize carcerality in all its forms (until Trump's election) and continues to mark World War II and now 9/11 as states of exception catalyzed by the attacks on Pearl Harbor and the World Trade Center. However, because of this renewed commitment to "never again," Japanese Americans did establish important relational organizing that would need to be utilized once Trump signed his infamous Muslim Ban (EO 13769). For example, Japanese American community organizations in Los Angeles began to work with "the Southern California Shura Council, the Muslim Public Affairs Council, and the Council on American Islamic Relations."[6] And, since 9/11, they have "held workshops, went to Manzanar Pilgrimages [together], broke[n] bread at Ramadan 'Break the Fast' events, spoke at each other's programs," and "created a program called Bridging Communities to help our young people get to know each other's history, values, and communities better."[7] These sites of relationality and the metaphorical "bridges" built by Japanese Americans and Arab Americans in the aftermath of 9/11 would continue to be necessary fifteen years later.

The Haunting of Executive Orders

Issued on January 27, 2017, Executive Order 13769, Protecting the Nation from Foreign Terrorist Entry into the United States, sought to restrict refugee admission and deny visas to immigrants from seven Muslim-majority countries under the guise of national security. The election of Donald Trump and the issuing of the executive order coincided with the seventy-fifth anniversary of Executive Order 9066, and the organizations featured in *Carceral Entanglements* have sought to strengthen their relationships to Muslim Americans by reinforcing the lessons of the Japanese American incarceration through calls to action.[8] In a cowritten *Time* magazine article, Norman Mineta and Ann Burroughs (the current president of the Japanese American National Museum) wrote a response to the election of Donald Trump that worried about a dangerous return of "hatred and fear" that promises to "punish people based on race and religion."[9] In March 2017, Densho issued a statement that narrated the United States' long history of immigration exclusion while urging its readers to "speak out, protest, support refugee legal defenses, use whatever skills you have to fight the fight, and mean it when you say 'Never Again.'"[10] The Manzanar Committee's 2017 pilgrimage entitled "Never Again, to Anyone, Anywhere!" stated that the Japanese American community "has a moral responsibility to speak out now" and "stand with those civil rights and civil liberties groups speaking out against Islamophobia and the persecution of Muslim people."[11] The executive order instilled a renewed sense of urgency within the memory work of these community organizations that simultaneously relied on a discourse of "never again" but also pushed to critique the United States as a carceral state.

The 2016 presidential election and Trump's executive orders have shifted this temporality from "on the cusp of occurring" to "it is happening right now." Japanese American memories were mobilized to "ensure that the most tragic civil rights chapters in our history remain where they belong—in history books and museums, and not part of our future."[12] The Manzanar Committee characterizes the aftermath of the presidential election as "unleash[ing] thoughts, feelings, and acts that are antithetical to our democracy," where "blatant racism and xenophobia are on the rise."[13] In a post–2016 election moment, the progressive temporality of "never again" collides with this rise in "blatant" racism. Here, Trump's overt racist attacks on communities of color via his "Make America Great" campaign ignite a shift in Japanese American memory production. In 2017, Executive Order 13769 produces a particular kind of haunting for Japanese Americans who are simultaneously commemorating seventy-five years of Executive Order 9066 in which their memories gain new life. Memories of World War II incarceration are resurrected and recentered to challenge what feels like a return to a racist past that had already been redressed three decades ago. However, as Densho reminds us,

> We have not been entirely successful in weeding out America's xenophobic and racist tendencies. Shades of our wartime suffering persist:

from the systemic profiling and mass incarceration of African Americans and Latinx men, women, and youth, to the National Security Entry-Exit Registration System (NSEERS), to the detention of immigrant families.[14]

Highlighting the unfinished business of "never again" through a comparative carceral lens, Densho makes visible the contradictory location of Japanese Americans that recognizes both the privilege of Japanese Americans in a post-redress era and their lingering carceral experiences. As I have argued, the contradictory location becomes an important point of interrogation and critique of Japanese American privilege established through masculinist, patriotic narratives of worth that sustain carceral and settler colonial logics. In the era of Donald Trump, "never again" is transforming—or, at the very least, existing alongside—other ways of remembering and thus organizing. To conclude, I want to feature the organization Vigilant Love for its feminist, interracial, and intergenerational organizing model that prioritizes solidarity over privileging Japanese American memories in the name of community safety. This organization inherently challenges the masculinist, patriotic narratives of worth that often sustain Japanese American community memories and instead offers another way to form meaningful and ethical solidarities.

Vigilant Love is a Los Angeles–based "solidarity community" that "actively creates spaces for connection and grassroots movement to ensure safety and justice of communities impacted by Islamophobia and violence."[15] The organization formed in the aftermath of the San Bernardino, California, mass shooting in 2015 in response to the growing wave of Islamophobic backlash in Southern California. Although the organization situates itself within the legacies of Muslim American and Japanese American solidarity since 9/11, it departs from it in many ways. First, the organization's vision identifies "the embodiment of vigilant love amongst generations of multi-ethnic and interspiritual community who create pathways to liberation and healing together" in the face of "cyclical violence."[16] In order to do this, they employ a "creative organizing model that integrates grassroots organizing, policy advocacy, political education, the arts, and healing practices within the culture of everything we do."[17] Vigilant Love is not about Japanese American incarceration as an exception to U.S. democracy, and it is not centered in its vision or projects. Instead, the organization prioritizes partnership over the kind of national and community memories exemplified by Norman Mineta.

In response to the first Muslim Ban, Vigilant Love and South Asians for Justice–Los Angeles utilized the space of the candlelight vigil as an active space of solidarity and resistance. Vigilant Love argues that "racialized and gendered

Islamophobia creates a hostile environment where Muslim Americans, Sikh, South Asian, Black and Arab American communities are harassed, targeted, and abused."[18] Therefore, the purpose of the vigil is to create alternative spaces of community safety and resistance in times of crisis, drawing from diverse communities in the Los Angeles area. In the face of Trump's executive orders to restrict, ban, and create walls in the name of national security, the vigil seeks to "redefine security as care, support, and protection for each other."[19] This redefinition is significant because it poses a community definition of safety that points to the ways national security rests on racialized and gendered harm and punishment. It demands "the city of Los Angeles and the state of California to remain a sanctuary space for all immigrants, refugees, and DACA-mented young people" and stipulates that "California, its cities, and law enforcement agencies refuse collaboration with ICE [U.S. Immigration and Customs Enforcement]."[20]

At the "No Ban No Wall Vigil" held on January 26, 2017, there were a variety of speakers that included a former Japanese American incarceree, an Iraqi refugee, an immigrants' rights advocate from the ICE out of LA Coalition, a tenants' rights advocate, and cultural performances that included a hip-hop artist and poetry performances. Japanese American incarceration as one of the many historical precedents for the current political climate exists to fuel the work of Vigilant Love, but it is not central to its organizing, its strategies, or its tactics. This is important because Japanese American incarceration and organizing are no longer exemplary or a model to be followed. Vigilant Love recognizes the limitations of utilizing Japanese American memories in this way, and their decentering of Japanese American incarceration is rooted in feminist approaches to organizing and relating to one another that inherently challenge masculinist and patriarchal narratives that unintentionally uphold the neoliberal racial order.

Vigilant Love is organized by four women activists: traci kato-kiriyama, a queer, third-generation Nikkei writer and performer; Sahar Pirzada, a Pakistani American Muslim community organizer and a Master of Social Welfare candidate; Traci Ishigo, a Nikkei, Buddhist, nonbinary femme, community organizer, trauma-informed yoga teacher, and Master of Social Welfare candidate specializing in mental health; and Kathy Masaoka, a community activist since the 1970s who has organized around issues related to youth, workers, housing in Little Tokyo, and redress.[21] Vigilant Love, while continuing to build relationships between Japanese Americans and Muslim Americans, is also centrally about the solidarities that are formed around female relationships based in their shared experiences as women of color. Pirzada notes that Vigilant Love's leaders are "all women," which for her means that women are "here and we will lead the resistance."²² Ishigo agrees with her and extends this analysis to think about how "women from a lot of communities of color have different, but shared experiences."²³ She then comments that, while "there are so many experiences to talk about it [which] makes it hard to break it down," we "need to consider all experiences and not just those that fit into cookie-cutter narratives."²⁴ Ishigo argues that "we need to resist the patriarchy in all its forms."²⁵

This linking of patriarchy to the security state thinks about the ways gendered discipline and violence are central to systems of oppression. Unlike the masculinist narratives of worth that come out of redress in order to make oneself visible to the state, Vigilant Love's intersectional approach to organizing and understanding history opens up the possibility for these meaningful relationships to persist. The organization recognizes intersectionality as a strength of their movement and states that "there is no future without intersectionality."²⁶ In this formulation of solidarity, Japanese Americans understand that it is "the responsibility of those who have privilege to center those who do not."²⁷ Here, decentering Japanese American narratives is about understanding Japanese American privilege as an important strategy of maintaining cross-racial alliances. The relationality of women of color experiences and histories allows Vigilant Love to open up spaces of safety for those who do not possess it in their everyday lives. I argue, then, that a vigilant love is a feminist love that is constantly keeping watch for possible danger that happens in and to marginalized communities. It has its eyes turned to the state (as a perpetrator of violence) and seeks to hold it accountable. This kind of radical feminist care work in movement building is not always visible or at the forefront of organizing models within the Japanese American community. I believe that Vigilant Love is actively working to change how Japanese Americans relate to other communities of color.

On January 29, 2017, Vigilant Love coordinated a nonviolent sit-in and rally at the Los Angeles International Airport where thousands of protestors showed up. Vigilant Love made calls to U.S. Customs and Border Protection, organized safety teams for protestors, and held an unapologetic healing group prayer in the airport. In a short film entitled *A Vigilant Love*, directed by filmmaker and activist Tani Ikeda, we are given a glimpse into Pirzada's and Ishigo's thoughts, fears, hopes, and friendship as they were preparing for the direct action.²⁸ In an interview with Ishigo, she tells the camera about Japanese American World War II incarceration as it relates to the current moment, but rather than establishing a progressive temporality, Ishigo states, "How can that be in this country? And at the same time makes total sense. And that's exactly why we Japanese Americans need to show up."²⁹ Ishigo articulates a temporality of no surprise, one that can acknowledge multiple forms of violence that happen at different historical moments. The emotional juxtaposition of "how can that be" and "at the same time" opens up a comparative space that allows Japanese Americans to provide support rather than take up space. The duty of Japanese American memories is to "show up." At the end of the film, Ishigo and Pirzada are in the car on the way home, and in an emotionally tender moment, Pirzada tears up and tells Ishigo, "What is going to happen if that happens, what is going to happen to me?"[30] She pauses and then says, "But then I'm like, but it won't because I have you. And I have others."[31] For Pirzada it was comforting and "healing to know that if anything goes down, Traci will have my back."[32] The emphasis on community building and healing that Vigilant Love incorporates demonstrates how this organization challenges state violence past, present, and future. Its efforts to reconceptualize safety in the face of bans and walls offer a model that reveals how Japanese American memories can be mobilized for ethical and meaningful cross-racial solidarities.

Shifting Futures: Abolition and Japanese American Memory

In addition to organizing around intersectionality and feminist critiques of national security, Japanese American memory has continued to expand its relational organizing to consider not just the relationship between Islamophobia and World War II incarceration but also how to mobilize against settler colonialism, antiblack racism, and immigration detention and deportation. There are several factors I see as contributing to this relational mobilization of memory that is happening. First, the development of Japanese American organizing has shifted significantly since the beginning of this project over a decade ago. Due to the shifting as well as aging populations within the Japanese American community, the organizations have become overwhelmingly intergenerational, where Sansei, Yonsei, Gosei, Shin-Issei, and Shin-Nisei collaborate. Generational distinctions are still important, as they inform one's experiences and how they connect to a Japanese American past and hold memories. However, the collaboration among generations has significantly shifted conversations and thus altered power dynamics. Rather than positing the youth as the future where lineage and heteronormative transfers of memory are solidified, these community spaces are organized around critiques of state violence through intergenerational conversation where all generations can learn from each other to participate in larger political actions, from abolishing the police to supporting Black reparations. Second, as I previously mentioned, Trump's presidency and his overt white supremacist discourse pushed many Japanese Americans into anxious action around the idea that there was a "recognition of the need to offer support and resistance" by "building solidarity with other communities of color that have experienced forced removal, detention, deportation, separation of families, and other forms of racial and state violence."[33] And third, in 2020, the murder of George Floyd by Minneapolis police officers resulted in outrage and protest during a global pandemic that catapulted abolition into the political mainstream. Like many other organizations, abolition officially entered Japanese American community spaces for the first time, enabling a reckoning with Japanese Americans' participation and maintenance in antiblackness. These three major shifts are not meant to imply that relational organizing is somehow suddenly free of antiblackness and settler desires but that, on a much larger scale, Japanese American memory work is actively working against those logics that *Carceral Entanglements* makes visible. A decade ago, abolition and alternative relationships to World War II incarceration lingered in the shadows, but today, Japanese American organizations and events actively seek to incorporate abolitionist and Native American stories and strategies of resistance into their work. This shift is one I could only have imagined and hoped for when this book started. It is not perfect or always readily accepted, but it is there.

I began with Inouye's "look how far we've come speech" because it started this entire project. While everyone stood to applaud Inouye for his success that also belonged to the entire community, I sat there uncomfortable, confused, and upset. The inability to celebrate placed me in a familiar place of unbelonging, the place where I often found myself in relation to Japanese American memory, community, and historiography. As the granddaughter of a family who replied "no, no" to the Loyalty Questionnaire and almost "repatriated" to Japan, I could never fit my family's experiences or their responses to incarceration into the existing narratives. As a Japanese American, I found myself simultaneously an outsider and an insider to Japanese American community spaces. Because of my familial history, I found myself located outside proper Japanese American history and geographically distant from epicenters of community-building spaces like Los Angeles, but I also had unique access to Japanese American spaces due to my own family's rise within the community via board memberships and sizable donations made to the spaces that preserved Japanese American history. However, my positionality allowed me to see how these narratives do not serve any of us. Attending this event forced me to see how Japanese American narratives were carefully crafted around racialized notions of worth and success that ultimately participated in the continued harm against other groups of color and functioned to exclude me as well. *Carceral Entanglements* is a deeply personal project to hold Japanese American memory practices, and those that are similar, accountable. These practices are generationally embedded within what Inouye sees as "our success," and *Carceral Entanglements* seeks to pay attention to what memories cannot be named, discussed, or celebrated and cherished. This book elaborates on the consequences of state recognition and visibility as a cautionary tale.

In the face of a global pandemic and the visibility of anti-Asian sentiment and violence with the spread of the COVID-19 virus, we see these familiar narratives of worthiness and respectability enter conversations advocating for hate crime legislation that are steeped in antiblackness, a dismissal of the settler state, and a securitization of safety that relies on the police. *Carceral Entanglements* is reminder of the dangers that exist when one relies on the state to recognize and repair racial harm through gendered respectability. It is an exploration of how carceral logics seep into acts of resistance, preservation, and celebration even when there is an active repelling of "never again." It is a dangerous future. We must resist the temptation to protect ourselves and each other through these measures that have failed us over and over again.

Notes

INTRODUCTION

1. James Kyung-Jin Lee, "Multiculturalism," in *Keywords for Asian American Studies*, ed. Cathy J. Schlund-Vials, K. Scott Wong, and Linda Trinh Võ (New York: New York University Press, 2015). *Carceral Entanglements* avoids reducing Japanese American history and memory to multicultural narratives of success and belonging as demonstrated by Inouye's speech. Multiculturalism is inherently assimilationist and actively participates in the maintenance of generational reproduction of heteronormative narratives that participate in antiblackness and settler logics that do not consider power in the celebration of Asian American life. Also see Candace Fujikane and Jonathan Y. Okamura, *Asian Settler Colonialism: From Local Governance to the Habits of Everyday Life in Hawaii* (Honolulu: University of Hawaii Press, 2008), 6.

2. William Minoru Hohri, *Repairing America: An Account of the Movement for Japanese-American Redress* (Pullman: Washington State University Press, 1988); Mitchell T. Maki, Harry H. L. Kitano, and S. Megan Berthold, *Achieving the Impossible Dream: How Japanese Americans Obtained Redress* (Urbana: University of Illinois Press, 1999). Many of these narratives come from community spaces like the Manzanar Committee, observations of the Day of Remembrance, and the Japanese American National Museum.

3. Maki, Kitano, and Berthold, *Achieving the Impossible Dream*.

4. Roderick Ferguson, *Aberrations in Black: Toward a Queer of Color Critique* (Minneapolis: University of Minnesota Press, 2003), 3. Like Hong and Ferguson in *Strange Affinities*, my work draws on a genealogy of women of color feminism and queer of color critique whose work "emerges to name the material conditions of racial and colonial violence" and is organized around "difference, the difference between and within racialized, gendered, sexualized collectivities." Grace Kyungwon Hong and Roderick A. Ferguson, eds., *Strange Affinities: The Gender and Sexual Politics of Comparative Racialization* (Durham, NC: Duke University Press, 2011), 9.

5. I pay attention to the discourses that refuse to and cannot be mobilized by the state to justify criminalization in the carceral and settler state. Examining the memories of incarceration that are not/cannot be resolved by redress are better situated to hold the state accountable for past and current state violences. Please see Cathy Cohen's critique of a queer political activism rooted in identity politics or a single oppression framework and the possibilities of "theoretical conceptualizations of queerness" that attempt to broaden "queerness" to encompass the systems of oppression that interact "to regulate and police the lives of most people" (440, 441). My usage of "normative" is in reference to the kinds of histories that emerge when narratives are constructed around punitive notions of state belonging: proper gendered, heteronormative behavior vs. a questioning of this historical production of knowledge. Cathy J. Cohen, "Punks, Bulldaggers, and Welfare Queens: The Radical Potential of Queer Politics?" *GLQ* 3, no. 4 (1997): 437–465.

6. Please see: Ellen D. Wu, *The Color of Success: Asian Americans and the Origins of the Model Minority* (Princeton, NJ: Princeton University Press, 2014).

7. Ferguson, *Aberrations in Black*, 3.

8. Grace Kyungwon Hong, "'Something Forgotten Which Should Have Been Remembered': Private Property and Cross-Racial Solidarity in the Work of Hisaye Yamamoto," *American Literature* 71, no. 2 (1999): 302.

9. Lisa Lowe, *Immigrant Acts: On Asian American Cultural Politics* (Durham, NC: Duke University Press, 1996), 22.

10. Lowe, 7.

11. Lowe, 13

12. Ronald Takaki, *Strangers from a Different Shore* (Boston: Little, Brown, 1998), 40.

13. Takaki, 40.

14. Lowe, *Immigrant Acts*, 11.

15. Takaki, *Strangers from a Different Shore*, 46

16. Takaki, 47.

17. Takaki.

18. Lowe, *Immigrant Acts*, 12.

19. Michael Warner, "Introduction: Fear of a Queer Planet," *Social Text*, no. 29 (1991): 9.

20. Yuji Ichioka, *Before Internment: Essays in Prewar Japanese American History*, ed. Gordan Chang and Eiichiro Azuma (Stanford, CA: Stanford University Press, 2006), 10.

21. 1790 Nationality Act.

22. Eiichiro Azuma, introduction to *Before Internment: Essays in Prewar Japanese American History*, by Yuji Ichioka, ed. Gordan Chang and Eiichiro Azuma (Stanford, CA: Stanford University Press, 2006), xix, xx.

23. And as I explain later, these memories are often problematically narrated as exceptional, where Japanese American World War II incarceration is an aberration of U.S. democratic principles.

24. There are many works, both scholarly and community based, that revolve around the experiences of a generation, such as Yuji Ichioka's *The Issei: The World of the First Generation*, Bill Hosokawa's *Nisei: The Quiet American*, and Mei Nakano's *Japanese American Women: Three Generations, 1890–1990*. However, a lot of the works that explicitly rely on the familial as regeneration utilize an oral history methodology or storytelling. Please see such works as Paul Howard Takemoto's *Nisei Memories: My Parents Talk about the War Years*. In addition, I further elaborate on this in later chapters in relation

to Densho: The Japanese American Legacy Project, Manzanar at Dusk by the Manzanar Committee, and Nikkei Student Unions.

25. Please see Tritia Toyota, who argues that the changing demography of the U.S. Nikkei community presents a narrative of community that is shifting and in transition where new conditions for membership remain undefined. Tritia Toyota, "The New Nikkei: Transpacific Shin Issei and Shifting Borders of Community in Southern California," *Amerasia* 38, no. 3 (2012): 2–27.

26. Commission on Wartime Relocation and Internment of Civilians, *Personal Justice Denied* (Seattle: University of Washington, 1997), xi.

27. Clyde Woods, "Les Miserables of New Orleans: Trap Economics and the Asset Stripping Blues, Part 1," *American Quarterly* 61, no. 3 (2009): 774.

28. Ruth Wilson Gilmore, *Golden Gulag: Prisons, Surplus, Crisis, and Opposition in Globalizing California* (Berkeley: University of California Press, 2007), 28.

29. Mae Ngai, *Impossible Subjects: Illegal Aliens and the Making of Modern America* (Princeton, NJ: Princeton University Press, 2004), 183.

30. Here, statelessness functions as a state of citizen nonbeing where Japanese immigrants lack any protections from the United States as "enemy aliens" and must forswear allegiance to Japan.

31. Immediately after Pearl Harbor, many already in the army were released except for those in the Hawaii National Guard. Takashi Fujitani, "Right to Kill and Right to Make Live: Koreans as Japanese and Japanese as Americans during World War II," *Representations* 99, no. 1 (2007): 13.

32. Commission on Wartime Relocation and Internment of Civilians, *Personal Justice Denied*, 258.

33. Commission on Wartime Relocation and Internment of Civilians, 258.

34. Takashi Fujitani, "Go for Broke, the Movie: Japanese American Soldiers in the US National, Military, and Racial Discourses," in *Perilous Memories: The Asia-Pacific War(s)*, ed. Takashi Fujitani, Geoffrey M. White, and Lisa Yoneyama (Durham, NC: Duke University Press, 2001), 244.

35. Jodi Kim, *Ends of Empire: Asian American Critique and the Cold War* (Minneapolis: University of Minnesota Press, 2010), 99.

36. Alien Land Law of 1913.

37. Kim, *Ends of Empire*, 99.

38. Kim, 113.

39. Kim, 99.

40. Kim, 33.

41. George Lipsitz, "'Frantic to Join . . . the Japanese Army': Black Soldiers and Civilians Confront the Asia Pacific War," in *Perilous Memories: The Asia-Pacific War(s)*, ed. Takashi Fujitani, Geoffrey M. White, and Lisa Yoneyama (Durham, NC: Duke University Press, 2001).

42. Kim, *Ends of Empire*, 103.

43. Grace Kyungwon Hong, *Death beyond Disavowal: The Impossible Politics of Difference* (Minneapolis: University of Minnesota Press, 2015), 7.

44. Hong, 7.

45. Hong, 7.

46. Please see Commission on Wartime Relocation and Internment of Civilians, *Personal Justice Denied*. This published report includes historical research, testimonials, and

the committee's recommendations. The report is divided into four parts: the Nisei and Issei, the Aleuts, recommendations, and papers for the commission. In the section on the Nisei and Issei, the report creates a linear historical timeline and divides the section into parts: pre–Pearl Harbor life to Executive Order 9066, exclusion and evacuation, economic loss, assembly centers, relocation centers, loyalty: leave and segregation, ending the exclusion, protest and disaffection, military service, Hawaii, Germans and German Americans, after camp, and an appendix on Latin Americans. The report was published because of the Civil Liberties Public Education Fund.

47. Commission on Wartime Relocation and Internment of Civilians, *Personal Justice Denied*, xxvii.

48. Wendsor Yamashita, "What She Remembers: Remaking and Unmaking Japanese American Internment" (M.A. thesis, University of California, Los Angeles, 2010), 7.

49. Commission on Wartime Relocation and Internment of Civilians, *Personal Justice Denied*, 133.

50. Yamashita, "What She Remembers," 60.

51. Commission on Wartime Relocation and Internment of Civilians, *Personal Justice Denied*, 254, 260.

52. Commission on Wartime Relocation and Internment of Civilians, 253.

53. Commission on Wartime Relocation and Internment of Civilians, xiii.

54. "About the Museum: A Living Memorial to the Holocaust," United States Holocaust Memorial Museum, accessed March 20, 2017. available at https://www.ushmm.org/information/about-the-museum.

55. And at the same time, Japanese Americans have a complicated history with Holocaust commemorations of genocide. In 1998, the Japanese American National Museum was invited to "mount an exhibit called 'America's Concentration Camps: Remembering the Japanese American Experience' at Ellis Island Immigration Museum" but was met with controversy over the usage of "concentration camp." The National Museum received pushback from the National Park Service over this terminology, citing that the phrase could be misunderstood by or offend the Jewish community in New York. Japanese American and Jewish groups met and reached a compromise that allowed the National Museum to use "concentration camp" if it explained the differences from Nazi death camps. In this complicated battle over correct terminology, the differences between the Holocaust and Japanese American incarceration disrupt the carceral exception that the discourse of "never again" allows. Aiko Herzig-Yoshinaga, "Words Can Lie or Clarify: Terminology of the World War II Incarceration of Japanese Americans," https://nps.gov/tule/learn/education/upload/Words-Can-Lie-or-Clarify-FINAL-Rev-8-15-10.pdf.

56. Bruce Embrey, "Message from Manzanar Committee Co-Chair," *44th Annual Manzanar Pilgrimage Program*, April 27, 2013, 5.

57. George Bush, "Letter from President George Bush to Internees," California State University Japanese American Digitization Project. CSU Dominguez Hills Department of Archives and Special Collections. 1991. Available at https://cdm16855.contentdm.oclc.org/digital/collection/p16855coll4/id/6715.

58. Gilmore, *Golden Gulag*. Victor Bascara, "The Cultural Politics of Redress: Reassessing the Meaning of the Civil Liberties Act of 1988 after 9/11," *Asian American Law Journal* 10, no. 2 (2003): 185–214.

59. Inouye articulates "afterlife" as a "lingering experience" that people "are breathing life back into" in "order to make it immediate and recognizable to other people." In the case of Japanese American incarceration, she argues they do so "to avert complacency in the face of continuing injustice." She draws on Avery Gordon's theorizations of "haunting" but distinguishes herself from this methodology by instead focusing on "concrete action" and things that are "purposefully detectable." While my work looks at the concrete actions that move Japanese American incarceration memories into the present moment, I am also theorizing about trauma. Drawing on the works of Grace M. Cho, Avery Gordon, Diana Taylor, and Ann Cvetkovich, I am not only looking at how trauma became recognizable and heard during Japanese American redress and reparations but at what could not be translated into state injury and what continues to be misheard, misread, and misremembered. My book, then, pays attention to the critiques these traumas make about family, cultural nationalism, and state violence. I seek to do a tracing of that which cannot be contained by redress. For more, please see: Karen M. Inouye, *The Long Afterlife of Nikkei Wartime Incarceration* (Stanford, CA: Stanford University Press, 2016), 10–12. Please also see: Grace M. Cho, *Haunting the Korean Diaspora: Shame, Secrecy, and the Forgotten War* (Minneapolis: University of Minnesota Press, 2008); Ann Cvetkovich, *An Archive of Feelings: Trauma, Sexuality, and Lesbian Public Cultures* (Durham, NC: Duke University Press, 2003); Diana Taylor, *The Archive and the Repertoire: Performing Cultural Memory in the Americas* (Durham, NC: Duke University Press, 2003).

60. Nuremberg trials, Germany (1945–1946); Truth and Reconciliation Commission, South Africa (1996); Testimonios, Latin America (1960s–1990s).

61. Bascara interrogates the Civil Liberties Act as an end point to make visible "the interests and limits of the nation-state." Drawing on Derrick Bell's theory of interest convergence, Bascara thinks about the passing of the Civil Liberties Act in conjunction with the dismantling of the welfare system. Bascara, "The Cultural Politics of Redress," 186.

62. Japanese American Citizens League Legislative Education Committee, *Redress! The American Promise* (Los Angeles, CA: JACLS Pacific Southwest District Council, 1986). Please see: Daniel Patrick Moynihan, *The Negro Family: The Case for National Action* (Washington, D.C.: Office of Policy Planning and Research, U.S. Department of Labor, 1965).

63. Bascara, "The Cultural Politics of Redress." Please also see: Lisa Marie Cacho, *Social Death: Racialized Rightlessness and the Criminalization of the Unprotected* (New York: New York University Press, 2012).

64. Cacho, *Social Death*, 4.

65. Alice Yang Murray, *Historical Memories of the Japanese American Internment and the Struggle for Redress* (Stanford, CA: Stanford University Press, 2008), 438.

66. William Bradford, "Beyond Justice: An American Indian Theory of Justice" (paper 217, Aboriginal Policy Research Consortium International, 2004), 64.

67. Bradford.

68. "What forms should reparations take?," N'Cobra (legacy website), accessed December 21, 2023, available at https://ncobra.org/default.

69. Gilmore, *Golden Gulag*, 83, 88.

70. Gilmore, 88.

71. Gilmore, 26.

72. Beth Richie, *Arrested Justice: Black Women, Violence, and America's Prison Nation* (New York: New York University Press, 2012), 3.

73. Patrick Wolfe, "Settler Colonialism and the Elimination of the Native," *Journal of Genocide Research* 8, no. 4 (2006): 388.

74. Alyosha Goldstein, *Formations of United States Colonialism* (Durham, NC: Duke University Press, 2014), 2.

75. Diane Fujino, "The Indivisiblity of Freedom: The Nisei Progressives, Deep Solidarities, and Cold War Alternatives," *Journal of Asian American Studies* 21, no. 2 (June 2018): 171.

76. Fujino, 172.

CHAPTER 1

1. Akemi Kikamura-Yano, Lane Ryo Hirabayashi, and James A. Hirabayashi, *Common Ground: The Japanese American National Museum and the Culture of Collaborations* (Boulder: University Press of Colorado, 2005), 3.

2. Kikamura-Yano, Hirabayashi, and Hirabayashi, 3.

3. Kikamura-Yano, Hirabayashi, and Hirabayashi, 1.

4. Kikamura-Yano, Hirabayashi, and Hirabayashi, 2.

5. Kikamura-Yano, Hirabayashi, and Hirabayashi, 11.

6. Kikamura-Yano, Hirabayashi, and Hirabayashi, 175.

7. Incite!, *The Revolution Will Not Be Funded* (Cambridge, MA: South End Press, 2007), xvi and xvii.

8. Incite!, xvi.

9. Karl Marx, "The Eighteenth Brumaire of Louis Bonaparte," in *The Marx-Engels Reader*, ed. Robert C. Tucker (New York: Norton, 1978), 597.

10. Marx, 595.

11. This is a sentence of Ann Cvetkovich that I have reworked to fit into thinking about the dinner. Ann Cvetkovich, *An Archive of Feelings: Trauma, Sexuality, and Lesbian Public Cultures* (Durham, NC: Duke University Press, 2003), 21.

12. Audre Lorde, *Sister Outsider* (Trumansburg, NY: Crossing Press, 1982), 55.

13. Dylan Rodriguez, "The Dreadful Genius of the Obama Moment: Inaugurating Multiculturalist White Supremacy," *Colorlines*, November 10, 2008, available at https://www.colorlines.com/articles/dreadful-genius-obama-moment.

14. Japanese American National Museum, *Continuing Family Stories: The Expanding Nikkei Community*, program, 2011, 10.

15. Japanese American National Museum, 7.

16. Japanese American National Museum, 2.

17. Tricia Toyota, "The New Nikkei: Transpacific Shin Issei and Shifting Borders of Community in Southern California," *Amerasia Journal* 38, no. 3 (2012): 3.

18. Toyota, 3.

19. Toyota, 3.

20. Toyota, 3, 19.

21. Toyota, 3.

22. Japanese American National Museum, *Continuing Family Stories*, 2.

23. Japanese American National Museum, 1.

24. Japanese American National Museum, 7.

25. I demonstrate how this will later happen at the Day of Remembrance panel event.

26. Japanese American National Museum, *Continuing Family Stories*, 13.

27. The Japanese American community can be linked to Japan in regard to business relations, culture, and crisis but not in relation to the legacies of Japanese colonialism. Japanese Americans can selectively choose which histories and presents they want to inherit from Japan.

28. Japanese American National Museum, *Continuing Family Stories*, 1.

29. Japanese American National Museum, 10.

30. Japanese American National Museum, 10.

31. Victor Bascara, "The Cultural Politics of Redress: Reassessing the Meaning of the Civil Liberties Act of 1988 after 9/11," *Asian American Law Journal* 10, no. 2 (2003): 108.

32. Roderick Ferguson, "Administering Sexuality," *Radical History Review* 100 (Winter 2008): 158.

33. Aihwa Ong, *Flexible Citizenship: The Cultural Politics of Transnationality* (Durham, NC: Duke University Press, 1999).

34. Japanese American National Museum, *Continuing Family Stories*, addendum schedule.

35. Japanese American National Museum, 11.

36. Japanese American National Museum, 11.

37. This is very different to how Sansei women filmmakers Rea Tajiri and Janice Tanaka are choosing to think about and remember internment.

38. Japanese American National Museum, *Continuing Family Stories*, 11.

39. There is also a shift from economies of scale (or Fordism) to small economies; however, this topic is not covered in depth in this book.

40. "Generation and Museum Tea Collection," Japanese American National Museum Store, accessed June 6, 2011, available at http://janmstore.com/genteas.html.

41. "Generation and Museum Tea Collection," Japanese American National Museum Store. Gaman and Ganbatte are often discussed in relation to incarceration experiences and survival.

42. "Generation and Museum Tea Collection," Japanese American National Museum Store.

43. "Generation and Museum Tea Collection," Japanese American National Museum Store.

44. *Continuing Family Stories: The Expanding Nikkei Community* (Japanese American National Museum, 2011), DVD.

45. Japanese American National Museum, *Continuing Family Stories*, 14.

46. *Continuing Family Stories: The Expanding Nikkei Community*.

47. *Continuing Family Stories: The Expanding Nikkei Community*.

48. *Continuing Family Stories: The Expanding Nikkei Community*.

49. *Continuing Family Stories: The Expanding Nikkei Community*.

50. *Continuing Family Stories: The Expanding Nikkei Community*.

51. This is further explored in Chapter 2.

52. Ferguson, "Administering Sexuality," 161.

53. *Continuing Family Stories: The Expanding Nikkei Community*.

54. *Continuing Family Stories: The Expanding Nikkei Community*.

55. *Continuing Family Stories: The Expanding Nikkei Community*.

56. Japanese American National Museum, "Continuing Family Stories," 72.

57. In other words, when the Nisei are no longer alive to fund the museum (as a huge portion of their funding comes from Nisei donors).

58. Japanese American National Museum, "Continuing Family Stories," 72.

59. In the "Eighteenth Brumaire of Louis Bonaparte," Karl Marx is critical of the relationship of revolutions to the past, present, and future, warning that "the social revolution of the nineteenth century cannot draw its poetry from the past, but only from the future." As I have argued, Japanese American nationalism constantly utilizes the past to legitimize the present moment and build a "successful" future. This relationship to the past is problematic for the way it allows for the policing and surveillance of "unworthy" populations through the positioning of Japanese Americans in opposition to such deviancy. Marx, "The Eighteenth Brumaire of Louis Bonaparte," 597.

60. *Continuing Family Stories: The Expanding Nikkei Community.*

61. *Continuing Family Stories: The Expanding Nikkei Community.*

62. *Continuing Family Stories: The Expanding Nikkei Community.*

63. Thank you to Grace Hong for this.

64. Again, thank you to Grace Hong.

65. Wahneema Lubiano, "Black Feminism and Black Common Sense," in *The House That Race Built* (New York: Pantheon, 1997), 235.

66. Day of Remembrance Committee, *2015 Day of Remembrance: EO 9066 and the [In]Justice System Today*, program, February 21, 2015, 1.

67. Day of Remembrance Committee, 1.

68. Manzanar Committee, *2015 Los Angeles Day of Remembrance: E.O. 9066 and the [In]Justice System Today*, accessed December 22, 2023, https://manzanarcommittee.org/2015/02/02/los-angeles-day-of-remembrance-2015-e-o-9066-and-the-injustice-system-today/#more-23549.

69. Manzanar Committee.

70. Day of Remembrance Committee, *2015 Day of Remembrance*, program, 1. Helen Ota, "2015 Day of Remembrance: EO 9066 and the [In]Justice System Today," event, February 21, 2015.

71. Helen Ota and Curtiss Takada Rooks, "2015 Day of Remembrance: EO 9066 and the [In]Justice System Today," event, February 21, 2015.

72. Ota, "2015 Day of Remembrance."

73. Ota and Rooks, "2015 Day of Remembrance."

74. Ota and Rooks.

75. Ota and Rooks.

76. Ota and Rooks.

77. Ota and Rooks.

78. Ota and Rooks.

79. Ota and Rooks.

80. Ota and Rooks.

81. Ota and Rooks.

82. Ota and Rooks.

83. Ota and Rooks.

84. Ota and Rooks.

85. Ota and Rooks.

86. Ota and Rooks.

87. Grace Kyungwon Hong, "'Something Forgotten Which Should Have Been Remembered': Private Property and Cross-Racial Solidarity in the Work of Hisaye Yamamoto," *American Literature* 71, no. 2 (1999): 304.

88. Hong, 292.

89. Hong, 293.

90. Hisaye Yamamoto, "A Fire in Fontana," in *Seventeen Syllables and Other Stories* (New Brunswick, NJ: Rutgers University Press, 2001), 137. Hong, "Something Forgotten Which Should Have Been Remembered," 301.

91. Hong, "Something Forgotten Which Should Have Been Remembered," 302.

92. Densho Encyclopedia, "Redress Movement," last updated August 24, 2020, available at http://encyclopedia.densho.org/Redress_movement/.

93. Alice Yang Murray, *Historical Memories of the Japanese American Internment and the Struggle for Redress* (Stanford, CA: Stanford University Press, 2008), 438.

94. Murray, 438, emphasis added.

95. In 2021, Japanese American community organizations (JACL, the Japanese American National Museum, NCRR, the Manzanar Committee, etc.) began mobilizing for African American reparations with about three hundred written testimonies from Japanese Americans submitted for HR 40, a bill that will create the Commission to Study and Develop Proposals for the African Americans Act.

96. Curtiss Takada Rooks, "2015 Day of Remembrance: EO 9066 and the [In]Justice System Today," event, February 21, 2015.

97. Rooks.

98. Ota and Rooks, "2015 Day of Remembrance."

99. Ota and Rooks.

100. Day of Remembrance Committee, *2015 Day of Remembrance*, program, 4.

101. Rey Fukuda, "2015 Day of Remembrance: EO 9066 and the [In]Justice System Today," panel, February 21, 2015.

102. Fukuda.

103. Fukuda.

104. Fukuda.

105. Fukuda.

106. Tina Takemoto, "Looking for Jiro Onuma: A Queer Mediation on the Incarceration of Japanese Americans during World War II," *GLQ* 20, no. 3 (2014): 245, 246.

107. Takemoto, 245.

108. Wendsor Yamashita, "What She Remembers: Remaking and Unmaking Japanese American Internment" (M.A. thesis, University of California, Los Angeles, 2010).

109. Valerie Matsumoto, "Japanese American Women during World War II," *Frontiers: A Journal of Women's Studies* 8, no. 1 (1984): 3.

110. Chiyoko Nishimori, personal interview, January 31, 2010, emphasis added.

111. Often these works argue that cultural patterns that produce gender-specific roles inadvertently work to justify the need for incarceration. This discussion of incarceration as a vehicle for improved women's rights implies that Japanese American women would still be subject to "patriarchal Japanese culture" without the intervention of the government. It is in this moment that the production of the Japanese American woman becomes essential to the construction of internment as benevolent and necessary for their insertion into modernity.

112. This does not mean that the Japanese American community ignores queer stories, as work has been occurring to incorporate these voices and histories. In 2014, Los Angeles–based Okaeri, a "group made up of LGBTQ Nikkei, parents of LGBTQ Nikkei, and allies of LGBTQ people," organized the "first-ever conference focused on LGBTQ Nikkei" called Okaeri: A Nikkei LGBTQ Gathering. It not only garnered two hundred attendees but also inspired similar events in Seattle, Sacramento, and San Francisco. It held a second conference in 2016 and in 2020 launched an oral history project, "Coming Out, Coming Home," to document queer Japanese American stories. Okaeri seeks to build an "inclusive Nikkei community" because "too many LGBTQ Nikkei are still estranged from [their] families and the Nikkei community." They articulate the "need for acceptance, healing, and the undoing of homophobia and transphobia" as central to their work. Please see: "About Okaeri," Okaeri, available at https://www.okaeri-losangeles.org/about-okaeri. In 2020, Amy Sueyoshi and Stan Yogi curated the virtual exhibit *Seen and Unseen: Queering JA History before 1945* to address how queer Nikkei are nonexistent in Japanese American history by bringing them into view. Named after the queer Issei poet Yone Noguchi's book, *Seen and Unseen* attempts to explore how "queer Nikkei might have felt being simultaneously queer, immigrant, and Asian in America" in order to remind us that "queer Americans continue to be seen and unseen today." *Seen and Unseen* makes it clear that queerness can be found in the archive, if one is purposely looking (implying that historical retrieval remains heteronormative). In this exhibit queerness is historicized as a Japanese tradition where same-sex sexuality and female impersonation are an inherent part of Japanese culture. By situating queerness as belonging to Japanese people, queerness is then read in archival documents as nonnormative performances of gender and sexuality in cultural productions, immigrant labor, and community formation. Jiro Onuma figures prominently in the archive with his photographs and his collection of male bodybuilding memorabilia. The exhibit articulates the inability to see queerness as well as the modality of "queerness under duress" not only as the result of a "growing white American anxiety around sexual and gender deviation in the first half of the twentieth century" but also as a result of race, gender, and sexual policing that occurred both within the family and the nation (via the carceral). For example, the first appearances of the generational term "Issei" were in a San Francisco–based Japanese-language newspaper (1917) that praised "permanent settlers who entered heterosexual marriages and had children." Generational growth was naturalized, while nonheteronormative living was becoming undesirable. And similar to Takemoto, *Seen and Unseen* identifies "queerness under duress" during World War II where not only the "government's racial fears of Nikkei but also sexual anxieties" are subject to camp regulations of "military surveillance and lack of privacy" where "any deviation from sexual and gender norms" were subject to community purview. As a result, queerness is articulated as becoming increasingly unmoored from Japanese culture, as "pejorative views around same-sex sexuality become explicit among increasingly Americanized Nikkei." Please see: Amy Sueyoshi and Stan Yogi, *Seen and Unseen: Queering JA History before 1945*, Digital Exhibit hosted by J-Sei from October 11, 2020 to June 30, 2021.

113. Povi-Tamu Bryant, "2015 Day of Remembrance: EO 9066 and the [In]Justice System Today," panel, February 21, 2015.

114. Bryant.

115. Bryant.

116. Bryant.
117. Bryant.
118. Bryant.
119. Murase is an "attorney, activist, administrator, writer, and photographer" who was part of the "core group who founded the Little Tokyo Service Center (LTSC), a social service and community economic development agency serving Little Tokyo and [the] greater Japanese American community throughout Los Angeles." See: "Mike Murase," Discover Nikkei, August 2021, available at http://www.discovernikkei.org/en/interviews/profiles/146/.
120. Mike Murase, "2015 Day of Remembrance: EO 9066 and the [In]Justice System Today," panel, February 21, 2015.
121. Murase.
122. Murase.
123. Alex Kanegawa, "2015 Day of Remembrance: EO 9066 and the [In]Justice System Today," call to action, February 21, 2015.
124. Kanegawa.
125. Mariko Fujimoto Rooks, "2015 Day of Remembrance: EO 9066 and the [In]Justice System Today," call to action, February 21, 2015.
126. On August 9, 2014, Michael Brown was fatally shot by Officer Darren Wilson in Ferguson, Missouri. His murder and the failure to indict Wilson sparked massive protests against police brutality and the carceral state.
127. Rooks, "2015 Day of Remembrance," call to action.
128. In their piece, "Mixed Race Asian American Identity on Display," Lily Anne Welty Tamai, Cindy Nakashima, and Duncan Ryuken Williams argue that Japanese American history has been presented as "heterosexual, endogamous, homogenous, and perfectly aligned to the Issei-Nisei-Sansei generations" where a "pervasive anxiety" exists around interracial or interethnic relationships that could potentially "lead to the demise of the Japanese American community." Those who are multiracial and/or multigenerational even have historically been left out of Japanese collective memory because of the heteronormative generational transfer of memory that structures Japanese American history. It is interesting that both events (gala dinner and Day of Remembrance) attempt to incorporate those outside the generational structure (Shin-Issei and Nisei and multiracial Asian Americans) by honoring, incorporating, and valuing their voice/stories. And they are incorporated by expanding the language of family to include them. In contrast, queer critiques cannot be incorporated since generational narratives are hinged upon the maintenance of nonnormative gender and sexuality. As a result, queer critiques that push for abolition are heard but do not become a part of communal memory. Lily Anne Welty Tamai, Cindy Nakashima, and Duncan Ryuken Williams, "Mixed Race Asian American Identity on Display," *Amerasia Journal* 43, no. 2 (2017): 178, 179.
129. Rooks, "2015 Day of Remembrance," call to action.
130. Rooks.
131. Rooks, emphasis added.
132. Takemoto, "Looking for Jiro Onuma," 248.
133. I would argue that in 2015, Japanese American community organizations were not necessarily ready to hear the queer disruptions and calls for abolition. By 2020, it was a different story. In 2020, the Trump administration galvanized many activist groups

to comparative action: sparking the formation of new organizations, interracial solidarity organizing, and a decentering of Japanese American World War II history. An abolitionist future is centered as groups seek disruption as part of their call to action.

CHAPTER 2

1. Densho, "Executive Director Message," in *2018 Annual Report*, 1, accessed September 18, 2019, available at https://www.flipsnack.com/densho/densho-2018-annual-report.html.

2. In a COVID-19 world, the Japanese American National Museum has become more digitally accessible with their online events.

3. Arthur A. Hansen, "Oral History and the Japanese American Evacuation," *Journal of American History* 82, no. 2 (1995): 628.

4. Hansen, 629.

5. Hansen, 629.

6. Hansen, 630.

7. Hansen, 630.

8. Densho, "About Densho," accessed January 5, 2018, available at https://densho.org/about-densho/.

9. Densho, "About Densho."

10. Densho, "About Densho."

11. Densho Encyclopedia, "War Relocation Authority," last updated May 6, 2015, available at https://encyclopedia.densho.org/War_Relocation_Authority/.

12. Mae Ngai, *Impossible Subjects: Illegal Aliens and the Making of Modern America* (Princeton, NJ: Princeton University Press, 2004), 177.

13. Ngai, 179.

14. Ngai, 183.

15. Brenda L. Moore, *Serving Our Country: Japanese American Women in the Military during World War II* (New Brunswick, NJ: Rutgers University Press, 2003).

16. Moore.

17. Richard Drinnon, *Keeper of Concentration Camps: Dillion S. Myer and American Racism* (Berkeley: University of California Press, 1987), 157.

18. Drinnon, 158.

19. Leslie A. Ito, "Japanese American Women and the Student Relocation Movement, 1942–1945," *Frontiers: A Journal of Women's Studies* 21, no. 3 (2000): 10.

20. Ito, 2.

21. Ito, 3.

22. Ito, 3.

23. Please see: Valerie Matsumoto, "Japanese American Women during World War II," *Frontiers: A Journal of Women's Studies* 8, no. 1 (1984); Mei Nakano, *Japanese American Women: Three Generations, 1890–1990* (San Francisco: Mina Press Publishing, 1990).

24. Matsumoto, "Japanese American Women during World War II," 3.

25. Please see Lisa Yoneyama's and Lila Abu Lughod's work for colonial and imperial contexts where gendered liberation becomes a vehicle or justification for war. Lisa Yoneyama, "Liberation under Siege: U.S. Military Occupation Japanese Women's Enfranchisement," in "Legal Borderlands: Law and the Construction of American Borders,"

special issue, *American Quarterly* 57, no. 3 (September 2005): 885–910. Lila Abu-Lughod, "Do Muslim Women Really Need Saving? Anthropological Reflections on Cultural Relativism and Its Others," *American Anthropologist* 104, no. 3 (September 2002): 783–790.

26. Commission on Wartime Relocation and Internment of Civilians, *Personal Justice Denied*, 255.

27. Commission on Wartime Relocation and Internment of Civilians, 258.

28. Fujitani, "Right to Kill and Right to Make Live," 23.

29. Victor Bascara, "The Cultural Politics of Redress: Reassessing the Meaning of the Civil Liberties Act of 1988 after 9/11," *Asian American Law Journal* 10, no. 2 (2003): 108.

30. Achille Mbembe, "Necropolitics," *Public Culture* 15, no. 1 (2003): 11–40.

31. Ann Cvetkovich, *An Archive of Feelings: Trauma, Sexuality, and Lesbian Public Cultures* (Durham, NC: Duke University Press, 2003), 270.

32. Densho, "About Densho," February 21, 2007, YouTube video, 9:28, available at https://www.youtube.com/watch?annotation_id=annotation_824558583&feature=iv&src_vid=hq4sBSsuJDQ&v=_lBKndA1vP4.

33. Densho.

34. Densho.

35. Densho.

36. Rainmakers TV, "Densho, Japanese American Legacy Project," August 3, 2014, YouTube video, 28:30, available at https://www.youtube.com/watch?v=3I_1WR1m1c4.

37. Rainmakers TV.

38. Rainmakers TV.

39. Rainmakers TV.

40. Grace M. Cho, *Haunting the Korean Diaspora: Shame, Secrecy, and the Forgotten War* (Minneapolis: University of Minnesota Press, 2008), 7.

41. Densho, "About Densho."

42. Densho.

43. Densho.

44. Densho.

45. Densho.

46. Densho.

47. Densho.

48. Densho.

49. Densho.

50. Densho.

51. Densho.

52. Densho.

53. Densho, emphasis added.

54. Densho.

55. Densho.

56. Densho.

57. Densho.

58. Densho.

59. I explore this more in the conclusion.

60. This includes their official website/archive, Facebook page, and blog—a variety of digital technologies to make life/death accessible to the public.

61. Densho's Facebook page, available at https://www.facebook.com/denshoproject.

62. John Lok, "Saving Densho Memories," *Seattle Times*, December 26, 2006.

63. Densho, "Pioneer Generation: Remembering the Issei," from Densho's Archives on Discover Nikkei, December 1, 2010, available at http://www.discovernikkei.org/en/journal/2010/12/1/pioneer-generation/.

64. Densho.

65. Densho.

66. Although this chapter centers oral history and the digital archive, there are cultural productions that utilize forgetting outside of the binaries of life/death and remembering/forgetting. In my M.A. thesis, "What She Remembers," I analyze Rea Tajiri's *History and Memory* film, which centers on the filmmakers' "frustration with her mother's lack of memories which prompts her to investigate silences, forgetting, and lies. Tajiri deals with the gaps by drawing on paranormal and ghostly feelings to point to the discomfort and violence of having to fit into the already established historical narratives." I argue that "Tajiri's nuanced exploration of this process of forgetting examines both how her mother was made to forget and how she needed to forget. Instead of casting her mother's silence and forgetfulness negatively, Tajiri resignifies the void in her mother's memories as not necessarily being something that needs to be filled. Rather her forgetting becomes a narrative itself." Through the medium of film, Tajiri is able to play with forgetting in ways that oral history methodology, archiving, and preservation cannot. As she gives shape to her mother's losses (including memories), she makes visible the ways historical narratives as truth violently erase her mother. The film itself is a journey to make sense of loss and ghosts as Tajiri grapples with the relationship between history and memory. Wendsor Yamashita, "What She Remembers: Remaking and Unmaking Japanese American Internment" (M.A. thesis, University of California, Los Angeles, 2010).

67. Giving To Densho, accessed December 26, 2023, available at https://densho.org/give/.

68. Giving to Densho.

69. Densho Planned Giving, accessed December 26, 2023, available at https://densho.org/give/planned-giving/,

70. Densho Planned Giving.

71. Other units in the Civil Liberties Curriculum include "Introduction: World War II Incarceration of Japanese Americans," "Dig Deep: Media and the Incarceration of Japanese Americans during World War II," "Causes of Conflict: Issues of Immigration," and "Immigration Journeys: Changes and Challenges." These three-week units, designed for different levels, contain curriculum packages and oral history video clips.

72. Densho and National Park Service, "Constitutional Issues: Civil Liberties, Individuals, and the Common Good," in *Civil Liberties Curriculum and Resource Guide for High School*, 3. Available at https://densho.org/wp-content/uploads/2021/12/Constitutional_Issues.pdf.

73. Densho and National Park Service, 1.

74. Densho and National Park Service, 6.

75. Densho and National Park Service, 12.

76. Densho and National Park Service, 12.

77. Densho and National Park Service, 54.

78. Densho and National Park Service, 13.
79. Densho and National Park Service, 13.
80. Jack Halberstam, *The Queer Art of Failure* (Durham, NC: Duke University Press, 2011), 69.
81. Densho and National Park Service, "Constitutional Issues," 60.
82. Densho and National Park Service, 60.
83. Densho and National Park Service, 57.
84. Judith Butler, "Afterword: After Loss, What Then?," in *Loss: The Politics of Mourning*, ed. David Eng and David Kazanjian (Berkeley: University of California Press, 2003).
85. Densho and National Park Service, "Constitutional Issues," 15.
86. Densho and National Park Service, 15.
87. Clyde Woods, "Les Miserables of New Orleans: Trap Economics and the Asset Stripping Blues, Part 1," *American Quarterly* 61, no. 3 (2009): 774.
88. Densho and National Park Service, "Constitutional Issues," 15.
89. Densho and National Park Service, 15.
90. Densho and National Park Service, 37.
91. Densho and National Park Service, 37.
92. Densho and National Park Service, 17.
93. Densho and National Park Service, 18.
94. Densho and National Park Service, 70.
95. Densho and National Park Service, 70.

CHAPTER 3

1. Manzanar Committee, *A Memory . . . A Monument . . . A Movement*, program, April 26, 2014, 13.
2. Manzanar Committee, 13.
3. Manzanar Committee, 13.
4. Victor Bascara, "The Cultural Politics of Redress: Reassessing the Meaning of the Civil Liberties Act of 1988 after 9/11," *Asian American Law Journal* 10, no. 2 (2003): 185–214.
5. This conceptualization of the "contradictory location" comes from Grace Kyungwon Hong's reading of "A Fire in Fontana." Grace Kyungwon Hong, "'Something Forgotten Which Should Have Been Remembered': Private Property and Cross-Racial Solidarity in the Work of Hisaye Yamamoto," *American Literature* 71, no. 2 (1999): 291–310.
6. Abbie Lynn Salyers, "The Internment of Memory: Forgetting and Remembering the Japanese American World War II Experience" (Ph.D. diss., Rice University, 2009), ProQuest/UMI (publication number: 3362399), 248.
7. "Who We Are," Manzanar Committee, accessed December 27, 2023, available at https://manzanarcommittee.org/who-we-are/. . Despite thinking this was their first pilgrimage, they realized later that two reverends had made the trek every year since the site had been closed in order to honor the two hundred people who died there.
8. "Who We Are."
9. "Who We Are."
10. "Who We Are."
11. Salyers, "The Internment of Memory," 249.

12. While this list represents those schools that commonly participate every year, it sometimes includes California State University, Fullerton (CSUF), which unfortunately had to drop out of the planning committee in 2015 and 2016. The NSUs involved as of 2021 include CSUF again as well as University of California, Riverside.

13. Gann Matsuda, "2015 Manzanar at Dusk: Sharing the Japanese American Incarceration Experience among Different Generations, Diverse Groups," Manzanar Committee, April 8, 2015, available at http:/manzanarcommittee.org/2015/04/08/2015-manzanar-at-dusk-040815/.

14. Candace Fujikane and Jonathan Y. Okamura, *Asian Settler Colonialism: From Local Governance to the Habits of Everyday Life in Hawaii* (Honolulu: University of Hawaii Press, 2008), 6.

15. Alyosha Goldstein, *Formations of United States Colonialism* (Durham, NC: Duke University Press, 2014), 2.

16. Sherene Razack, ed., *Race, Space, and the Law: Unmapping a White Settler Society* (Toronto: Between the Lines, 2002). Mona Oikawa, *Cartographies of Violence: Japanese Canadian Women, Memory, and the Subjects of Internment* (Toronto: University of Toronto Press, 2012).

17. Oikawa, *Cartographies of Violence*.

18. Eichiro Azuma, *Between Two Empires: Race, History, and Transnationalism in Japanese America* (Oxford: Oxford University Press, 2005), 65.

19. Patrick Wolfe, "Settler Colonialism and the Elimination of the Native," *Journal of Genocide Research* 8, no. 4 (2006): 387–409.

20. Wolfe, 388.

21. Wolfe, 388.

22. This is not to equate Indigenous experiences with those of other groups of color because their dispossession is contingent upon the figure of the settler. The purpose is to consider how containment and dispossession operate together in the racial state.

23. The Interpretive Center at Manzanar does have a small section devoted to the Owens Valley prior to incarceration that discusses Indigenous experiences with settlers, but this is the first time that Japanese Americans actively acknowledge the colonial.

24. Bruce Embrey, "A Memory . . . A Monument . . . A Movement," closing remarks speech, April 26, 2014.

25. Embrey.

26. This film was a collaboration among the Owens Valley Committee, Deepest Valley, the Manzanar Committee, the Lone Pine Paiute Shoshone Reservation, and the Big Pine Tribe of the Owens Valley. The executive producer was Angela Mooney D'arcy.

27. Seventh Generation Fund for Indigenous Peoples and Graven Image Films, "Saving *Payahüüpuü*: The Owens Valley Solar Story," April 25, 2014, YouTube video, 14:42, available at https://www.youtube.com/watch?v=mTV9Pd6AaNk.

28. Seventh Generation Fund for Indigenous Peoples and Graven Image Films.

29. Seventh Generation Fund for Indigenous Peoples and Graven Image Films.

30. Seventh Generation Fund for Indigenous Peoples and Graven Image Films.

31. Seventh Generation Fund for Indigenous Peoples and Graven Image Films.

32. Seventh Generation Fund for Indigenous Peoples and Graven Image Films.

33. Seventh Generation Fund for Indigenous Peoples and Graven Image Films.

34. Seventh Generation Fund for Indigenous Peoples and Graven Image Films.

35. Seventh Generation Fund for Indigenous Peoples and Graven Image Films.

36. Chantal R. Walker, "*Piyahu Nadu*: Land of Flowing Waters: The Water Transfer from Owens Valley to Los Angeles 1913–1939" (M.A. thesis, University of California, Los Angeles, 2014).

37. Jenna Cavelle, "A Paiute Perspective on the LA-Owens Valley Water Story: Jenna Cavelle in Conversation with Alan Bacock and Harry Williams," *Arid: A Journal of Desert Art, Design and Ecology* 3, no. 2 (Fall 2013), available at http://aridjournal.com.

38. Walker, "*Piyahu Nadu*: Land of Flowing Waters," 2. The California Volunteers were militia groups who protected territories and thus white settlers under threat by Indigenous populations.

39. Walker, 2.

40. A land exchange in 1937 between the Department of the Interior and the City of Los Angeles established the current land base for the Bishop, Lone Pine, and Big Pine Reservations—where water was also supposed to be exchanged. However, an agreement about the water could not be reached because the LA City Charter would not allow the sale of the water without two-thirds of the city's votes. In 1939, the city agreed to provide four acre-feet of water per year to the reservations. The tribes of these reservations feel that the federal government did not fulfill its trust responsibilities and ignored the federally reserved Native American water rights when they entered this agreement on their behalf. Owens Valley Indian Water Commission, "History of Water Rights," available at http://www.oviwc.org/water-crusade/... Walker. "*Piyahu Nadu*: Land of Flowing Waters," 46–48.

41. Manzanar Committee, "Letter to Mayor Eric Garcetti," addition to *A Memory . . . A Monument . . . A Movement*, program, April 26, 2014.

42. Manzanar Committee.

43. Manzanar Committee, emphasis added.

44. Harry Williams, personal interview, July 9, 2015.

45. Williams.

46. Williams.

47. Williams.

48. Williams.

49. Williams.

50. Gann Matsuda, personal interview, October 1, 2014.

51. Williams, interview.

52. Williams.

53. Williams.

54. Williams.

55. Williams.

56. Matsuda, interview.

57. Matsuda.

58. Sally Manning, *Big Pine Paiute Newsletter*, April 2015.

59. Matsuda, interview.

60. The first two Katari cohorts were generously funded through a GoFundMe campaign and the third (disrupted by COVID-19) by the UCLA Aratani CARES grant. Initially, the Katari cohorts consisted of Manzanar at Dusk NSU representatives from UCLA, UCSD, CSULB, CSUF, and CPP. One year later, University of California, Riverside joined. Key planning members of Katari are Gann Matsuda, Bruce Embrey, Jason Fujii, and Wendi Yamashita of the Manzanar Committee and Rose Masters, Alisa Lynch

Broch, and Sarah Bone of the National Park Service. In 2021, two former students of Katari have joined the Katari Planning Committee: Seia Watanabe and Justin Fujii.

61. "Katari: Keeping Japanese American Stories Alive," Manzanar Committee, accessed on May 23, 2023, available at https://manzanarcommittee.org/katari/.

62. In this case, not read as apathy (which I discuss in Chapter 4) but as a gap in knowledge.

63. "Katari: Keeping Japanese American Stories Alive," Manzanar Committee.

64. Former incarcerees of Katari have included Pat Sakamoto, Yoshiye Okimoto Hayashi, Minoru Tonai, Hiroshi Shimizu, and Nancy Oda. Redress activists have included Bruce Embrey and Gann Matsuda.

65. "Katari: Keeping Japanese American Stories Alive," Manzanar Committee.

66. Erica Wei, "Manzanar: One Weekend, One Incredible Experience." Manzanar Committee, April 19, 2018, available at https://manzanarcommittee.org/2018/04/19/erica-wei/.

67. Seia Watanabe, "What Resonates With Me the Most Is the Refusal for This History to Be Forgotten, Erased, or Overlooked," Manznar Committee, May 10, 2021, available at https://manzanarcommittee.org/2021/05/10/watanabe-ref/.

68. Watanabe.

69. Sean Gasha, "Being at Manzanar Makes All the Difference in the World," Manzanar Committee, December 10, 2019, available at https://manzanarcommittee.org/2019/12/10/sean-gasha/.

70. And like the Densho digital archive, Katari does seek to banish death by bringing Manzanar and those who experienced it back to life. However, this chapter is less interested in the biopolitical management of life and more interested in how reprosexuality and generational responsibility push for a different connection to land and place.

71. Maile Arvin, Eve Tuck, and Angie Morrill, "Decolonizing Feminism: Challenging Connections between Settler Colonialism and Heteropatriarchy," *Feminist Formations* 25, no. 1 (Spring 2013): 25.

72. Kevin Amemiya, "We Have a Duty to Them to Keep Their Stories Alive," Manzanar Committee, January 30, 2019, available at https://manzanarcommittee.org/2019/01/30/amemiya-reflection/.

73. "New Exhibit: Button Family's History at Manzanar," Sierra Wave Media, September 11, 2017, available at https://sierrawave.net/new-exhibit-button-familys-history-manzanar/.

74. Hayley Yamamoto, "History Can Never Be Fully Discovered When Only Looking at the Surface," Manzanar Committee, March 13, 2021, available at https://manzanarcommittee.org/2021/03/13/yamamoto-ref/.

CHAPTER 4

1. "Uniting Nikkei for the Future," *Rafu Shimpo*, July 8, 2011, available at http://www.rafu.com/2011/07/uniting-nikkei-for-the-future/.

2. "Uniting Nikkei for the Future," *Rafu Shimpo*.

3. Kizuna, "About Kizuna," accessed December 28, 2023, available at https://gokizuna.org/about.

4. Michael Warner, "Introduction: Fear of a Queer Planet," *Social Text*, no. 29 (1991): 9.

5. erin Khuê Ninh, introduction to *Ingratitude: The Debt-Bound Daughter in Asian American Literature* (New York: New York University Press, 2011).
6. Warner, "Introduction: Fear of a Queer Planet," 9.
7. Chris Eng, "Queer Genealogies of (Be)Longing: On the Thens and Theres of Asian America in Karen Tei Yamashita's I Hotel," *Journal of Asian American Studies* 20, no. 3 (2017): 349.
8. Gann Matsuda, "The Constitution of the University of California, Los Angeles Nikkei Student Union," authored March 17, 1984, reprinted April 2, 1989.
9. Alan Nishio, "Awards Nomination UCLA Nikkei Student Union," no date.
10. Nikkei Student Union, *The Last Generation*, Cultural Night program, February 21, 2001, 3.
11. At UCLA there are a variety of Cultural Nights such as Vietnamese Student Union, Chinese American Student Association, Hanoolim (Korean American), Samahang Pilipino, Taiwanese Cultural Night, and United Khmer Students. But there also such groups as the East African Student Association, and in 2017 there was the first Queer Cultural Night.
12. Please see: Theodore S. Gonzalves, *The Day the Dancers Stayed: Performing in the Filipino/American Diaspora* (Philadelphia: Temple University Press, 2010); Barbara Gaerlan, "In the Court of the Sultan: Orientalism, Nationalism, and Modernity in Philippine and Filipino American Dance," *Journal of Asian American Studies* 2, no. 3 (1999): 251–287; Neal Matherine, "Bayan Nila: Pilipino Cultural Nights and Student Performance at Home in Southern California," *Asian Studies: Journal of Critical Perspectives on Asia* 49, no. 1 (2013): 105–127.
13. Eng, "Queer Genealogies of (Be)Longing," 346.
14. I attended the 2011 NSU Cultural Night and received a copy of *The Last Generation* script.
15. Nikkei Student Union, *The Last Generation*, 1.
16. Eng, "Queer Genealogies of (Be)Longing," 349.
17. Eng, 349.
18. Nikkei Student Union, *The Last Generation*, 1.
19. Nikkei Student Union, 1.
20. Nikkei Student Union, 4.
21. Nikkei Student Union, 4.
22. Nikkei Student Union, 4.
23. Eng, "Queer Genealogies of (Be)Longing," 348.
24. Diana Taylor, *The Archive and the Repertoire: Performing Cultural Memory in the Americas* (Durham, NC: Duke University Press, 2003), 2, 3.
25. Nikkei Student Union, *The Last Generation*, 6.
26. Warner, "Introduction: Fear of a Queer Planet," 9.
27. Ann Cvetkovich, *An Archive of Feelings: Trauma, Sexuality, and Lesbian Public Cultures* (Durham, NC: Duke University Press, 2003), 22.
28. "No-No" is in reference to the 1943 WRA Loyalty Questionnaire that attempted to determine which incarcerees were "loyal" or "disloyal" in order to segregate them. About "12,000 out of the 78,000 people over the age of 17" had "either refused to answer, gave qualified answers, or answered negatively." Those who answered "no" were sent to Tule Lake and for many years were "shunned by a Japanese American community [especially the JACL] that emphasized loyalty and military service after the war." Brian

Niiya, "No-No Boys," Densho Encyclopedia, last updated July 15, 2020, available at https://encyclopedia.densho.org/No-no_boys/. It was not until 2000 that the JACL National Council issued an apology to the Nisei draft resisters of Heart Mountain who refused to join the military unless their rights as U.S. citizens were restored. And it was not until 2019, at the fiftieth JACL National Convention, that an apology was issued to Tule Lake resisters. J. K. Yamamoto, "JACL National Council Passes Resolution Apologizing to Tule Lake Resisters," *Rafu Shimpo*, September 2, 2019.

29. Eng, "Queer Genealogies of (Be)Longing," 346.
30. Nikkei Student Union, *Our [I]dentity*, Cultural Night program, February 20, 2012, 2.
31. Nikkei Student Union, 6.
32. Eng, "Queer Genealogies of (Be)Longing," 364.
33. ACLU, "SB 1070 at the Supreme Court: What's at Stake," accessed on March 8, 2021, available at https://www.aclu.org/sb-1070-supreme-court-whats-stake.
34. ACLU.
35. Nikkei Student Union, *Our [I]dentity*, Cultural Night performance, February 20, 2012.
36. Nikkei Student Union.
37. Nikkei Student Union.
38. Nikkei Student Union.
39. Nikkei Student Union.
40. Nikkei Student Union.
41. Nikkei Student Union, *Senbazuru*, Nikkei Student Union Cultural Night video recording, February 15, 2016.
42. Nikkei Student Union.
43. Japanese Village Plaza website, accessed March 4, 2017, available at http://japanesevillageplaza.net/.
44. Samuel Mori, "Shopping Mall in Little Tokyo," Discover Nikkei, November 16, 2016, available at http://www.discovernikkei.org/en/journal/2016/11/16/shopping-mall/.
45. Nikkei Student Union, *Senbazuru*.
46. Nikkei Student Union.
47. Nikkei Student Union.
48. Huping Ling and Allan W. Austin, eds., *Asian American History and Culture: An Encyclopedia* (New York: Routledge, 2010), 1–2:434, 435.
49. Huping Ling and Allan W. Austin, eds., *Asian American History and Culture: An Encyclopedia* (New York: Routledge, 2010), 1–2:434, 435.
50. Ling and Austin, 435.
51. Ling and Austin, 435.
52. Evelyn Nakano Glenn, "From Servitude to Service Work: Historical Continuities in the Racial Division of Paid Reproductive Labor," *Signs* 18, no. 1 (1992): 4.
53. Glenn, 1.
54. Glenn, 1.
55. Eng, "Queer Genealogies of (Be)Longing" 345, 346.
56. Nikkei Student Union, *Senbazuru*.
57. Nikkei Student Union.
58. Nikkei Student Union.

59. Nikkei Student Union.
60. Warner, "Introduction: Fear of a Queer Planet," 9.
61. Nikkei Student Union, *Senbazuru*.
62. Nikkei Student Union.
63. Nikkei Student Union.
64. Nikkei Student Union.
65. Thanks to Emiko Kranz for this interview. Kranz also served as UCLA NSU's external vice president in her sophomore year, participated in NSU Drama, and performed in two Cultural Night productions. In her role as NSU president, she also served as a representative for the Manzanar at Dusk Committee. Emiko Kranz, personal interview, November 11, 2016.
66. Kranz.
67. Kranz.
68. Nobuko Miyamoto, "The Evolution of FandangObon," *Discover Nikkei*. January 21, 2016, available at https://discovernikkei.org/en/journal/2016/1/21/fandangobon/#:~:text=FandangObon%20is%20a%20project%20that,order%20to%20celebrate%20mother%20earth.
69. Kranz, interview.
70. Kranz, emphasis added.
71. Kranz, emphasis added.
72. Kranz.
73. "JACL History," Japanese American Citizens League, accessed April 14, 2021, available at https://jacl.org/history.
74. Kranz, interview.
75. Kranz.
76. Kranz.
77. Kranz.

CONCLUSION

1. Dylan Rodriguez, "The Pitfalls of (White) Liberal Panic," *Abolition Journal*, November 18, 2016, available at https://abolitionjournal.org/the-pitfalls-of-white-liberal-panic/.
2. Frances Kai-Hwa Wang, "Virginia Mayor Cites Japanese Internment in Statement on Barring Refugees," *NBC News*, November 18, 2015, available at https://www.nbcnews.com/news/asian-america/virginia-mayor-compares-barring-syrian-refugees-japanese-american-internment-n465877.
3. Densho, "A Cabinet Meeting the Day after 9/11—Norman Mineta," April 9, 2015, YouTube video, 2:00, available at https://www.youtube.com/watch?v=VH7rGPXGicM.
4. Densho.
5. Marlon Romero, "Finding Aid for the Civil Liberties Public Education Fund Grant Program Records," Online Archive of California, 2010, available at https://oac.cdlib.org/findaid/ark:/13030/kt3c6033q1/entire_text/.
6. J. K. Yamamoto, "Message of Tolerance in Little Tokyo," *Rafu Shimpo*, December 14, 2015, available at https://rafu.com/2015/12/message-of-tolerance-in-little-tokyo/.
7. Yamamoto.

8. UCLA NSU did not participate, although, as mentioned in Chapter 4, the NSU president wanted to address it via their 2017 Cultural Night but was unable to do so due to time constraints.

9. Norman Y. Mineta and Ann Burroughs, "I Was Imprisoned in a U.S. Internment Camp. Bigotry Put Me There," *TIME*, November 21, 2016, available at http://time.com/4579182/japanese-internment-bigotry/.

10. Tom Ikeda, "This Is Not a Test," Densho, January 28, 2017, available at https://densho.org/this-is-not-a-test/.

11. Manzanar Committee, "Presidential Election and Its Aftermath," from *Never Again, to Anyone, Anywhere!*, program, April 29, 2017, 18.

12. Mineta and Burroughs, "I Was Imprisoned in a U.S. Internment Camp."

13. Manzanar Committee, "Presidential Election and Its Aftermath," 18.

14. Ikeda, "This Is Not a Test."

15. "Who We Are," Vigilant Love, accessed January 15, 2017, available at https://www.vigilantlove.org/who-we-are/.

16. "Who We Are," Vigilant Love.

17. "Who We Are," Vigilant Love.

18. "What We Do," Vigilant Love, accessed January 15, 2017, available at https://www.vigilantlove.org/what-we-do/.

19. Angry Asian Man [Phil Yu], "No Ban, No Wall: A Resistance and Solidarity Vigil," advertisement, *Angry Asian Man* (blog), January 25, 2017, available at http://blog.angryasianman.com/2017/01/no-ban-no-wall-resistance-solidarity.html.

20. Angry Asian Man.

21. Vigilant Love also consists of fourteen leaders and advisors as well as partnering organizations such as Asian Americans Advancing Justice, NCRR, the Council on American-Islamic Relations (CAIR), the California Immigrant Policy Center, the Tuesday Night Project, Jewish Voice for Peace Los Angeles, Af3irm: A Transnational Feminist Organization, Kabataang Maka-Bayan: Pro-People Youth, the National Queer Asian Pacific Islander Alliance (NQAPIA), Aware-LA, the Muslim Anti-Racism Collaborative (ARC), Sila Consulting, Bend the Arc: A Jewish Partnership for Justice, the Japanese American Cultural and Community Center, Muslim Student Association West, Southwest Asian and North Afrikan–Los Angeles, 18 Million Rising, White People 4 Black Lives, Uplift, American Friends Service Committee, Heart, Mpower Change: Muslim Grassroots Movement, Nikkei Democracy Project, Justice Warriors for Black Lives, Harness, and Social Venture Partners (SVP). See: "Who We Are," Vigilant Love.

22. Massoud Hayoum, "Muslim Ban: Japanese and Muslim Americans Join Forces," *Al Jazeera*, February 1, 2017, available at https://www.aljazeera.com/indepth/features/2017/02/muslim-ban-japanese-muslim-americans-join-forces-170201055155362.html.

23. Massoud Hayoum, "Japanese-Americans Unite with Muslims against Trump's Immigration Plans," *New Arab*, January 27, 2017, available at https://www.alaraby.co.uk/english/society/2017/1/27/japanese-americans-unite-with-muslims-against-trumps-immigration-plans.

24. Hayoum.

25. Hayoum.

26. Hayoum.

27. Hayoum.

28. The film is produced for the Nikkei Democracy Project, "a multi-media collective that uses the power of the Japanese American imprisonment story to expose current threats to Constitutional rights." "About" Renee Tajima Peña, accessed December 29, 2023, available at https://www.reneetajimapena.com/about.

29. Nikkei Democracy Project, "A Vigilant Love," directed by Tani Ikeda, produced by Tadashi Nakamura and Renee Tajima-Pena, 2017, video, 6:14, available at https://vimeo.com/254789121.

30. Nikkei Democracy Project.

31. Nikkei Democracy Project.

32. Nikkei Democracy Project.

33. Nikkei Progressives, available at https://www.nikkeiprogressives.org, and Tsuru for Solidarity, available at https://tsuruforsolidarity.org.

Selected Bibliography

Angry Asian Man [Phil Yu]. "No Ban, No Wall: A Resistance and Solidarity Vigil." Advertisement. *Angry Asian Man* (blog). January 25, 2017. Available at http://blog.angry asianman.com/2017/01/no-ban-no-wall-resistance-solidarity.html.

Azuma, Eiichiro. *Between Two Empires: Race, History, and Transnationalism in Japanese America*. Oxford: Oxford University Press, 2005.

Bascara, Victor. "The Cultural Politics of Redress: Reassessing the Meaning of the Civil Liberties of 1988 after 9/11." *Asian American Law Journal* 10, no. 2 (2003): 101–130.

Bradford, William. "Beyond Justice: An American Indian Theory of Justice." Paper 217, Aboriginal Policy Research Consortium International, 2004.

Bush, George H. W. "Letter from President George Bush to Internees." 1991.

Cacho, Lisa Marie. *Social Death: Racialized Rightlessness and the Criminalization of the Unprotected*. New York: New York University Press, 2012.

Cavelle, Jenna. "A Paiute Perspective on the LA-Owens Valley Water Story: Jenna Cavelle in Conversation with Alan Bacock and Harry Williams." *ARID*, 2013. Available at http://aridjournal.com/a-paiute-perspective-owens-valley-water-jenna-cavelle/.

Cho, Grace M. *Haunting the Korean Diaspora: Shame, Secrecy, and the Forgotten War*. Minneapolis: University of Minnesota Press, 2008.

Commission on Wartime Relocation and Internment of Civilians. *Personal Justice Denied*. Seattle: University of Washington, 1997.

Cvetkovich, Ann. *An Archive of Feelings: Trauma, Sexuality, and Lesbian Public Cultures*. Durham, NC: Duke University Press, 2003.

Day of Remembrance Committee. *2015 Day of Remembrance: EO 9066 and the [In]Justice System Today*. Program. February 21, 2015.

Densho. "About Densho." February 21, 2007. YouTube video, 9:28. Available at https://www.youtube.com/watch?annotation_id=annotation_824558583&feature=iv&src _vid=hq4sBSsuJDQ&v=_lBKndA1vP4.

———. "A Cabinet Meeting the Day after 9/11 – Norman Mineta." April 9, 2015. YouTube video, 2:00. Available at https://www.youtube.com/watch?v=VH7rGPXGicM.
———. "Pioneer Generation: Remembering the Issei." From Densho's Archives on Discover Nikkei. December 1, 2010. Available at http://www.discovernikkei.org/en/journal/2010/12/1/pioneer-generation/.
Densho and National Park Service. "Constitutional Issues: Civil Liberties, Individuals, and the Common Good." In *Civil Liberties Curriculum and Resource Guide for High School*, 2009.
Drinnon, Richard. *Keeper of Concentration Camps: Dillion S. Myer and American Racism*. Berkeley: University of California Press, 1987.
Embrey, Bruce. "Message from Manzanar Committee Co-Chair." *44th Annual Manzanar Pilgrimage Program*, April 27, 2013.
Eng, Chris. "Queer Genealogies of (Be)Longing: On the Thens and Theres of Asian America in Karen Tei Yamashita's I Hotel." *Journal of Asian American Studies* 20, no. 3 (2017): 345–372.
Ferguson, Roderick. *Aberrations in Black: Toward a Queer of Color Critique*. Minneapolis: University of Minnesota Press, 2003.
———. "Administering Sexuality." *Radical History Review* 100 (Winter 2008): 158–169.
Fujikane, Candace, and Jonathan Y. Okamura. *Asian Settler Colonialism: From Local Governance to the Habits of Everyday Life in Hawaii*. Honolulu: University of Hawaii Press, 2008.
Fujino, Diane. "The Indivisiblity of Freedom: The Nisei Progressives, Deep Solidarities, and Cold War Alternatives." *Journal of Asian American Studies* 21, no. 2 (June 2018): 171–208.
Fujitani, Takashi. "Go for Broke, the Movie: Japanese American Soldiers in U.S. National, Military, and Racial Discourses." In *Perilous Memories: The Asia Pacific War(s)*, edited by T. Fujitani, Geoffrey M. White, and Lisa Yoneyama, 239–266. Durham, NC: Duke University Press, 2001.
———. "Right to Kill and Right to Make Live: Koreans as Japanese and Japanese as Americans during World War II." *Representations* 99, no. 1 (2007): 13–39.
Gilmore, Ruth Wilson. *Golden Gulag: Prisons, Surplus, Crisis, and Opposition in Globalizing California*. Berkeley: University of California Press, 2007.
Goldstein, Alyosha. *Formations of United States Colonialism*. Durham, NC: Duke University Press, 2014.
Hayoum, Massoud. "Japanese-Americans Unite with Muslims against Trump's Immigration Plans." *New Arab*, January 27, 2017.
———. "Muslim Ban: Japanese and Muslim Americans Join Forces." *Al Jazeera*, February 1, 2017. Available at https://www.aljazeera.com/indepth/features/2017/02/muslim-ban-japanese-muslim-americans-join-forces-170201055155362.html.
Herzig-Yoshinaga, Aiko. "Words Can Lie or Clarify: Terminology of the World War II Incarceration of Japanese Americans." August 15, 2010. Available at https://nps.gov/tule/learn/education/upload/Words-Can-Lie-or-Clarify-FINAL-Rev-8-15-10.pdf.
Hong, Grace Kyungwon. *Death beyond Disavowal: The Impossible Politics of Difference*. Minneapolis: University of Minnesota Press, 2015.

———. "'Something Forgotten Which Should Have Been Remembered': Private Property and Cross-Racial Solidarity in the Work of Hisaye Yamamoto." *American Literature* 71, no. 2 (1999): 291–310.
Hong, Grace Kyungwon, and Roderick A. Ferguson, eds. *Strange Affinities: The Gender and Sexual Politics of Comparative Racialization*. Durham, NC: Duke University Press, 2011.
Ichioka, Yuji, with Gordan Chang and Eiichiro Azuma. *Before Internment: Essays in Prewar Japanese American History*. Stanford, CA: Stanford University Press, 2006.
Ikeda, Tom. "This Is Not a Test." Densho. January 28, 2017. Available at https://densho.org/this-is-not-a-test/.
Inouye, Karen M. *The Long Afterlife of Nikkei Wartime Incarceration*. Stanford, CA: Stanford University Press, 2016.
Japanese American National Museum. *Continuing Family Stories: The Expanding Nikkei Community*. DVD. Los Angeles, Japanese American National Museum, 2011.
———. *Continuing Family Stories: The Expanding Nikkei Community*. Program, 2011.
Kikamura-Yano, Akemi, Lane Ryo Hirabayashi, and James A. Hirabayashi. *Common Ground: The Japanese American National Museum and the Culture of Collaborations*. Boulder: University Press of Colorado, 2005.
Kim, Jodi. *Ends of Empire: Asian American Critique and the Cold War*. Minneapolis: University of Minnesota Press, 2010.
Lee, James-Kyung-Jin. "Multiculturalism." In *Keywords for Asian American Studies*, edited by Cathy J. Schlund-Vials, K. Scott Wong, and Linda Trinh Võ, 169–173. New York: New York University Press, 2015.
Lipsitz, George. "'Frantic to Join . . . the Japanese Army': Black Soldiers and Civilians Confront the Asia Pacific War." In *Perilous Memories: The Asia-Pacific War(s)*, edited by Takashi Fujitani, Geoffrey M. White, and Lisa Yoneyama, 347–377. Durham, NC: Duke University Press, 2001.
Lorde, Audre. *Sister Outsider*. Trumansburg, NY: Crossing Press, 1982.
Lowe, Lisa. *Immigrant Acts: On Asian American Cultural Politics*. Durham, NC: Duke University Press, 1996.
Lubiano, Wahneema. "Black Feminism and Black Common Sense." In *The House That Race Built*. New York: Pantheon, 1997.
Manning, Sally. Earth Day Is April 22. *Twa Gwa Tu Zu Way (We All Count . . . Everybody)*. Big Pine Paiute Newsletter. April 2015.
Manzanar Committee. *A Memory . . . A Monument . . . A Movement*. Program. April 26, 2014.
———. "Presidential Election and Its Aftermath." From *Never Again, to Anyone, Anywhere!* Program, 2017.
Marx, Karl. "The Eighteenth Brumaire of Louis Bonaparte." In *The Marx-Engels Reader*, edited by Robert C. Tucker, 594–617. New York: Norton, 1978.
Matsuda, Gann. "The Constitution of the University of California, Los Angeles Nikkei Student Union." Authored March 17, 1984, reprinted April 2, 1989.
Matsumoto, Valerie. "Japanese American Women during World War II." *Frontiers: A Journal of Women's Studies* 8, no. 1 (1984): 6–14.
Mbembe, Achille. "Necropolitics." *Public Culture* 15, no. 1 (2003): 11–40.

Mineta, Norman Y., and Ann Burroughs. "I Was Imprisoned in a U.S. Internment Camp. Bigotry Put Me There." *TIME*, November 21, 2016. Available at http://time.com/4579182/japanese-internment-bigotry/.

Murray, Alice Yang. *Historical Memories of the Japanese American Internment and the Struggle for Redress*. Stanford, CA: Stanford University Press, 2008.

N'Cobra. "What Forms Should Reparations Take?" Accessed December 21, 2023. Available at https://ncobra.org/default.

Ngai, Mae. *Impossible Subjects: Illegal Aliens and the Making of Modern America*. Princeton, NJ: Princeton University Press, 2004.

Nikkei Democracy Project. "A Vigilant Love." Directed by Tani Ikeda. Produced by Tadashi Nakamura and Renee Tajima-Pena. 2017. Video, 6:14. Available at https://vimeo.com/254789121.

Nikkei Student Union. *The Last Generation*. Culture Night program. February 21, 2011.

———. *Our [I]dentity*. Culture Night program. February 20, 2012.

———. *Senbazaru*. Culture Night video recording. February 15, 2016.

Nishio, Alan. "Awards Nomination UCLA Nikkei Student Union." No date.

Rainmakers TV. "Densho, Japanese American Legacy Project." August 3, 2014. YouTube video, 28:30. Available at https://www.youtube.com/watch?v=3I_1WR1m1c4.

Richie, Beth. *Arrested Justice: Black Women, Violence, and America's Prison Nation*. New York: New York University Press, 2012.

Rodriguez, Dylan. "The Dreadful Genius of the Obama Moment: Inaugurating Multiculturalist White Supremacy." *Colorlines*, November 10, 2008.

Salyers, Abbie Lynn. *The Internment of Memory: Forgetting and Remembering the Japanese American World War II Experience*. Ph.D. diss., Rice University, 2009. ProQuest/UMI (publication number: 3362399).

Seventh Generation Fund for Indigenous Peoples and Graven Image Films. "Saving *Payahuupu*: The Owens Valley Solar Story." April 25, 2014. YouTube video, 14:42. Available at https://www.youtube.com/watch?v=mTV9Pd6AaNk.

Takaki, Ronald. *Strangers from a Different Shore*. Boston: Little, Brown, 1998.

Takemoto, Tina. "Looking for Jiro Onuma: A Queer Mediation on the Incarceration of Japanese Americans during World War II." *GLQ* 20, no. 3 (2014): 241–275.

Taylor, Diana. *The Archive and the Repertoire: Performing Cultural Memory in the Americas*. Durham, NC: Duke University Press, 2003.

Toyota, Tricia. "The New Nikkei: Transpacific Shin Issei and Shifting Borders of Community in Southern California." *Amerasia* 38, no. 3 (2012): 2–27.

United States Holocaust Memorial Museum. "About the Museum: A Living Memorial to the Holocaust." Accessed March 20, 2017. Available at https://www.ushmm.org/information/about-the-museum.

Walker, Chantal R. "*Piyahu Nadu*: Land of Flowing Waters: The Water Transfer from Owens Valley to Los Angeles 1913–1939." M.A. thesis, University of California, Los Angeles, 2014.

Warner, Michael. "Introduction: Fear of a Queer Planet." *Social Text*, no. 29 (1991): 3–17.

Wolfe, Patrick. "Settler Colonialism and the Elimination of the Native." *Journal of Genocide Research* 8, no. 4 (2006): 387–409.

Woods, Clyde. "Les Miserables of New Orleans: Trap Economics and the Asset Stripping Blues, Part 1." *American Quarterly* 61, no. 3 (2009): 769–796.

Yamamoto, Hisaye. "A Fire in Fontana." In *Seventeen Syllables and Other Stories*, 150–157. New Brunswick, NJ: Rutgers University Press, 1994.
Yamamoto, J. K. "Message of Tolerance in Little Tokyo." *Rafu Shimpo*, December 14, 2015.
Yamashita, Wendsor. "The Colonial and the Carceral: Building Relationships between Japanese Americans and Indigenous Groups in the Owens Valley." *Amerasia* 42, no. 1 (2016): 121–138.
———. "What She Remembers: Remaking and Unmaking Japanese American Internment." M.A. thesis, University of California, Los Angeles, 2010.

Index

abolition, 20, 80; increased receptivity to calls for, 149n133; memory and, 135–137; of prisons, 46, 53
"abstract citizens," 5
African Americans. *See* Blacks
afterlife of Japanese American incarceration, 16, 17, 143n59
Akutsu, Gene, 70
Alien Land Laws, 89, 109, 115–116
All People's Christian Church, 41
allyship, 44, 126; by Manzanar organizations, 97–98, 102; prison abolition and, 53; privilege assessment and, 49
Always Welcome, Never for Sale (play), 107
Amemiya, Kevin, 100, 101
American Airlines, 26
American Civil Liberties Union, 60
"Americanness," 58, 59
"America's Concentration Camps: Remembering the Japanese American Experience" (exhibit), 142n55
Another Inmate Gold Star Mother (WRA promotional still), 60
antiblackness, 2, 3, 17, 29, 137; abolitionism and, 135, 136; Day of Remembrance on, 21, 38, 46–47, 48, 49, 50, 52, 53
apartheid, 16
apocalyptic futurity, 117–120

apology for Japanese American incarceration, 12, 15, 16, 17, 36, 63, 68, 87; as a technology for neocolonialism and neoliberalism, 18; worthiness criteria, 32–33, 62
Arab Americans, 70, 130
Archive and the Repertoire, The: Performing Cultural Memory in the Americas (Taylor), 109
Archive of Feeling, The (Cvetkovich), 65
Arizona v. United States, 115
Asian Pacific Coalition, 125
Asian Pacific Islanders, 125
Asian Settler Colonialism (Fujikane and Okamura), 88–89
assimilationism, 7, 35, 58, 61, 139n1
Azuma, Eichiro, 89

Bacock, Alan, 93, 102
Bascara, Victor, 33, 63
Besig, Ernest, 60
Bid for Education Fund, 35–36, 45
Big Pine Paiute Tribal Council, 94
Big Pine Paiute Tribe, 84, 85, 91, 93, 98, 155n40
biopolitical logic of Densho archive, 64–65, 69, 72, 73
biopolitical management of memory, 74, 75, 76, 77, 78, 83

biopower, 58, 64
Bishop Paiute Tribe, 84, 85, 91, 92, 96, 155n40
Black Lives Matter, 45, 53
Blackness, 29, 38, 39. *See also* antiblackness
Black Power movement, 41, 49
Blacks, 24–25, 54; Day of Remembrance and, 21, 24, 39–53; in Little Tokyo district, 118; military service of, 10; murder of, 24, 39, 45, 50 (*see also* death, of Blacks); NSU cultural events and, 125; reparations struggle, 17–19, 44, 135, 147n95; statistics on devaluation of lives of, 45
Bowers, David, 129
Boyle Heights, Los Angeles, 40
Bridging Communities, 130
Bronzeville, 118
Brothers Miyazaki (play), 107
Brown, Michael, 39, 50, 149n126
Brown, Wendy, 13
Bryant, Povi-Tamu, 39, 45–46, 48–50, 51–52, 53
Burroughs, Ann, 131
Bush, George W., 129–130
Butler, Judith, 78
Button, Irene, 102

Cacho, Lisa, 17
California, 10
California State Historic Landmark #850 (Manzanar), 86
California State Polytechnic University, Pomona (CPP), 88
California State University, Fullerton, 56
California State University, Long Beach (CSULB), 88
California State University, Sacramento, 56
California Volunteers, 93
Camp Harmony, 77
capitalism, 3, 26, 96
Central Avenue, Los Angeles, 40
Chado, 34
Children's Day, 125
Chinese Exclusion Act of 1822, 6
Chinese immigration, 5–6
Chirashi, 127
Cho, Grace M., 143n59
Citizen Isolation camps, 40
citizenship: "abstract citizens," 5; denial of, 3, 9, 17, 43, 59, 89; spectralization of, 58; status of Issei *vs.* Nisei, 7

citizen-subjects, 27, 48, 53, 124; in the global economy, 32; ideal, 3, 17; incarceration as an interruption to, 13–14; military service and, 14
civil liberties, limits of, 73–75
Civil Liberties Act of 1988, 12, 15–16, 18, 69, 87, 130, 143n61
Civil Liberties Public Education Fund, 15, 130, 142n46
civil rights movement, 41
Cleaver, Eldridge, 49
Clinton, Bill, 44
coalitional intimacies, 114, 116, 117
Cold War, 20
colonialism: Cultural Night performance on, 106–107; Indigenous groups of Owens Valley and, 22, 85, 86, 88–94, 97; neo-, 16, 18; recognizing violence of, 90–94. *See also* settler colonialism
Commission on Wartime Relocation and Internment of Civilians, 8, 9–10, 16, 44, 50; hearings of, 62–64; Inouye's role in establishing, 15; Manzanar Committee testimony at, 87; report of, 63, 141n46; significance of creation, 12–13
common good, limits of, 73–75
Constitution, US, 79–80
constitutional value, limits of, 73–75
containment, 8, 18, 20, 21, 90, 95
"Continuing Family Stories: The Expanding Nikkei Community" (Gala Dinner 2011), 1, 27, 31
contradictory location, 4–5, 25, 86, 132, 153n5
Council on American Islamic Relations, 130
COVID-19 pandemic, 23, 100, 101, 136, 137
Creative Visionary Award, 31
Crenshaw district, Los Angeles, 40, 41
Crossover (documentary), 27
Cultural Ambassador Award, 31
cultural ambassadors, as the new subjects of history, 31–33
cultural nationalist history, gendered limits of, 111–114
Cultural Night performances, 22–23, 104–127; *The Last Generation: Every Generation Needs a Regeneration*, 107–114; *Our [I]dentity: It's More Than Blood*, 114–117; *Senbazuru*, 117–124; variety of, 157n11
Customs and Border Protection, US, 134
Cvetkovich, Ann, 65, 143n59

D'arcy, Angela Mooney, 92
Day of Remembrance (DOR) (2015), 21,
  24, 25, 38, 39–53; discourse of proximity
  as shared history, 42–44; on Nikkei
  futurity, 50–53; organizations hosting, 39;
  queering the conversation, 45–50, 52–53;
  as a starting point in carceral connections,
  39–42
death, 2–3, 62; of Blacks, 24, 39, 44, 45, 50
  (*see also* Blacks, murder of); the Densho
  archive on, 21–22, 55, 56, 57, 64–66, 67,
  70–72, 73, 83; erasure and, 59; forgetting
  as, 36; as Gala Dinner theme, 27–28,
  31, 38; of groups of color (non-Japanese),
  37; immigration and, 33; of Indigenous
  groups, 92, 96; of Isssei, 71; Japanese
  American National Museum on, 36; of
  Nisei, 2, 7, 22–23, 29–30, 32, 58, 60, 70,
  83, 99, 101, 104, 109, 120; premature,
  8–9, 12, 16; visibility and, 8, 9–10, 59, 72
debt-creditor relationship, 105
debt-obligation, 108, 109–111
December 7, 1941. *See* Pearl Harbor bombing
Declaration of Independence, 79–80
Dellums, Ron, 42
democracy. *See* liberal democracy
democratic ideals: comparative historical
  methodology within confines of, 79–83;
  establishing, 74, 75
Densho: The Japanese American Legacy
  Project, 21–22, 54, 55–57, 64–83, 129;
  biopolitical logic of, 64–65, 69, 72, 73;
  comparative historical methodology in,
  79–83; on continuing racist tendencies,
  131–132; on death, 21–22, 55, 56, 57,
  64–66, 67, 70–72, 73, 83; described,
  55–56; financial contributions to, 72;
  on forgetting, 73, 76–79; immigration
  exclusion protest urged by, 131; Katari
  compared with, 100; on life, 22, 55,
  56, 57, 64, 65, 66, 70–72, 73, 83; on
  memory (*see* memory, the Densho archive
  on); mission of, 57; "Ongoing Injustice"
  assigment, 81–83; on redress, 64–65, 66,
  69, 72, 82; teaching Japanese American
  incarceration in, 73–75; "Town Meeting"
  activity, 80–81; translation of name, 57,
  71; YouTube channel, 65, 66, 75
Día de los Niño, 125
disappearance: of Indigenous groups, 92; for
  racialized belonging, 57–59

Distinguished Service Cross, 60
DOR. *See* Day of Remembrance (2015)
Douglass, Frederick, 79–80
Dymally, Mervin, 42

East LA Community Corporation, 45
Eastside Los Angeles, 40
economic loss (due to incarceration), 13
education, 28; Gala Dinner on, 27, 35–38;
  World War II era, 61
"Eighteenth Brumaire of Louis Bonaparte"
  (Marx), 146n59
El Tejon Reservation, 93
Embrey, Bruce, 84, 91, 98, 156n64
Embrey, Sue Kunitomi, 86
Emi, Frank, 27
Ends of Empire (Kim), 10
"enemy alien" status, 10, 11, 19, 48, 61, 62, 86
"EO 9066 and the [In]Justice System
  Today" (DOR event), 39. *See also* Day of
  Remembrance (2015)
erasure, 4, 8, 11, 17, 101; death and, 59; the
  Densho archive on, 64; Japanese American
  National Museum on resisting, 36; for
  racialized belonging, 57–59
Executive Order 9066, 8, 13, 39, 40, 52;
  Densho archive on, 68; EO 13769 issued
  on 75th anniversary of, 131; Manzanar
  Committee on, 86, 94; Week of
  Remembrance on, 106
Executive Order 13769 (Muslim Ban),
  130–135

family: author's, 47; as Gala Dinner theme,
  31; heteronormative formation of, 45, 46,
  47–48, 52, 53, 105, 114; immigration
  loopholes and, 5–6; nuclear, 6, 7, 21, 100,
  105
FandangObon, 125
FBI, 58, 67, 68
Ferguson, Roderick, 4, 36
Fiesta Matsuri, 125
financial contributions: to the Densho
  archive, 72; to the Japanese American
  National Museum, 26, 27, 29, 34
"Fire in Fontana, A" (Yamamoto), 41, 43–44
Floyd, George, 136
Ford, Ezell, 39
forgetting: as death, 36; Densho archive on,
  73, 76–79; Gala Dinner on refusal of,
  35–37

Fort Independence Indian Community of Paiute Indians, 84
Fort Tejon, 93, 102
Foucault, Michel, 57–58, 64
442nd Regimental Combat Team, 10, 14, 63
Fujikane, Candace, 88–89
Fujino, Diane, 20
Fujitani, Takashi, 9, 10, 63
Fukuda, Rey, 39, 45–48, 49–50, 51–52, 53
Fukushima Daiichi nuclear disaster, 33
Furutani, Warren, 86
futurity: apocalyptic, 117–120; Day of Remembrance on, 50–53; Gala Dinner on, 35–38

Gala Dinner of Japanese American National Museum (2011), 1, 21, 24, 25, 26; cultural ambassadors at, 31–33; Day of Remembrance compared with, 39, 47; on education and the future, 27, 35–38; generationality theme at, 31, 33–35; language of lineage and legacy at, 30–31; parameters of, 27–29
gaman, 35
ganbatte, 35
Garcetti, Eric, 94
Garner, Eric, 39, 50
gendered behavior, 3, 17
gendered liberation, 61–62
gendered limits, of cultural nationalist history, 111–114
gendered normative visibility, 62–64
gendered racial rehabilitation, 10, 11
gender roles: incarceration and switching of, 47–48, 61; Nisei, 59–62
generational debt: continuing limits of, 124–127; *The Last Generation on*, 107–114; *Senbazuru* on, 117–124
generational history, 107–109
generationality, 2–3, 19, 31; defined, 5; heteronormative logic of, 5–8; rupture and reification in, 33–35
generational narratives, Shin-Nisei disruption of, 114–117
generational reproduction, 75, 83, 101, 116
generational storytelling, 99–102
Generation Teas, 34–35
Gentlemen's Agreement of 1907–1908, 6
gentrification, 121, 126, 127
Giant Robot Exhibition, 37
Gilmore, Ruth Wilson, 8, 19

Glenn, Evelyn Nakano, 119
Glorious Excess (exhibit), 37
Golden Gulag (Gilmore), 8
Goldstein, Alyosha, 20, 89
Gordon, Avery, 143
Gosei, 34, 99; defined, 50, 105; intergenerational collaboration and, 135
Graven Image Films, 91
groups of color (non-Japanese), 63–64, 126; Cultural Nights and, 124–125; death of, 37; as "deserving" of punishment, 91; heteronormative discourse and, 63; redress predicated on devaluation of, 44; reparations struggle, 17–19; Trump and, 131
Guanier, Lani, 80
Guantanamo Bay, 130

hakujins, 116
Halberstam, Jack, 76
Hansen, Art, 56
haunting: of executive orders, 130–135; Gordon's theorization, 143n59; transgenerational, 67
Hawaii, 6, 89
Hayakawa, S. I., 14
Hayashi, Yoshiye Okimoto, 156n64
Hero's Welcome Home, A (play), 107
heteronormativity, 3, 4, 17, 25, 100, 140n5; family formation and, 45, 46, 47–48, 52, 53, 105, 114; generationality and, 5–8; groups of color seen through discourse of, 63; Inouye's demonstration of, 2; of memory transmissions, 21, 45, 47, 76, 107, 135
Hirano, Irene Y., 25–26, 37
history: cultural ambassadors as the new subjects of, 31–33; cultural nationalist, 111–114; discourse of proximity as shared, 42–44; generational, 107–109
History and Memory (film), 152n66
Hohri, William, 27
Holiday Bowl, 40
Holocaust memorialization, 15, 16, 142n55
Holocaust Memorial Museum, 15
home: Little Tokyo as, 118–119; Owens Valley as, 96
Hong, Grace Kyungwon, 11–12, 43
housing covenants, 40
housing discrimination, 40, 118
HR 543, 87
Hunter, Roberta, 94

ICE (Immigration and Customs Enforcement, US), 133
Ichioka, Yuji, 6–7
Ikeda, Tani, 134
Ikeda, Tom, 55, 66, 68, 69
immigration: Chinese, 5–6; Cultural Night performances on, 114–117; EO 13769 and, 130–135; Japanese (*see* Japanese immigration); Trump-era policies on, 70, 128
Immigration Act of 1924, 32, 33, 89
Immigration Act of 1965, 32, 33
Immigration and Customs Enforcement, US (ICE), 133
Independence, California, 84
Indigenous groups of Owens Valley, 22, 84–103. *See also* Owens Valley
individuals, limits of, 73–75
Inouye, Daniel, 1–2, 7, 14–15, 24, 28, 35–36, 37–38, 45, 136, 137
Inouye, Karen M., 16, 143n59
Inyo County, 85
Ishigo, Traci, 133, 134–135
Islamophobia, 131, 132, 133, 135. *See also* Muslim Americans
Issei, 6–7, 10, 104; citizenship denied to, 7, 9, 17, 59; cultural death of, 58; Cultural Night performances on, 107, 109, 115–116, 117; Day of Remembrance on, 39; death of, 71; defined, 5; the Densho archive on, 67, 71–72; era of immigration, 5; family narratives of, 47; first appearances of term, 148n112; gender roles and, 61; Japanese American National Museum on, 25, 29, 33, 34, 35; land purchases by, 89; oral history on, 56
Issei Oral History Project, 56
Ito, Leslie A., 60–61

JACCC. *See* Japanese American Cultural and Community Center
JACL. *See* Japanese American Citizens League
Japan: Japanese American community linkages to, 145n27; natural disasters in, 33; US occupation of, 10
Japanese American Citizens League (JACL), 17, 39, 56, 126
Japanese American Cultural and Community Center (JACCC), 40, 125
Japanese American National Museum, 15, 24–38, 131; as community archive, 25–27; Day of Remembrance hosted by, 39; Densho compared with, 55; financial contributions to, 26, 27, 29, 34; national medal awarded to, 28, 29; opening of, 25; use of term "concentration camp" by, 142n55; Young Professionals Network, 37, 104–105. *See also* Gala Dinner of Japanese American National Museum (2011)
Japanese American privilege, 44, 46, 49, 52, 53, 125–126, 134
Japanese American Project at Cal State Fullerton, 56
Japanese American Research Project at UCLA, 56
"Japanese American Women and the Student Relocation Movement, 1942–1945" (Ito), 60–61
Japanese immigration: barriers to, 3, 89; the Densho archive on, 67; by generation, 5; Japanese American National Museum on, 32, 33; loopholes allowing for family creation, 5–6; "new" immigrants, 30; recent population of, 99, 101
Jones, Genevieve "Gina," 98
Jung, Soya, 48
Justice Department detention centers, 40

Kanai, Noitoshi, 32, 33
Kanegawa, Alex, 50–51
Katari: Keeping Japanese American Stories Alive, 99–102, 105, 155n60, 156n64, 156n70
kato-kiriyama, traci, 133
Khuê Ninh, erin, 105
Kibei Nisei, 58
Kim, Jodi, 10
King, Martin Luther, Jr., 50
Kizuna, 105
Kochiyama, Yuri, 41–42
Kodomo no Hi, 125
Kranz, Emiko, 117, 123, 124–127, 159n65

LA Coalition, 133
"Ladies Agreement," 6
LADWP. *See* Los Angeles Department of Water and Power
land ownership, denial of, 3, 10, 90, 116. *See also* property rights, denial of
Last Generation, The: Every Generation Needs a Regeneration (play), 107–114
Latinos, 114–115

legibility, 6, 15; Day of Remembrance on, 53; the Densho archive on, 54, 67; Indigenous groups and, 86; Japanese American National Museum and, 26; military service and, 14, 60, 61; through redress and testimony, 2; unintended consequences of, 16
lesbian public cultures, 65
LGBTQ Nikkei, 148n112
liberal democracy, 11, 13, 20, 69, 90
life: the Densho archive on, 22, 55, 56, 57, 64, 65, 66, 70–72, 73, 83; truth and, 36
Lifetime Achievement Award, 32
Little Tokyo, Los Angeles, 21, 40, 107, 117–124
Little Tokyo People's Rights Organization, 87
Little Tokyo Service Center (LTSC), 45, 149n119
Lone Pine, California, 84
Lone Pine High School, 88
Lone Pine Paiute-Shoshone Tribe, 84–85, 91, 155n40
"look how far we've come" temporality, 27–29
"Looking for Jiro Onuma" (Takemoto), 47
Los Angeles, California: housing in, 40; land purchases in Owens Valley, 93–94; water diversion to, 22, 94, 95, 96
Los Angeles Aqueduct, 94
Los Angeles Department of Water and Power (LADWP), 22, 84, 95, 96, 97, 98, 99, 101, 102; groups standing against valley destruction by, 85; land transfer by, 87; Owens Valley stakeholders and, 90–94
Los Angeles International Airport sit-in and rally, 134
Los Angeles Tribune, 41, 43
"loss of loss," 78
Lowe, Lisa, 4
loyalty, 58–59, 60, 61
Loyalty Questionnaire, 9, 57, 59, 136, 157n28
Loyola Marymount University, 40

MacBeth, Hugh, 40
"Make America Great" campaign, 131
Maki, Lane, 35–37, 38
Maki, Mitch, 35
Malcolm X, 41, 49
Mandela, Nelson, 50

Manzanar at Dusk, 88, 99
Manzanar Committee, 84, 90–91, 92, 96, 103, 105; author's membership in, 99; coalition building and, 97–99; Day of Remembrance hosted by, 39; generational storytelling preserved by, 99–102; letter on incarceration drafted by, 94–95; membership of, 88; mission of, 85; redress and reparations struggle and, 86–87; on Trump election, 131
Manzanar National Historic Site, 22, 84, 85, 99–100, 101, 102; historic site designation, 86, 87, 95; preservation of Japanese American experience by, 86–90; settler colonial desires and, 94–95
Manzanar pilgrimages, 84, 102, 130; history and current manifestation of, 86–88; "Never Again, To Anyone, Anywhere," 131; overlap with incarceration memorialization, 85; Owens Valley tribal representatives and, 98
Manzanar Project (later named Manzanar Committee), 86
Manzanar Reward Road, 84
Marx, Karl, 146n59
Masaoka, Joe Grant, 56
Masaoka, Kathy, 133
Matsuda, Gann, 92, 93, 97, 98, 99, 156n64
"maybe if I did" temporality, 122–124
"Meaning of July Fourth for the Negro, The" (Douglass), 79–80
memory, 1–5, 20; abolition and shifting futures of, 135–137; biopolitical management of, 74, 75, 76, 77, 78, 83; Commission hearings and, 16; the Densho archive on, 22, 55, 56, 57, 64–70, 72, 73, 74, 83; the Densho archive on combating loss of, 65–70; the Densho archive on failure of, 75–76; EO 13769 triggering of, 131; as Gala Dinner theme, 35–37; heteronormative transmission of, 21, 45, 47, 76, 107, 135; performances of, 4–5, 11 (*see also* Cultural Night performances); public, 2–5, 19, 25, 45; strategies for organizing and mobilizing, 128; understanding of historical, 5–8
Mexico, 125
"military necessity" justification for incarceration, 2, 8, 40, 62
military service, 2, 9–10, 32, 59–60; of Blacks, 10; casualties in, 10, 63; 442nd

Regimental Combat Team, 10, 14, 63; honors awarded for, 60, 63; of Native Americans, 11; "No-No" boys, 112, 157n28; 100th Infantry Battalion, 63; redress and, 9, 14–15, 59; segregation in, 9, 10, 35–36, 59, 63, 107; of women, 60
Mineta, Norman, 129, 131, 132
Minidoka (camp), 77
Minidoka National Historic Site, 73
Mirikitani, Janice, 110
"Mixed Race Asian American Identity on Display" (Tamai, Nakashima and Williams), 149n128
mochi, 120–122
model minority discourse, 10, 11, 38, 48–49; Japanese American National Museum and, 34; welfare program dismantling justified by, 44, 63
Moore, Brenda, 60
Morihiro, George, 77–78
Moynihan, Daniel Patrick, 17
multiculturalism, 21, 28; as assimilationist, 139n1; Day of Remembrance on, 42–44
Murase, Mike, 39, 45, 49–50, 149n119
Murray, Alice Yang, 17–18
Muslim Americans, 70, 128; Cultural Nights and, 120, 121, 126, 127; Executive Order 13769 and, 130–135; racial profiling of, 129–130
Muslim Public Affairs Council, 130
Mutual Trading Company, 32

Nakanishi, Don, 106
Nakashima, Cindy, 149n128
National Coalition for Redress and Reparations, 87
National Council for Japanese American Redress, 86–87
National Japanese American Student Relocation Council, 61
National Medal for Museum and Library Services, 28, 29
National Park Service, 20, 22, 73, 86, 87, 94, 99, 101
National Security Entry-Exit Registration System (NSEERS), 130, 132
Native Americans: abolitionist movement and, 136; the Densho archive on, 81; military service of, 11; reparations struggle, 18. *See also* Indigenous groups of Owens Valley

NCRR. *See* Nikkei for Civil Rights and Redress
Negro Family, The: The Case for National Action (Moynihan), 17
neocolonialism, 16, 18
neoliberalism, 3, 21, 25, 64, 66, 126, 129; normalization and justification of, 5; redress and, 4, 11–16; redress as disavowal of racial order of, 16–20; testimony as a technology of, 16
"Never Again, To Anyone, Anywhere" (Manzanar pilgrimage theme), 131
"never again" discourse, 15, 25, 26, 128, 137; Densho archive and, 70, 80, 132; EO 13769 and, 130; Holocaust *vs.* incarceration use of, 142n55; of relationality, 129–130
"New Nikki, The: Transpacific Shin Issei and Shifting Borders of Community in Southern California" (Toyota), 30
Ngai, Mae, 58
Nikkei, 26; Blacks and, 45; Civil Liberties Act significance for, 15–16; complications of identity in, 114; futurity of, 37, 38, 50–53, 117–120; integrating new immigrants into identity of, 30; LGBTQ, 148n112; Manzanar organizations and, 88; political complacency attributed to, 125–126; transforming apathy in, 109–111
Nikkei Democracy Project, 161n28
Nikkei for Civil Rights and Redress (NCRR), 39, 42, 106
Nikkei Progressives, 128
Nikkei Student Unions (NSUs), 88, 99, 101, 105–127. *See also* Cultural Night performances
Nisei, 100; Blacks and, 41; Cultural Night performances on, 22–23, 109; Day of Remembrance on, 39; death of, 2, 7, 22–23, 29–30, 32, 58, 60, 70, 83, 99, 101, 104, 109, 120; defined, 2, 5; the Densho archive on, 57, 66, 67, 70; era of immigration, 5; family narratives of, 47; as focal point of community identity, 6–7; gender roles of, 59–62; Japanese American National Museum on, 25, 29–30, 33, 34–35; military service of (*see* military service); oral history on, 56
Nisei Progressives, 20
Nisei Week, 118
Nishio, Alan, 106

"No Ban No Wall Vigil," 133
Noguchi, Yone, 148n112
"No-No" boys, 112, 157n28
normativity, 2–3, 19, 62–64, 140n5. *See also* heteronormativity
NSEERS. *See* National Security Entry-Exit Registration System
NSUs. *See* Nikkei Student Unions
nuclear family, 6, 7, 21, 100, 105
number of Japanese American incarcerees, 68, 99

Obama, Barack, 28–29
Obama, Michelle, 28
Oda, Nancy, 156n64
Oikawa, Mona, 89
Okaeri, 148n112
Okamura, Jonathan Y., 88–89
Omori, Chizuko, 71
Omori, Emiko, 71
100th Infantry Battalion, 63
Onuma, Jiro, 53, 148n112
oral history, 64, 65, 68, 69, 71, 73; the Densho archive positioning of, 75–76; Katari's use of, 100; long trajectory of, 56
Ota, Helen, 40
Our [I]dentity: It's More Than Blood (play), 114–117
Owens River, 94
Owens Valley, 22, 84–103; centering, 96–97; coalition building in, 97–99; as "home" to Indigenous groups, 96; Indigenous tribes of, 84–85; location of, 84; Paiute name for, 93; reexamining "isolation" and "desolation" in, 94–95; solar ranch proposal (*see* Southern Owens Valley Solar Ranch); stakeholders in, 90–94; water rights in (*see* water rights (Owens Valley))
Owens Valley Committee, 85, 98

Page Act of 1875, 5–6
PATRIOT Act, 130
Paya (documentary), 97
Pearl Harbor bombing, 6, 8, 57; the Densho archive on, 67–68, 71, 81, 82; September 11 attacks compared with, 81, 129–130
performances of memory, 4–5, 11. *See also* Cultural Night performances
Personal Justice Denied (report), 13–14, 141n46
picture bride system, 6
Pilipino Cultural Nights, 106–107

Pirzada, Sahar, 133–134, 135
Piyahu-Nadu, 93
police: abolition movement, 135; brutality of, 24, 39, 45
Princeton University, 27
prison industrial complex, 4, 82
prison nation, 19, 20
prison system/incarceration, 19, 46–47, 53
private property, 90
privilege. *See* Japanese American privilege
progressive temporality, 15, 18, 19
progress narratives, 35
property rights, denial of, 4, 43, 44, 89–90. *See also* land ownership, denial of
Protecting the Nation From Foreign Terrorist Entry into the United States. *See* Executive Order 13769
"protection" justification for incarceration, 8, 57
proximity as solidarity, 41, 42–44, 48, 49, 53
public memory, 2–5, 19, 25, 45
Purple Hearts, 63
Puyallup Assembly Center, 77–78

queerness/queering: Day of Remembrance conversation and, 45–50, 52–53; Japanese American stories of, 148n112; of memory transmission, 21
queer of color critique, 3–4, 139n4

Rabbit in the Moon (documentary), 71
racialized social-spatial enclosures, 8–9, 11, 80, 81–82
racism: the Densho archive on, 131–132; disavowal of, 3, 7, 9–10, 16–20, 32, 58, 67, 86
"Racism and the Glass Ceiling" (presentation), 106
Rafu Shimpo, 104, 105, 109, 118
Rainmakers TV, 66
Ramadan, 130
Razack, Sherene H., 89
redemption narratives. *See* state redemption narratives
redress, 2, 3, 5, 7–8, 32–33, 56, 91, 126; court case for, 27; Day of Remembrance on, 42, 44, 52, 53; the Densho archive on, 64–65, 66, 69, 72, 82; limits of gendered normative visibility and, 62–64; Manzanar Committe advocacy for, 86–87; military service in relation to, 9, 14–15,

59; neoliberalism and, 4, 11–16; neoliberal racial order disavowal and, 16–20; Trump and crumbling logic of, 128
regeneration, temporality of, 109–111
relocation, 58–59, 60–61
reparations, 2, 8, 15, 56, 91; Blacks' struggle for, 17–19, 44, 135, 147n95; Day of Remembrance on, 42, 52, 53; as a defining historical moment, 12–13; the Densho archive and, 66, 69, 72; limits of gendered normative visibility and, 62–64; "living victims" stipulation, 18, 44; Manzanar Committee's advocacy for, 86–87; military service in relation to, 59; monetary amount of, 12, 16, 87; Native Americans' struggle for, 18
reprosexuality, 6, 105
Richie, Beth, 19
Rodriguez, Dylan, 128
Rohwer, Arkansas, 35
Rooks, Curttis Takada, 24, 40, 45, 51
Rooks, Mariko Fujimoto, 51–52
Roosevelt, Franklin D., 8, 39

sacrifice, 14, 32, 50, 60, 61, 62, 63, 105, 108, 124
Sakai, Stan, 31, 33
Sakamoto, Pat, 156n64
San Bernardino, California mass shooting, 132
San Francisco State College strike, 14
Sansei, 7, 25, 41, 49, 100, 104; Cultural Night performance on, 109; defined/era of immigration, 5; family narratives of, 47; Japanese American National Museum and, 30, 32, 34
Santa Anita Assembly Center, 40
Santa Monica, California, 92
Saving Payahüüpüü: The Owens Valley Solar Story (film), 91–94
SB 1070. *See* Support Our Law Enforcement and Safe Neighborhoods Act
Seen and Unseen (Noguchi), 148n112
Seen and Unseen: Queering JA History before 1945 (virtual exhibit), 148n112
self-determination, 18, 19
Senbazuru (play), 117–124
September 11 attacks, 23, 26, 70, 120, 132; the Densho archive on, 69, 79, 80–81; Pearl Harbor bombing compared with, 81, 129–130

Serving Our Country (Moore), 60
settler colonialism, 3, 4, 20, 132; Indigenous groups of Owens Valley and, 85, 86, 89, 91, 96, 97, 101, 102; Japanese Americans as settlers, 90; Manzanar National Historic Site and, 94–95; memory and mobilization against, 135
Seventeen Syllables (Yamamoto), 27
Seventh Generation Fund for Indigenous Peoples, 91
sharing space narrative, 42–44
Shimizu, Hiroshi, 156n64
Shin-Issei, 30; defined, 7; intergenerational collaboration and, 135
Shin-Nisei, 30; defined, 7; generational narratives disrupted by, 114–117; intergenerational collaboration and, 135
Shinoda, Mike, 37
slavery, 79, 80, 81, 82
social reproduction, 119
solar ranch proposal (Owens Valley). *See* Southern Owens Valley Solar Ranch
solidarity: family responsibility and, 52; via proximity, 41, 42–44, 48, 49, 53
"Something Forgotten Which Should Have Been Remembered" (Hong), 43
South Africa, 50
South Asians for Justice-Los Angeles, 132
Southern California NSUs, 99
Southern California Shura Council, 130
Southern Owens Valley Solar Ranch, 22, 84–85, 102; coalition building by opponents of, 97–99; described, 84; Owens Valley stakeholders and, 90–94; tabling of plans for, 98
South Los Angeles, 40
Spoonhunter, Topah, 102
statelessness, 9, 59, 141n30
state redemption narratives, 7–8, 32–33, 63, 65, 73, 130
States of Injury: Power and Freedom in Late Modernity (Brown), 13
state violence, 1, 52, 62; against Blacks, 50; the Densho archive on, 57, 66, 82; groups of color "deserving" of, 91; Manzanar Committee education on, 86, 87; in Owens Valley, 85
Stewart Indian school, 102
Stone, Cheyenne, 102
storytelling: generational, 99–102; visualizing, 111–114

success narratives, 2, 17, 24, 63, 64; Black community abandonment and, 44, 54; at Gala Dinner, 27, 28, 29, 31, 37–38; Japanese American National Museum and, 26
Sueyoshi, Amy, 148n112
Support Our Law Enforcement and Safe Neighborhoods Act (SB 1070), 114–115, 126
Supreme Court, US, 115
Syrian refugees, 129

taiko, 87, 106
Tajiri, Rea, 152n66
Takaezu, Toshiko, 27
Takaki, Ronald, 6
Takarabe, Heihachiro, 567
Takemoto, Tina, 47, 52–53
Tamai, Lily Anne Welty, 149n128
Taylor, Diana, 109, 143n59
temporality, 4; of "look how far we've come/where we are going," 27–29; of "maybe if I did," 122–124; progressive, 15, 18, 19; of regeneration, 109–111
Terasaki Family Foundation, 1
testimony, 3, 15, 62–64; at Gala Dinner, 36; legibility through, 2; as a technology of neocolonialism and neoliberalism, 16
Thirty-Ninth Street Elementary School, 41
Till, Emmett, 50
Time magazine, 131
Tōhoku earthquake and tsunami, 33
Tonai, Minoru, 156n64
Toyota, Tritia, 30
transgendered women, 24, 45. *See also* Fukuda, Rey
trauma, 143n59; Commission testimony on, 64; the Densho archive on, 66, 67, 69, 76–79, 83
Trump, Donald, 23, 70, 126–127, 128–129, 135–136; election of, 128, 130–131; executive orders of, 130–133
truth: Commission hearings and, 16; the Densho archive on, 22, 56, 69, 76, 83; life and, 36
Tsuru for Solidarity, 128
Tule Lake, 9, 59, 157n28

University of California, Los Angeles (UCLA), 23, 27, 49, 105–127; Japanese American Research Project, 56; Manzanar organizations and, 86, 88. *See also* Cultural Night performances
University of California, San Diego (UCSD), 88, 100
unmapping, methodology of, 89

Vigilant Love, 128, 132–135, 160n21
Vigilant Love, A (film), 134
violence of value, 17
visibility, 6, 15, 126; Day of Remembrance on, 53; death and, 8, 9–10, 59, 72; the Densho archive on, 57, 64, 65, 72; gendered normative, 62–64; of Indigenous groups, 86; Nisei gender roles and, 59–62; *Our [I]dentity* on, 117; unintended consequences of, 16, 17

Wakayama, Ernest, 40
Wakayama, Toki, 40
Walker, Chantal, 93
Walking against the Wind (play), 107
War Department, 9
Warner, Michael, 6, 105
War Relocation Authority (WRA), 8, 9, 56; *Another Inmate Gold Star Mother*, 60; creation and purpose of, 57; historical narratives and their impact, 57–59
Watanabe, Masao, 77, 100
water rights (Owens Valley), 22, 87, 92, 93–94, 95, 96, 97, 155n40
Watts Riots, 43
Week of Remembrance, 106
Wei, Erica, 100
welfare policies, 3, 17, 19, 44, 63
Wells Fargo, 26
Westside Los Angeles, 40
"What She Remembers" (Yamashita), 152n66
"where we are going" temporality, 27–29
white supremacy, 34, 36, 70, 74, 90, 102, 128, 135–136
"Who Is Singing This Song" (Mirikitani), 110
Williams, Duncan Ryuken, 149n128
Williams, Harry, 92–93, 96–98
"Will to Institutionality, The" (Ferguson), 36
Wilson, Darren, 149n126
Wolfe, Patrick, 20, 90
woman of color feminism, 139n4
women: Black/transgendered, 24, 45; Chinese immigrant, 5–6; Japanese immigrant, 6; military service of, 60; Nisei, 59–62

Women's Army Corps (WAC), 60
Wood, Clyde, 8, 80
Wooden, John, 27
World Trade Center attack, 130
worthiness narratives, 2, 26, 59, 60, 62–64, 137
WRA. *See* War Relocation Authority

Yamamoto, Hisaye, 27, 41, 43–44, 71
Yamano, Jane Aiko, 31–32, 33
Yamasaki, Frank, 77

Yellow Brotherhood, 41
Yogi, Stan, 148n112
Yonamine, Wally, 27
Yonsei, 25, 34, 99; Cultural Night performances on, 107, 108, 109, 110, 115; defined, 5, 105; era of immigration, 5; intergenerational collaboration and, 135; Japanese American National Museum on, 30; Manzanar pilgrimages and, 88
YouTube channel of Densho archive, 65, 66, 75

Wendi Yamashita is Assistant Professor of Ethnic Studies at California State University, Sacramento. She is coeditor of *Asian Americans & Pacific Islanders: A Historical Community Overview*.

www.ingramcontent.com/pod-product-compliance
Lightning Source LLC
Chambersburg PA
CBHW020800160426
43192CB00006B/393